"A compelling, persuasive book to which attention must be paid...A summons that is filled with hopeful possibility for new peace-making initiatives beyond old ideologies."

—**Walter Brueggemann**, Columbia Theological Seminary

"I have much in common with my wise, loving Jewish friend, Mark Braverman—including our shared belief that Jesus calls us to be peacemakers. This is a beautifully written, thought-provoking, important book."

—**Lynne Hybels**, advocate for Global Engagement

"Braverman demands from church and synagogue a new level of accountability to the religious message of liberation found in Abrahamic traditions...In doing so, he affirms a pathway of loving resistance to occupation."

—**Rabbi Lynn Gottlieb**, author of *Trail Guide to the Torah of Nonviolence*

"*A Wall in Jerusalem* is what we call 'political theology' and it is a shining example of how it can be done well."

—**Gary M. Burge**, Ph.D., Professor of New Testament, Wheaton College and Graduate School

"Compassionate, intelligent, and laying a groundwork for both courage and healing."

—**Fr. Richard Rohr**, Franciscan priest and author

"Mark's voice is unique and desperately needed today. I especially urge my fellow Christians, and most especially sincere Christian Zionists, to read *A Wall in Jerusalem* with an open mind and heart." —**Brian D. McLaren**, author/speaker/ activist (brianmclaren.net)

ALSO BY MARK BRAVERMAN

Fatal Embrace: Christians, Jews, and
the Search for Peace in the Holy Land

A WALL IN JERUSALEM

HOPE, HEALING, AND THE STRUGGLE FOR
JUSTICE IN ISRAEL AND PALESTINE

MARK BRAVERMAN

JERICHO
BOOKS™

New York • Boston • Nashville

Scripture quotations are taken from the New Revised Standard Version Bible, copyright © 1989 the Division of Christian Education of the National Council of the Churches of Christ in the United States of America. Used by permission. All rights reserved.

Jericho Books
Hachette Book Group
237 Park Avenue
New York, NY 10017

www.JerichoBooks.com

Book design by Sean Ford
Printed in the United States of America

RRD-C

First Edition: November 2013
10 9 8 7 6 5 4 3 2 1

Jericho Books is an imprint of Hachette Book Group, Inc.
The Jericho Books name and logo are trademarks of Hachette Book Group, Inc.

The Hachette Speakers Bureau provides a wide range of authors for speaking events. To find out more, go to www.HachetteSpeakersBureau.com or call (866) 376-6591.

The publisher is not responsible for websites (or their content) that are not owned by the publisher.

ISBN 978-1-4555-7420-9 (paperback)

Library of Congress Control Number: 2013950127

For Susie, again.

CONTENTS

As he was leaving the temple, one of his disciples said to him, "Look, Teacher! What massive stones! What magnificent buildings!"

"Do you see all these great buildings?" replied Jesus. "Not one stone here will be left on another; every one will be thrown down."

Mark 13:1–2

Vox victimarum vox Dei: The cries of the victims are the cries of God.

Chapter 1

THE CHALLENGE TO THE CHURCH

Sixty-eight years ago, the Christian world stood before the ovens of Auschwitz and said, "What have we done?"

Luther scholar Aarne Siirala wrote that "his visit to the death camps...overwhelmed him with shock and revealed to him that something was gravely sick at the very heart of our tradition. Auschwitz has a message that must be heard: it reveals an illness operative not on the margin of our civilization but at the heart of it, in the very best that we have inherited...It summons us to face up to the negative side of our religious and cultural heritage."[1]

The decades that followed the attempted extermination of the Jewish people in the heart of Christian Europe saw a determined effort to cleanse Christianity of the pernicious anti-Jewish doctrine that had poisoned the faith over the two thousand years of Christian-Jewish history. This focus on reconciliation with the Jewish people has motivated theological thinking, preaching, and church policy since that time, and it continues to this day. "Anti-Jewishness," wrote Protestant theologian Robert T. Osborn, "is the Christian sin."[2] Notice that Osborn doesn't call anti-Jewishness *a* sin of which Christians are guilty. Rather, it has taken first place. Correcting it would require a fundamental overhaul of the faith.

The wake-up call began, not surprisingly, in Germany. In the aftermath of the war, church leaders contemplated with horror how the German church, with some heroic exceptions, had collaborated actively, even eagerly, with the Nazi regime. "How," wrote Hans Joachim Iwand, a member of the German Confessing Church, the small group that had opposed Nazism and that included the martyred Dietrich Bonhoeffer, "can the German people that has initiated the fruitless rebellion against Israel and his God become pure? Who is going to take this guilt away from us and our theological fathers—because there it started?"[3] This penitent and confessing spirit spread to America, where the work of Protestant theologian Paul van Buren in the 1970s and '80s set the stage for a wide-ranging project of Christian-Jewish understanding and reconciliation. According to van Buren, forging a positive relationship with Judaism and the Jewish people was nothing less than the reimagining of what it meant to be Christian. "If the church stops thinking of the Jews as the rejected remnant of the people Israel," wrote van Buren, "if it starts speaking of the continuing covenantal relationship between this people and God, then it will have to rethink its own identity."[4]

The problem, said van Buren, was that Christianity had allowed itself to be built on a foundation of anti-Judaism. He set out to correct this theological error by framing God's covenant with the Jewish people as the basis for the Christian revelation. And this was no tweaking of some finer points of theology; this was a revolution in the way Christians were thinking about themselves. "Christianity must refer to Judaism in order to make sense of itself," wrote van Buren. This is in the service of the "church's reversal of its position on Judaism from that of anti-Judaism to that of an acknowledgement of the eternal covenant between God and Israel."[5] Only by deeply honoring the Jewish people, van Buren asserted, can Christians be truly Christian.

Strong stuff!

Anti-Jewishness, more commonly known as anti-Semitism, is an evil like any form of racism or discrimination. Given the huge burden of responsibility that the church bears for Jewish suffering throughout the ages, why shouldn't it put this at the top of its list? Is it not the heart of Christianity to, in the words of the apostle Paul, "destroy the barrier, the dividing wall of hostility" between the Gentile followers of Jesus and the Jewish people from whose midst the new faith had emerged? Theologians set to work to reject the erroneous and destructive doctrine of "replacement theology" (sometimes called supercessionism), which states that the Christian Church has replaced the Jewish people in God's love, and that as punishment for failing to accept Jesus as the Messiah, God rejected the Jews and condemned them to wander the earth until the end of time. Listen to Paul, Christians were now being instructed: he was not throwing the Jews out of the church! Rather, he was passionately committed to building one community, one *ecclesia*, to bring Jew, Gentile, and Greek; man and woman; slave and freeman, together in the church of Jesus Christ. "In him," wrote Paul in his Letter to the Ephesians, "the whole building is joined together and rises to become a holy temple in the Lord" (Ephesians 2:21). Rather than promoting a doctrine that says that

Christians have displaced the Jews as God's beloved people, we must reaffirm the special relationship between God and the Jewish people. Judaism would no longer be seen as Christianity's shadow. Instead, it would take its rightful place as the very foundation of Christian faith. In renouncing anti-Judaism, therefore, Christians were returning to the foundations of Christianity, to a mission of unity, not division; of love, not hatred. The Roman Catholic Church followed the lead of the Protestant churches with the Second Vatican Council (1963–1965), in which the Church "decrie[d] hatred, persecutions, displays of anti-Semitism, directed against Jews at any time and by anyone."[6]

Generations of theologians and clergy have been educated in this revised theology. No longer would anti-Jewish ideas and images be heard from the pulpits. Offending passages from the Gospels would increasingly be avoided, or reinterpreted as applying to only one group of Jews in a particular historical context, not to an entire people. Churches and synagogues sponsored interfaith seminars. Interfaith studies began to occupy a prominent place in the curricula and course offerings in seminaries, and in graduate school departments of religious studies. Organizations to educate Christians about Judaism and help fight anti-Semitism sprang up, bringing Jewish and Christian clergy and scholars to sit together on a single dais. While still acknowledging their differences, the two faith communities were finding ways to reconnect after two thousand years of enmity and distrust. It was a meeting, all hoped, in which both communities would gain a deeper understanding of their own particular richness and would affirm their common commitment to making the world a more just, compassionate, and loving place.

How good this has been, how healing and hopeful for the future!

But there is another theme here, one that we ignore at our peril. Let's return to Paul van Buren, the foremost Protestant spokesman for this powerful Christian-Jewish alliance. Why, asks van Buren, after eighteen centuries, should Christian leaders "turn Christian teaching on its head" with respect to the Jewish people? It was the trauma of the Nazi Holocaust of course, but just as powerful was the establishment of the State of Israel in 1948, and then the Israeli victory in the 1967 war in which Israel took control of the Old City of Jerusalem that changed the way Christians began to regard the Jewish people:

> [t]he Holocaust and the emergence of the state of Israel...are what impelled them to speak in a new way about Jews and Judaism...the Israeli Defense Force sweeping over the Sinai and retaking East Jerusalem was what could not possibly fit our traditional myth of the passive suffering Jew. The result is that events in modern Jewish history, perhaps as staggering as any in its whole history, have begun to reorient the minds of increasing numbers of responsible Christians.[7]

What a change this is from the idea of a suffering people who need to be rescued from persecution! This image of the Jewish fighter, proud and strong, no longer the helpless, servile "ghetto Jew," was and continues to be a dominant feature of the modern Zionist movement and a central theme in Israeli culture.

But let us pay close and thoughtful attention to this new

theme. Listen to the drumbeat of conquest and military triumph in this passage. Notice the biblical undertone in the two words *Sinai* and *Jerusalem.* Sinai was the mountain where God descended and gave us the Mosaic code, the divine commandments that form the basis of Judaism and the bedrock of Christianity. It is a code that requires above all equality, human dignity, and compassion for the most vulnerable in society. When did the image of a people redeemed from slavery and gathered at the foot of the mountain to receive the Ten Commandments morph into tanks rumbling over desert sands in a lightning war of conquest? How is it that Jerusalem, the very symbol of holiness and hope, has now become something that is "taken" by military force? Didn't Christians attempt that a thousand years ago, when the Crusaders set out with sword and shield to wrest Jerusalem from the infidel? Have we forgotten how Jesus entered Jerusalem on Palm Sunday, not with an army but with a small band of followers waving palm branches, not swords, singing Hosannah to God in the highest? This was the same Jesus who proclaimed to his followers that the temple of stone and gold would be destroyed and replaced by his body—a communion of all humankind. What happened to transform this vision of universal harmony to one of conquest and temporal power?

The Birth of a Dream

The State of Israel was the realization of a dream. It was the dream of a people who, despite having made enormous contributions wherever they had settled in the wide world, had nevertheless been driven out of many of those same societies.

When allowed to stay, they were merely tolerated, often confined to ghettoes and denied the rights afforded to others. At times this condition of marginalization and second-class status intensified to outright persecution and slaughter. The declaration of the State of Israel in 1948 was the culmination of the dream of the Jewish people to return to the condition of independence, self-determination, and security symbolized by the kingdoms of Judah and Israel described in the Old Testament, a national epic that told the story of liberation from bondage, inheritance of a Promised Land, exile, and return. Although many of the original European Zionist leaders and writers were not religious, and the historical validity of the biblical story has now been questioned, the Old Testament narrative remained a powerful source of national identity and justification for Zionist strivings.[8]

By the end of the nineteenth century, the ferocity of attacks against Jews in tsarist Russia had intensified, along with the increasing restrictions on their rights to live in Russian society as full citizens. Outbreaks of anti-Semitism, even in supposedly liberal central and western Europe, had also occurred, and the need to find a solution became urgent. To many, Zionism provided the answer. The First Zionist Congress—convened in 1897 in Basel, Switzerland, under the leadership of the Austrian Jewish journalist and intellectual Theodor Herzl—is considered the official birth of modern political Zionism.

Zionism is a form of nationalism that maintains that Jews are a people or national group like any other, and that Jewish identity and the survival and well-being of the Jewish people depends on the existence of an independent Jewish nation-state. Although the settlement of Palestine was not part of

Herzl's original vision—several other locations for a Jewish state were proposed in the early years of the Zionist movement—the claim to Palestine (called Eretz Yisrael, Hebrew for "the Land of Israel," by Zionists) was soon established as an essential element of the Jewish project to create a national homeland. Jews from eastern and central Europe began to come to Palestine as part of an organized project of immigration and settlement from Europe at the end of the nineteenth century, and this immigration continued into the twentieth century. Although how Jewish settlement might impact the local population of Palestine began to become apparent in the early years of the *yishuv,* as the Zionist settlement was called, the original Zionists did not conceive of their movement as a settler colonial project. An early Zionist slogan that identified Palestine as "a land without a people for a people without a land" illustrates the lack of awareness on the part of the early European settlers of the existence of a large Arab population in Palestine. This early failure on the part of Zionists to acknowledge and respect the rights of the indigenous people and culture set the stage for the modern political conflict.

Jewish settlement in Palestine was facilitated by the establishment in 1901 of the Jewish National Fund, a corporation created to raise money for the purchase of land, to organize immigration, and to establish agricultural settlements. The growth of Jewish settlement was encouraged by Great Britain, which took control of the territory after World War I and provided diplomatic support for the Zionist project, famously through a 1917 document that came to be known as the Balfour Declaration, after its author, Britain's foreign secretary Arthur Balfour. The document, which states "His Majesty's government view with favour the establishment in Palestine of a national home for the Jewish people," continues to be cited by supporters of Zionism as a primary source for the legitimacy of Zionism as a political program.

Although relations between Jewish settlers and the indigenous Christian and Muslim Arab population of Palestine were initially peaceful and amicable, trouble began in the early twentieth century. By the 1920s, Palestinians had begun to understand that the hardworking, idealistic settlers arriving from Europe since the 1880s, seeking to escape from marginalization and outright persecution, and who were followed by successive waves of immigration in the twentieth century, added up to a colonial project aimed at displacing the existing Palestinian society of farming communities, rural villages, and bustling cities. Conflicting British promises to both Arabs and Jews following the awarding of the mandate for Britain to govern Palestine at the close of World War I further fed the growing conflict between the Zionist push for a Jewish state and the desire of Palestinians for political autonomy and self-determination. After World War II, as the world reacted in horror over the near destruction of the Jews of Europe by the Nazi regime, the concept of dividing the territory between a Jewish and Arab state gained increasing support.

The United Nations decision in November 1947 to partition the territory into two states, one Arab and one Jewish, was a watershed event. The plan allocated 43 percent of Palestine for the Arab state and 57 percent to the Jewish state, with Jerusalem as an internationally administered zone. The Zionist leadership accepted this arrangement, and the State of Israel was declared on May 14, 1948, by David Ben-Gurion, head of the World Zionist Organization and the Jewish Agency for

Palestine. Palestinian leaders, supported by the governments of the neighboring Arab states, rejected the plan, arguing that the allocation of land violated the rights of the majority Arab population of the territory. (At the time, Jews accounted for 20 percent of the population and owned 6 percent of the land.) What followed was an armed conflict that ended with an armistice and the establishment of cease-fire lines that became the de facto borders of the State of Israel until 1967.

Conflicting Narratives

Here, again, mythology and historical facts clash. The Israeli narrative of the founding of the State of Israel, almost completely accepted by the Western world, is of hugely outnumbered Jewish forces prevailing against the massed power of five Arab armies who invaded the day the state was declared, determined to "push the Jews into the sea." But this picture does not match the reality of a well-prepared, well-armed Zionist military force prevailing against poorly equipped, disorganized, and inconsistently motivated forces from neighboring states. (There was no Palestinian state, hence no army, only local defensive militias in the individual villages, no match for the well-organized and professionally led Jewish forces.) This "David and Goliath" picture, with Israel as the young shepherd armed with only a slingshot and his faith against the Arabs, depicted as violent, powerful bullies determined to smash the small, brave, freedom-seeking nation, lends powerful support to what Jewish theologian Marc Ellis has described as the belief in Jewish innocence.[9] In this image, well supported by popular books, movies, and the media, Israel's war of 1948 was a war of self-defense—I grew up knowing it as both "the War of Independence" and the "War of Liberation"—rather than the campaign of conquest and ethnic cleansing that Israeli historians have now documented.[10]

What we Jews have called our war of liberation served as a way to carry out a carefully designed project by the Zionist movement to banish the indigenous Palestinians so that a Jewish state could be established. Records unearthed by Israeli historians reveal that the campaign to "transfer" the Palestinian population to make way for a Jewish state was in the planning by Zionist leaders as far back as the 1930s, and that the 1948 hostilities provided the opportunity to carry out this campaign of ethnic cleansing. In fact, actions by Jewish forces designed to expel Palestinians from villages throughout Palestine had been put into operation months before a single Arab soldier crossed into Palestine after the declaration of the State of Israel in May 1948. It resulted in the destruction of more than 500 Palestinian villages and the expulsion of 750,000 Palestinians from their villages and cities before the cessation of hostilities in March 1949.[11]

It is indisputable that the well-organized Jewish army that would go on to become the military of the State of Israel protected the Jewish population of Palestine from hostile Arab forces. Jewish soldiers fought courageously to defend their communities and their families, and Jewish losses were considerable where the army encountered stiff opposition, particularly in battles in and around Jerusalem. More than six thousand Israelis died in the 1947–48 hostilities, a huge number when you consider that this constituted 1 percent of the Jewish population of Palestine at the time. The deaths were not confined to combatants: two thousand of the Jewish dead were civilians. But it is also true that the conflict resulted in the dispossession and displacement of fully one half of the Palestinians living between the Jordan River and the Mediterranean Sea, whose descendants are now estimated to number ten million. Denied the right to return to their cities and villages, they now live in neighboring Arab countries and on every continent, with close to one and a half million remaining stateless, residing in refugee camps in Jordan, Syria, Lebanon, the West Bank, and the Gaza Strip.[12]

Occupation

The cessation of hostilities in 1949 left Israel in control of 78 percent of the territory of historic Palestine, with the West Bank of the Jordan River, including East Jerusalem, under Jordanian control and the Gaza Strip administered by Egypt. In June 1967, Israel attacked Egypt, Syria, and Jordan. As a result of its victories in these campaigns, commonly known as the Six-Day War, Israel occupied the Syrian Golan Heights, the Gaza Strip, and the West Bank, including East Jerusalem, which had been under Jordanian control.[13] Over the next three decades, negotiations over return of the occupied territories were unsuccessful. Once in control of these territories, Israel began almost immediately to establish settlements for the exclusive use of Jewish Israeli citizens.[14] As the pace of Jewish settlement building increased, Palestinian frustration and anger grew, resulting in the First Intifada (in Arabic, "shaking off"), a largely nonviolent uprising that was met with brutal repression by the Israeli military. As settlement activity accelerated, with settlements growing from small outposts to large blocs today totaling over half a million people, the urgency to find a negotiated peace based on the creation of a Palestinian state in the West Bank and Gaza gained momentum. In 1993 the Palestine Liberation Organization (PLO) was formally recognized as the legitimate representative of the Palestinian people, and the process was set in motion toward the creation of a Palestinian state. The 1993 Oslo Accords, or "Declaration of Principles," brokered through international channels, was the first agreement between Israel and political representatives of the Palestinians. It was meant to be the first step toward an autonomous Palestinian state in the West Bank and Gaza, and to normal relations with Israel. The Accords created the Palestinian Authority (PA), which would exercise various degrees of control over a portion of the area occupied by Israel. The Accords established three geographical zones: Area A, under complete control of the PA; Area B, under Palestinian civil control and Israeli military control; and Area C, completely controlled by Israel. Area C consists of Jewish-only settlements and "security zones," off-limits to Palestinians. Today, Area C is situated to the west of the separation barrier, encompassing the settlement blocs and effectively annexed to Israel. In Area B, under the military control of Israel, Palestinian movement and commerce are increasingly restricted, with the inhabitants of many villages undergoing transfer into the urban centers that make up Area A. Area A, amounting to about 11 percent of all of Palestine and consisting of separated enclaves surrounded by Israeli-controlled territory, is where the Palestinian population is increasingly concentrated.

A Peace Process Falters

The Oslo Accords, symbolized for many by the iconic photograph of PLO chairman Yasser Arafat shaking hands with Israeli prime minister Yitzhak Rabin on the White House Lawn under the beaming gaze of President Bill Clinton, were the cause of great optimism, especially on the part of Palestinians. But by 2000, the mood had changed, as the pace of land-taking, the proliferation of illegal settlements, the construction of Jewish-only roads, and restrictions on movement increased. Palestinians began to realize that they were farther from, not closer to, sovereignty and self-determination. Instead of withdrawing Israeli troops and taking steps toward the creation of a Palestinian state in the West Bank and Gaza, it was clear that Israel was using the military and civil control ceded in the agreement to increase its outright annexation of Palestinian lands and to build an extensive infrastructure of political and economic control over the remaining territory west of the Jordan River. The occupation was not ending; it was deepening.

The Al Aqsa Intifada (or Second Intifada) in September 2000 is generally understood as having originated from the Palestinians' deep frustration over the failure of the Olso Accords to achieve their promised goals. It was also a reaction to the enormous growth of Jewish-only settlements throughout the West Bank and Gaza and to the increasing restrictions imposed on Palestinian society. Although violence against Israel took many forms, the most well known were suicide bombings carried out by militant Palestinian resistance groups against civilian and military targets in Israel and in Gaza and the West Bank. These occurred at the rate of 2 to 5 per year between 1989 and 2000, and increased dramatically, to a total of 127 attacks at their peak for the period 2001–2004. Israel responded to these attacks with military incursions into the West Bank and Gaza Strip, in addition to erecting security checkpoints, conducting mass arrests, and imposing strict curfews for civilians in urban areas. In 2002, Israel began construction of the separation barrier, a twenty-eight-foot-high militarized concrete wall (in some areas it consists of parallel metal fences running along each side of a patrol road) that runs north to south through the entire West Bank, in effect creating a new border that incorporates large areas of existing and planned Israeli settlement development and extends deep into Palestinian territory. In 2005, Israel removed its six thousand Jewish settlers from the Gaza Strip. However, it still has authority over the northern, eastern, and, through control of the seacoast, western border of Gaza; maintains tight control over movement in and out of the Strip; and places restrictions on food, medical, and building supplies. As a result, Gaza suffers from cripplingly high levels of unemployment and a steady deterioration of physical infrastructure and overall living conditions. It has been compared to an open-air prison housing over one and half million people.

A False Note

A stalled peace process and a Jewish society that was intended to be a democracy ruling over a captive population of Palestinians is hardly the heroic picture drawn by van Buren. Conquest, sadly, is conquest. What do we make of a theology that links the colonization of a Middle Eastern territory by European settlers and the military actions of a modern nation-state to biblical prophecies and concepts of divine promise? The new theology about Jews, Judaism, and the role of "the land" that has dominated Christian beliefs and attitudes since World War II has come to support a program of conquest and dispossession. It is taught in the seminaries and in departments of theology and religious studies and is promoted in books and journals. Until very recently, nothing challenging the actions of the State of Israel or raising the issue of Palestinian suffering has been heard from the pulpits; nor has this discussion been permitted in the academy.

Not only fundamental Christian principles of equality and social justice are at stake here. The historic and ongoing injustice toward the Palestinians by the State of Israel presents a dire threat to the Israeli dream of a secure homeland and a vibrant, democratic society, because conquest is the fundamental barrier to peace. The dispossession of the Palestinians has created four generations of refugees and untold suffering and loss. Far from creating a "blessing" to the Jewish people, taking possession of the land is isolating Israel in the community of nations and poisoning its society. This is the grim reality I have seen with my own eyes, one that has become painfully apparent to a growing number of Americans who have visited the region and seen what is to be seen.

I know it's confusing. Given the shameful history of Christian persecution of Jews, isn't it incumbent on Christians to give the Jews the benefit of the doubt and to bless their national homeland project? Doesn't the Holocaust change everything? Isn't the creation of Israel and the seemingly miraculous picture, as van Buren writes, "of the Israelis holding out and winning their war of independence against the combined forces of five national armies" a miracle of heroism and rebirth that must be celebrated as evidence of God's blessing? In light of such momentous events of tragedy and triumph, should we not, like van Buren, support this redemption of the Jewish people, rising out of the ashes of the death camps? Evangelical as well as mainline American Christians believe that the Bible conveys the Jewish people's right to the land through God's promise to Abraham in the Book of Genesis, and furthermore that the New Testament tells us that the Jewish possession of the land, and of Jerusalem in particular, presages the End Times.

But this is precisely how this revised theology has gotten it wrong.

Yes, given the tragic history of Christian-Jewish relations, there has been a compelling need to break down the walls of hostility, to build a new house where all are equal in God's love. But instead of a new building, a new gathering, a congregation called *ecclesia* dedicated to love and compassion "for the least of these," the Church in the United States—albeit unwittingly and in good faith—has, in its uncritical support of the State of Israel, embraced conquest and the triumph of military might. "We trust violence," writes theologian Walter Wink, lamenting how committed we remain in our society to physical force to cope with our fears and to settle conflicts, "Violence 'saves,'" he writes. "It is 'redemptive.'"[15] As Christians rush to undo their sins against the Jews through an unconditional endorsement of the Jewish national homeland project, something precious and fundamental to Christianity has been lost, a legacy that is at the heart of Jesus' ministry and the timeless message of the Gospels. Reclaiming this legacy is what holds the key to peace for Israelis and freedom and self-determination for Palestinians.

Reclaiming a Precious Legacy

To understand how this is so, we need to look at the context of Jesus' ministry.

The Palestinians of Jesus' time were suffering horribly under the heel of the Roman Empire. Rome's method of domination was to replace the agrarian, community-based society of its colonial subjects with a system based on tribute to the empire. In the case of Galilee and Judea, devotion to the God of Abraham was to be supplanted by worship of the emperor. The Mosaic law that governed the everyday lives of the farmers and tradespeople of first-century Palestine—a civil code based on social equality, forgiveness of debts, and, most important, protection of the most vulnerable—was being pushed aside by the ancient equivalent of a national security state. Under this system, "peace"—the so-called Pax Romana—was secured by an army of soldiers and civil servants charged with maintaining an order that, through crushing taxation and overwhelming military force, secured wealth and power for a minority elite at the expense of an increasingly impoverished agrarian and urban population.

In his childhood in Galilee, Jesus saw popular revolts against Rome and its client rulers brutally suppressed. Villages were burned, people enslaved, and thousands of insurgents crucified. Jesus' ministry can be seen as a direct response to the cruelty of imperial rule, which included the client king and priestly class installed in Jerusalem to administer it. It was precisely this system that Jesus was challenging when he stationed himself in the temple courtyard after entering Jerusalem with his followers on that final week recorded in the Gospel accounts. Jesus' mission was to support his suffering people by reminding them that faithfulness to the enduring values of their tradition—rather than armed resistance or capitulation to the power structure—was the key to their survival. It was the original message of nonviolent resistance, based on keeping faith with God. "Do not trust in princes!" says the psalm (146:3), and to this Jesus adds: Or similarly transgress against God by taking up arms against them, for "All who take the sword will perish by the sword!" (Matthew 26:52). In so doing, Jesus was operating very much in the prophetic tradition by speaking the truth of God's law to the idolatry of earthly power. What sets Jesus apart from the prophets was that he was not a lone voice challenging the structures of authority, but a leader and a builder of community. Jesus not only confronted the powers but also presented an alternative way of living. And after his ultimate sacrifice, he sent his followers out to the ends of the earth to work for the creation of that kingdom, that alternative order: His church.

And that is why the Christian endorsement today of yet another earthly kingdom is a betrayal of that mission. There is much that is right about a revised theology that rejects Christian triumphalism and renounces hatred of Jews. But in their haste to help the Jewish people overcome oppression, Christians have enabled the Jews to fall into the very same sin from which Christians have tried to liberate themselves, by granting the now rehabilitated Jews the right, and the means, to seek their own redemption at the expense of another people.

We are not speaking here of the right of the citizens of Israel to live in peace and security—this is indisputable. But it is a tragic and startling irony that when you visit the Holy Land today, you see what Jesus saw. You see land taken through the imposition of illegal laws and the tread of soldiers' boots. You see attempts to destroy community and family through the disruption of the economic and social basis of village life. It was precisely this type of desperate crisis that motivated Jesus' message of compassion for the most vulnerable in society and his protest against the abuses of power. A similar crisis is unfolding in the story told in these pages. It's the story of Palestinian mothers and fathers nonviolently resisting the loss of their land and the theft of their children's future. It's the story of courageous Israelis calling their own society to account for its historic and present-day crimes against the Palestinian people—Israelis struggling heroically to rescue their country from the sickness that threatens the future of its own children. We are looking at a society very much like that of two thousand years ago: on the one hand, stricken by the illnesses brought on by the addiction to power; and on the other, blessed by the presence of prophets.

This book is my testimony as a Jew, passionately devoted to my tradition and to my people. It is written with an anger that burns at the injustice being suffered by innocent people on both sides of the Israeli-Palestinian divide. The Palestinians have lost their land and live under daily, crushing humiliation. The Jewish citizens of Israel live behind a wall of soul-killing racism. They do not know that this "enemy" is the best potential friend they have, if they can only learn to trust and to join the neighborhood to which they fled from a murderous and inhospitable Europe. I have also written this book in deep sadness—sadness over how my people have fallen into sin. We, even we, with the memory of our own persecution so fresh, so seared into our consciousness and our very identity, have become the tyrants. It's the story of how I, a Jew born at the midpoint of the twentieth century and heir to the legacy of vulnerability and of the deep sense of victimhood that now drives us, have by the grace of God crossed over to the other side of the wall my people have built to protect us from this "enemy." It is the story of how I, like Jacob reunited with Esau, have seen in the face of my estranged brother the face of God.

This book is also the story of the church, forged in the crucible of the worst evil the world had ever known, created to bring a message of hope and God's love to all humankind. The church affirmed this legacy in the twentieth century by giving birth to the civil rights movement in the United States and by playing a critical role in the struggle to end apartheid in South Africa. We will delve into the lessons learned from these earlier struggles for freedom and human dignity as we consider how the church is summoned once again to fulfill its calling—to strive, in every age, to confront tyranny and injustice, to renew itself and be reborn. We are now, as we are in every historical era, standing with the man from Nazareth, ready to answer the prophetic call:

> *The Spirit of the Lord is upon me,*
> *because he has anointed me*
> *to bring good news to the poor.*
> *He has sent me to proclaim release to the captives*
> *and recovery of sight to the blind,*
> *to let the oppressed go free,*
> *to proclaim the acceptable year of the Lord.*
>
> (Luke 4:18–19)

This book is about voices. Voices of women and men called to discipleship, unfurling their own scrolls of Isaiah, proclaiming that this is the year, this is the time. Voices crying out from their pain, their faith, and their hope. It is these voices that fill these pages. The rest, as a great rabbi once said, is commentary.

Chapter 2
THE WALL IN MY HEART

It wasn't going well. The people entering and leaving the building were not happy about our presence on the street outside the National Conference Center, in Washington, DC. No one would accept the printed information we were offering, and all efforts to engage anyone in conversation or even a brief verbal exchange failed—unless you count the occasional accusation of "Shame on you!" We were standing outside the annual conference of the American Israel Public Affairs Committee, more commonly known as AIPAC, or the "Israel lobby." We were protesting our government's massive, unconditional military aid to Israel and its blanket diplomatic protection of the Jewish state in the international arena.

My fellow protesters and I were arguing that, although we supported Israel's right to live in peace and security, the United States should call Israel to account for its human rights violations and its flouting of international law in its treatment of the Palestinians. In our printed flyer, we pointed out that changing U.S. policy of unconditional support for

Israel was not only the right thing to do, but was in our self-interest: its support of Israel's oppression of the Palestinians was isolating the United States globally, as awareness of and sympathy for the Palestinian cause was growing and awareness of Israel's human rights abuses was drawing increasing attention not only in the Arab world, but also in Europe, Asia, Africa, and Latin America. Since 1974, Israel has received $3 billion a year in direct aid from the United States, in addition to assistance for specific armament projects. It has been the largest single recipient of foreign aid since 1974, despite the fact that the United States has officially objected to many of Israel's policies in the territories occupied since 1967. Since 1972, the United States has exercised its veto in the case of twenty-nine United Nations resolutions and fourteen UN Security Council resolutions critical of Israel.

I had staked out my position outside the convention center that day in 2008 as a Jew who was heartbroken about and, frankly, horrified by Israel's actions and by the policies of a state that purportedly existed to keep me safe in a world that for millennia had persecuted my people. But I was also standing there as an American objecting to my country's failed policy in the Middle East. It had failed because rather than addressing the root cause of the Israel-Palestine conflict, which was the dispossession of the indigenous Arab population to make way for the Jewish state, the United States had supported and perpetuated the injustice. Since the founding of Israel in 1948, the United States has backed Israel diplomatically and financially, ignoring the plight of millions of Palestinians made refugees through the establishment of Israel; abetting the continued taking of land; and sanctioned these abridgements of human rights by blocking United Nations resolutions and appeals to the Geneva Conventions by the international community. I have a deep attachment to Israel: I lived there as a young man, I speak the language, and I have deep family roots in Jerusalem. But I could not be quiet in the face of such behavior. I knew that the path to peace would be found not through military force, the seizure of land, or walling out the Palestinians. The only way to secure peace was to share the land with the people who were already living there when the Jews of Europe, seeking a haven from persecution, began arriving in the late nineteenth century. I had been taught from an early age that the conflict that had plagued the Jewish state for its entire history arose out of the eternal hatred of the "Arabs" for the Jewish people. But I had just traveled to Israel and had met the Palestinians, and I knew that they didn't hate me.

In my hands that day was a stack of copies of a recent *Los Angeles Times* opinion piece in which a Palestinian American professor made an eloquent, balanced appeal for Palestinian rights. My goal was to get people entering the conference center to accept the handout and, even better, engage with me in conversation. After hours of having no luck on either score, I was considering giving up and going home when a well-dressed man on his way into the conference walked up to me, looked me in the eye, and said, "I'll take one."

"Great!" I said, and handed it to him. Taking it, he tore it into shreds, threw it in my face, and walked off without another word.

How, I have often asked myself in recalling that day, *did I get here?*

A Wall in Jerusalem

In the early spring of 2009, I was seated in the office of Lana Abu-Hijleh, in the city of Ramallah in Israeli-occupied Palestine. The country director for an international development agency, Lana is a Muslim woman from an old, respected Palestinian family. Like every Palestinian living under occupation, Lana has a story. She told me about the morning in October 2002 when her mother was gunned down by Israeli soldiers as she sat on the front porch of their home in Nablus, one of the largest and oldest cities in Palestine. "More tea?" she asked as she told me about this tragedy. These stories are not told for sympathy or to shock. They simply make the point: *We are Palestinians. This is our life.* Lana told me that she lives in Jerusalem now, commuting to Ramallah, a short drive if you don't consider the checkpoints. The twenty-eight-foot-high separation wall built by Israel—along the road dividing the northern suburbs annexed by Israel that will be part of Jewish "Greater Jerusalem" from what will remain, presumably, the Palestinian West Bank—accompanies you on the five-mile journey. One day, Lana's eight-year-old daughter, sitting with her in the car, turned to her and asked, "Mommy, why do they make the Jews live behind that wall?"

I knew that wall. It had been built to "protect" the Israelis, but this little girl understood that it was the builders of the wall, not the Palestinians, who were the prisoners. I agreed. My experience was that the Palestinians—trapped in their ever-shrinking walled-in enclaves; cut off from their farmlands, markets, and families; and forced to undergo humiliating and unpredictable delays at every turn—have not lost their dignity or even their hope. In contrast, the great majority of the Jewish citizens of Israel are prisoners of their own fear, fear created by their failure to know their Palestinian neighbors for who they truly are. When I stood before the wall for the first time, on a ruined street in East Jerusalem in the summer of 2006, dwarfed by its height and overwhelmed by its ugliness, something big turned over deep within me. I knew that wall. It lived inside me.

Group identity is a powerful force. It shapes national, ethnic, and organizational culture—and it has a dark side. Samuel Huntington, who published his theory of the "clash of civilizations" in 1993, wrote that "culture and cultural identities...are shaping the patterns of cohesion, disintegration, and conflict in the post–Cold War world."[1]

Citing Huntington, Douglas Johnston of the International Center for Religion and Diplomacy notes that "a conflict becomes intractable when identity is involved and takes the form of defining one's self in opposition to someone else."[2] Today, nations, religious communities, and ethnic groups, especially during periods of stress and change, continue to build and reinforce their identities by emphasizing the categories of "us" and "them." For Jews, a profound feeling of separateness and vulnerability has been a part of our collective experience for two thousand years. Forged over millennia of persecution and marginalization, and buttressed by a religiously based sense of being a special, chosen people, our strong sense of group identity has helped us survive as a people.

This self-image profoundly colored my upbringing and early experience. I was born into the safe, prosperous context of mid-twentieth-century Jewish America. I swam in the deep, protecting waters of an old and majestic tradition. My early life was enriched by beautiful rituals, splendid holidays, a monumental literature—and, perhaps most of all, the claiming of an illustrious history. As Jews, we feel well-deserved pride for having survived and, over the course of three thousand years, having made extraordinary contributions to civilization. But this upbringing had another side, and it was one with which, as I began as an adult to step out of my insular Jewish world, I grew increasingly uncomfortable. It was a paradox: growing up in the open, if rather bland and racially segregated culture of eastern metropolitan America in the 1950s, I never experienced anti-Semitism—but then, I never ventured very far into what I had learned to call the "non-Jewish world." The "dark side" of growing up Jewish was that I was taught to avoid and to fear the "goyim"—as my grandmother, born in Europe, and even my own American-born parents called the society surrounding the Jewish bubble in which we lived. *Goyim*, from the Old Testament Hebrew, means simply "the nations." They were "the other." But throughout the centuries, and right into mid-twentieth-century America, the word became freighted with a darker meaning. Although it was not always made explicit, one fact about the goyim was particularly clear to me: they were dangerous.

That's why we had Israel.

Having come into the world only three years after the end of World War II, and in the same year as the establishment of the State of Israel, I was raised in a potent combination of Rabbinic Judaism and political Zionism. I was taught that a miracle, born of heroism and bravery, had blessed my generation. The State of Israel was not a mere historical event; it was redemption from millennia of marginalization, demonization, and murderous violence. The legacy of this history was a collective identity of brittle superiority: we were special for having survived, despite the effort, "in every generation" (so reads the prayer we recite every Passover) to eradicate us. In order to survive in this hostile, murderous world of the goyim, we had to remain ever vigilant, mistrustful, and—in a not always obvious but nevertheless profound way—apart. Whether justified on a biblical basis by religious Jews or, as the Zionist founders of Israel claimed, simply by virtue of our history of suffering, the State of Israel existed to ensure our safety and to underscore our unique identity in a world that could never be trusted. So I treasured the miracle of the new State of Israel. It represented the end of our history of insecurity and suffering, a solution at last to our eternal vulnerability. My religious faith was completely bound up with this new political reality. Was not God surely at work here, fulfilling the promises made so long ago? In the words of our daily liturgy, the State of Israel was "the first flowering of our redemption." The story of the birth and survival of the young state spoke of our legacy of separateness, vulnerability, but also of our specialness. I embraced this legacy.

Until I saw the occupation. *at age 60*

The journey began for me in the summer of 2006. I found myself in Israel and the occupied Palestinian territories with Interfaith Peace-Builders, an organization that brings North Americans to the region to meet with Israelis and Palestinians and to see the "facts on the ground" firsthand. I had signed up for the trip because of a feeling that would not leave me alone: that there was another side to the story that I had been told as a Jew growing up in postwar America. I had assumed, since I wanted to connect with both Israelis and

Palestinians working for peace, that my outlook was progressive, even "left-wing." I was not prepared for how much even that perspective was to be tested.

As I toured the West Bank, meeting the Palestinians living under occupation and the Israeli soldiers who enforced it, and speaking with the courageous people from both sides working nonviolently to break the spiral of violence and mistrust, I experienced at close range the damage inflicted by the occupation on the Palestinian people and on Israeli society. I witnessed Israel's separation wall snaking through the West Bank on land taken in clear violation of international law; the humiliating checkpoints restricting Palestinian movement; the network of Jewish-only highways; the massive, continuing construction of illegal Jewish-only settlements and towns on Palestinian land; the vicious acts of ideological Jewish settlers destroying Palestinian orchards and physically assaulting farmers, housewives, and schoolchildren; and the destructive impact of militarization and ongoing conflict on Israeli society. I realized that a humanitarian crime was being committed, and that the role of occupier was leading Israel toward political disaster and the Jewish people down a road of spiritual peril.

As I stood before the huge barrier of concrete and steel, the grim consequences of our national homeland project became agonizingly clear to me. It wasn't that I didn't understand "the hope of two thousand years, to be a free people in our own land," as expressed in the Israeli national anthem, "Hatikvah." I felt it to my core. But my confrontation with the occupation of Palestine was pushing me to question the very concept of the Jewish state. I was beginning to understand that we had to move on, toward a renewed Jewish identity, where freedom from fear meant walls being dismantled, not built higher. On that day, the wall inside me began to come down.

A Divided City

That summer, I traveled daily between two worlds. I woke up every morning in the home of my uncle and aunt in the German Colony section of West Jerusalem, a neighborhood of stately homes that, until 1948, housed well-to-do Palestinian families, now displaced and living in the West Bank or abroad. The neighborhood is one of the most fashionable in West Jerusalem, and it is peopled entirely by Jews. None of them ever ventures into Arab East Jerusalem, except for the occasional shopping excursion to the Arab marketplace in the Old City or for a religious pilgrimage to the Western Wall, near the site of the Jewish temple destroyed in 70 CE. Between 1948 (when the Jewish forces retreated from the walled Old City and the eastern half of Jerusalem in the face of the Arab Legion) and 1967 (when the Israeli army recaptured the eastern side in the Six-Day War), a Berlin-type wall divided the city. That wall of wood and mortar that had bisected the city was now gone, but the ethnographic barrier remained. Every morning, I left Jewish West Jerusalem and walked to the east side for a day of meetings with Israeli and Palestinian organizations devoted to activism and education. I crossed the street that once marked the boundary wall and, in one step, as in a cinematic special effect, left the Jewish west side and entered Arab East Jerusalem. In contrast to sedate, devout, manicured, and ordered West Jerusalem, East Jerusalem was riotous in color and tempestuous in emotion.

Daily, I experienced the contrast between the two cultures. On the one hand, there was the indigenous Palestinian society: passionate, industrious, wise, connected deeply to the land. On the other was the new Israeli civilization: transplanted from Europe, carved into the ancient landscape, marvelously creative, hardworking, and hungry for life—and ignorant of the people it was displacing. One day, I stopped a distinguished-looking man in traditional Arab dress to ask for directions and almost began to address him in Hebrew. I had forgotten that I had crossed the invisible barrier that separated Jew from Palestinian.

I had visited Israel many times in the course of my life to that point, including living on a kibbutz for a year after college. But I had never before crossed the line that separated Jew from Palestinian. That summer, traveling in the West Bank—witnessing the separation wall, the checkpoints, the network of restricted roads (two sets of license plates: one for Jews, one for Arabs!), the house demolitions, the evictions of Arabs from their villages and neighborhoods, and the massive, continuing construction of illegal Jewish settlements and towns—words such as *apartheid* and *ethnic cleansing* sprang to my mind, unbidden but undeniable. Even though I had considered myself sympathetic to the Palestinian cause, I had always squirmed when I heard *Nakba,* or "catastrophe," the term the Palestinians use for the expulsion of three quarters of a million people from their cities, villages, and farms in 1948. I experienced this combination of fear and defensiveness not because I rejected the idea of a catastrophe for Palestinians, but because I thought it discounted the Jewish reality: Was not 1948 a war of self-defense, a war to prevent yet another slaughter of Jews? Hadn't they attacked us? Hadn't they rejected the 1947 United Nations plan partitioning the territory into a Jewish state and an Arab state, and by so doing, brought the catastrophe upon them themselves? Wasn't Israel there to protect us from the eternal, implacable hatred of our enemies? But when I began to learn the other story, the narrative of these so-called "enemies," I realized that our own actions had started the cycle of violence.

As I made this daily crossing, eastward in the morning and west at night, an extraordinary thing happened: I began to feel increasingly out of place in West Jerusalem, among my people, where I spoke the language and understood the traditions. In contrast, I felt increasingly comfortable in Arab East Jerusalem, among Muslims and Christians, in the midst of a culture that was new to me and where I didn't even speak the language. On the east side of town, I was welcomed into Palestinian homes, sat at their dinner tables, and learned about their history. They shared their sadness about the losses they had suffered, their dreams for the future, and their deepening despair. The language and cultural differences seemed to melt away. One day it dawned on me that it was in the east side that I was feeling at home, on the east side where I wanted to be. I was profoundly disturbed by this. What was happening to me?

What was happening was that I was encountering the "other" from which I had been walled off for my entire life. And this was not an exercise in cultural tourism or a research project to understand the roots of conflict. This was an urgent, painful journey of self-discovery, a search for the part of myself I had always felt was missing. What was ironic—and really quite wonderful—was that this journey was taking place in the midst of the very people I had been brought up to believe were my mortal enemies. What was happening, the miracle for me, was that the wall that had been installed in my heart, that same wall built from fear and mistrust that has sliced Jerusalem into a Jewish half and an Arab half and that represented the single greatest barrier to peace in this precious land, was crumbling. Stone by stone, section by section, the wall inside me was coming down.

Chapter 3

THE WALL COMES DOWN

One day, not long after my first confrontation with the wall, I sat in the offices of Sabeel, an organization of Christian Palestinians, in East Jerusalem. The Arabic word means "the way," and also "source of life-giving water." The people of Sabeel confront the challenges of life in Palestine today by emulating the mission and life of Jesus and by embracing nonviolence. A woman on the Sabeel staff named Nora Carmi spoke to us. Nora is a Jerusalemite, a refugee in her own land—her family lost their West Jerusalem home in 1948. The conflict has brought Nora (both a mother and a grandmother) pain, loss, and fear. Yet these troubles have only strengthened her faith. I asked Nora how she deals with being dispossessed and occupied, in a situation that was worsening every year. I will never forget her answer: "We follow Jesus."

Nora went on to explain: Who was Jesus? He was a Palestinian Jew living under Roman occupation. Faced with an empire that sought to destroy not only the physical but the ethical basis of first-century Jewish society in Palestine, he did not turn to hatred of his oppressors or to fomenting rebellion—in contrast, he taught love of all humankind, commitment to God's requirement to pursue social justice, and persistent, stubborn, nonviolent resistance to oppression. "Love your enemies," Jesus instructed his people: do not allow them to take away your dignity, or to come between you and your devotion to the commandments to love your neighbor and to be responsible stewards of the earth. "We follow Jesus," Nora said. "Empires come and empires go. We are here."

Another stone dislodged itself from the wall inside me. Here was a woman whose family had been driven from the neighborhood, perhaps the very street, where I was staying with my aunt and uncle in West Jerusalem, a woman whose faith and courage were inspiring me in a way I had never before experienced. Leaving Sabeel that day, I took with me a copy of *Justice and Only Justice: A Palestinian Theology of Liberation,* by Rev. Naim Stifan Ateek, the Palestinian Anglican priest who founded Sabeel. Ateek was eight years old in 1948, the year that Jewish forces expelled his family from their home, their church, and their village. His book recounts how his experience of dispossession and occupation had shaped his life and forged his faith. I read the book in one sitting, gripped by the story of this Palestinian who was dispossessed by my people the year I was born. I realized that I was reading my story—*my other story*—the one I had not been told but that was mine, nonetheless. After recounting his personal narrative, Ateek dives right into the theology that has guided his ministry, tracing a direct line from the Old Testament prophets to Jesus of Nazareth. The questions, and the answers, came quickly. Did I believe in the prophets' call for justice? Had I not been taught that the core of my Jewishness was a commitment to equality and to compassion for humankind? I realized that the outrage I was experiencing about the violations of human rights I had witnessed was the most Jewish thing I had ever felt, and that working for justice in Palestine was *the most Jewish thing that I could do.*

It was a beautiful, miraculous irony. Here I was, a Jewish man who as a child had been instructed not even to enter a church because Christians were dangerous, for whom the name Jesus evoked feelings not of joy and devotion, but of fear. Now I was discovering that in his ministry, Jesus exemplified what I as a Jew held as most valuable and sacred: respect for human rights and the dignity and equality of all humankind. And it was the suffering Palestinian Christians, and in particular the writings of an Anglican priest, that had opened me to this missing and precious part of myself!

Walking the ground of the Holy Land at this particular moment in its history, I could not avoid the striking parallels between our own time and the first-century context in which Jesus' ministry took place. The Palestine into which Jesus was born was a land in which an indigenous population of shepherds, farmers, tradespeople, scholars, and spiritual leaders suffered under the tyranny of the Roman Empire, where popular resistance was put down by brutal military force. It hit me, with a force as strong as the Mediterranean sun beating down on me as I walked those streets and those hills that summer, that this described the situation in Palestine today, but the oppressed were the Palestinians, and the oppressor was, ironically and tragically, the government of Israel, supported by the United States and its Western allies. I was not only "walking where Jesus walked," but also *seeing what he saw.* And I was coming to know him as a Jew who, out of love for his people, his tradition, and his God, led a movement to nonviolently oppose the power structure, both Roman and Jewish, that was acting in opposition to the core principles of his faith. I was coming to realize that we needed, urgently, to turn to his teachings. I understood now, perhaps for the first time, what I had read about theology being a response to the "signs of the times"—rooted in and responding to history. I realized that it is precisely when the political system fails to bring about the required changes in human affairs—in fact, when the political system *is* the problem—that we must look, as did the oppressed Jews of Jesus' time, not to military force or political maneuvering, but to the spiritual guidance of prophetic leaders. I realized that, reading the signs of our times, we needed Jesus now more than ever.

Looking in the Mirror

Jerusalem is a city of ancient stones. They speak powerfully. I confronted one such stone as I turned a corner in the labyrinth of the Old City's Jewish Quarter. Someone had painted the blue-and-white flag of the State of Israel on the wall enclosing the narrow street. Affixed to the wall just below this patriotic image was a plaque on which were engraved the following words:

ON THIS SPOT ELHANAN AARON ATTALI—MAY HIS MEMORY BE A BLESSING—
WAS MURDERED AT THE HANDS OF THE SONS OF EVIL.
IN HIS BLOOD WE WILL LIVE ON,
AND WE WILL REDEEM JERUSALEM.
"REMEMBER WHAT AMALEK DID TO YOU ON YOUR WAY OUT OF EGYPT!"

Elhanan Attali was a student at a yeshiva, a Jewish educational institution that focuses on study of traditional texts, who was murdered in the Old City in 1991. Israeli police believe that Attali was attacked by Palestinians, but no one has ever been formally charged. There had been anger and tension in this neighborhood around disputes over a nearby Palestinian property that had been taken over by a yeshiva. Palestinians claimed that this was part of a pattern of encroachment by Orthodox Jews into the Christian and Muslim neighborhoods of the Old City.

In traditional Judaism, the Amalekites are the symbol for evil, for the perpetual threat to our survival. Amalek represents the enemy that in every age seeks to destroy us. The reference is to an incident during the exodus, in which the Israelites were attacked from the rear and without warning by this Canaanite tribe. The full quote from Deuteronomy reads as follows:

Remember what Amalek did to you on the way as you came out of Egypt—how he attacked you on the way when you were faint and weary, and cut off your tail, those who were lagging behind you, and he did not fear God. Therefore when the Lord your God has given you rest from all your enemies around you, in the land that the Lord your God is giving you for an inheritance to possess, you shall blot out the memory of Amalek from under heaven; you shall not forget.

(Deuteronomy 25:17–19)

Apparently, Amalek was still with us, and I was never to forget. Who, I asked myself, were these people who were so thirsty for vengeance, so ready to project this ancient, iconic enmity onto the Palestinian people? How had the project to restore our dignity and independence as a people turned into a project driven by fear and hatred? What could expressions such as this have to do with "redeeming" Jerusalem? We seemed to be in the territory not of Sinai and the Mosaic covenant, but of the Book of Joshua—a narrative of war, conquest, and domination. And yet, in the midst of my shock and horror, I understood the sentiment all too well. What had stopped me in my tracks, what held me rooted to the spot in that narrow passage in the ancient city, was the realization that, staring at that message of hatred and fear, I was looking in the mirror. As a Jew raised on equal portions of the stories of victimhood (Egyptian bondage, millennia of persecution, Nazi genocide) and triumph (liberation from bondage, conquest of the Promised Land of Canaan, survival despite the millennia of persecution, establishment of the State of Israel), I understood the complex sources of the fearful message on that memorial. Furthermore, as an American schooled in our contemporary narrative of the "war on terror," I also recognized the message of fear of the Other. Were we not enjoined as Americans to wage war on a people who, we had been told, embrace a strange God and a dark, violent religion that teaches them to "hate our freedom"?

I was looking in the mirror at every turn. One evening, on a recent visit to the region, returning from a family gathering in the north of Israel, I arrived at the central bus station in West Jerusalem. I was bound for Ramallah, in the Palestinian West Bank, five miles to the north. The route lay through Arab East Jerusalem, via the Palestinian bus depot where I would catch the bus to Ramallah. I needed a taxi to get from the west to the east side, perhaps a half mile away. But it was not easy to find a West Jerusalem taxi driver who would take me across the line to the east side—enemy territory to most West Jerusalemites. I finally secured one, the dispatcher assuring him that he had only to travel one short block over that invisible border into the east side, deposit me there, and return to safety. On the short ride, I chatted with the driver, discovering that he was a recent Jewish immigrant from the former Soviet Union and that, given his birthplace, our grandparents could easily have been related. Then he changed the subject, asking me what I was doing in East Jerusalem. (Translation: *What business does a Jew like you have over "there"?*) I hadn't planned to get into politics with him—I was tired, and focused on getting to my destination—so I didn't tell him about Ramallah. Instead I concocted a story about meeting an international journalist at a popular gathering spot in East Jerusalem. But politics is a subject not easily avoided in the Holy Land. After a short silence, my driver said, "I don't like them, these cousins of ours." This was an interesting statement: he was referring, of course, to the Palestinians, but he identified them as family! Resigned now to this conversation, I asked him, "Why don't you like them?"

"They are dirty and they are thieves" was his reply.

Rather than directly challenge his statement, I took an indirect approach: "It's not easy for them," I pointed out. "After all, we came here and took their land." This statement was met with outrage by my Russian Israeli friend. This land, of course, was "ours"; it could not possibly be "their" land. Exiting the taxi, I made one last attempt: "You come from the Soviet Union. So you know what propaganda is, right?"

Right. "Have you considered that your current government is also feeding you propaganda?" Leaving him, fairly sure that this "cousin of mine" was not about to give this proposition serious consideration, I felt deep sadness. I was sad about what this man's worldview showed about what my people had come to in our search for security and safety. But crossing the street to the terminal and boarding the bus marked "Ramallah" ("Hills of God" in Arabic), I was comforted. I was greeted in Arabic by the bus driver and offered a cigarette. In my less-than-minimal Arabic, I exchanged greetings with women in head scarves carrying sacks of oranges on their way to the refugee camp three miles up the road. Having made it to the east side, I felt strangely, and improbably, at home. And then my sadness returned as I considered that my taxi driver, a Russian Jew who, but for an accident of history, could have been me, would no sooner have crossed that East Jerusalem street and entered that bus than he would have stepped off the edge of a cliff.

It is also true that six short years ago, apart from the overt racism he had expressed, the similarities between this man and me would have outweighed the differences. I might not have been as terrified as he, but I would have been reluctant to climb aboard that Palestinian bus, to enter that world of strangers and enemies. This attitude was still in evidence when I first began to interact with Palestinians on that initial visit to the West Bank in the summer of 2006. Sitting with individuals or a family group, I would open the conversation with "full disclosure": I'm a Jew, and I'm from "over there," the other side of that line. And the response would always be the same: "Why do you feel the need to tell us this? We know that you are a Jew. You are welcome here." Thank you for coming, they were saying to me, for crossing the line, for acknowledging our humanity and our presence here.

I remember one young man in particular, twenty-one-year-old Awad. He reminded me of my son Jacob: brown curly hair; wide, deep, intense eyes; a tall frame; strong hands. Awad was completing a degree in accounting at Bethlehem University. After he graduated, there would be virtually no chance for a job in occupied Palestine. He did not want to leave his family or his hometown, but he told me, "There is no future for me here." This young man was angry, frustrated, even bitter. *But he did not hate me.* And he did not fear me. This was not so, I realized, with most of my Jewish family and friends in Israel, who, informed that I would be traveling to Ramallah, or Bethlehem, or the hills of Jenin, told me that I was crazy, that I was at risk of being killed by the murderous people who lived on the other side of that line. (Otherwise, why the wall?)

Planting the Seeds

So how was it that I was sitting in a living room in Bethlehem and not safely "at home" in a café in Tel Aviv or in a Jewish home in West Jerusalem? What had brought me here? What had allowed me to cross over? At the time, in the midst of this stressful and miraculous transformation, it hadn't occurred to me to ask the question. Given time for reflection, however, I have come to understand that the seeds that had produced this fruit were planted long ago.

My family history as a Jewish American is unusual. The great majority of Jewish citizens of the United States today are descendants of the two million Jews who emigrated from eastern Europe between 1881 and 1924. My father's parents were part of this huge influx. But my mother's father was born in Palestine, in the Old City of Jerusalem around 1900, literally in the shadow of the Temple Mount, a site revered as holy by Jews for centuries. He was the fifth generation of a well-known Hasidic (ultra-Orthodox) family that had immigrated to the Holy Land in the nineteenth century. His arranged marriage to my grandmother, the daughter of a devout Jew from Philadelphia, was his ticket out of the poverty of Jerusalem. They proudly raised their four children as Americans, but instilled in them a deep connection to their Jewish roots. My grandfather may have left the Holy Land, but the heart of the family remained in Jerusalem. Two of his four children and several grandchildren have immigrated to Israel. My mother's younger sister Sylvia was the first, having emigrated to Palestine in 1947 as part of the wave of American Jews committed to the realization of the Zionist dream that was unfolding in the wake of the Nazi Holocaust. Sylvia joined Hashomer Hadati, a religious Zionist organization; adopted her Hebrew name, Yaffa; and hopped on a boat to become, in Zionist parlance, a *halutza*—a pioneer. There she met and married a Czech refugee, one of the few from his family to escape Hitler, and settled down to build the Jewish homeland.

It was the summer of 1965. I was seventeen, on my first visit to Israel as part of a Jewish youth group pilgrimage, and I was meeting my Israeli family for the first time. I was sitting on my aunt Yaffa's porch in K'far Haroeh, a religious agricultural village on a hill overlooking Israel's coastal plain. A large dome-roofed yeshiva situated at the highest point dominated the settlement, which was dotted with citrus groves and simple stucco homes. It was the Israel of the picture books and novels of my childhood. I had met my grandfather's brothers, who looked like him (and like me) and were warm and loving to the grandson of the one who had deserted the Holy Land for the "golden streets" of America. I was the boy who had "come home." Seventeen years of religious training and education in language, history, and culture had clicked into place. Proud of the miracle of modern Israel, of what my people had done to create this vibrant country out of the ashes of Auschwitz, I was—there is no better way to put it—in love.

My aunt, her three children, and I were sitting together eating a meal. They were talking about "the Arabs." I don't remember the context of the conversation. But I do remember the tone and the attitude: it was the way whites in Philadelphia talked about black people in the pre–civil rights era in which I had grown up. I knew there were Arabs in the land—we didn't talk about "Palestinians" then—but in the story I had been told, they figured only as the enemies who had been defeated in the war and who continued to threaten the security of the young state. And in that moment, hearing the racism, and understanding, at some level, the fear that lay under the surface, I knew there was more to the story. In that moment, in the midst of my flush of enchantment and delight at the miracle of the Jewish state, and in the midst of the warmest family love I had ever experienced, I knew there was a problem, a fatal flaw in the Zionist dream. The dream that had produced the storybook land of kibbutzim and cities of white stone and black-hatted men free to recreate their Old World of spirit and study was built on a shaky foundation, a foundation of denial. There were other people here; they were here when we arrived from the shores of an inhospitable, murderous Europe. I knew this, and I also could see that, in this ingathering of my blood, these "others" didn't count. And I knew somehow, even then, that this fundamental flaw would grow and ultimately overtake the dream of independence and security.

A seed had been planted.

Five years later, I took time off after college and lived for a year on a kibbutz in the Galilee. It was a wonderful way to connect with my Jewishness, embrace the Zionist dream, and reject the piety of my synagogue upbringing all at the same time. Like most kibbutzim, this one was officially secular: no evocation of the pious "ghetto Jew" of Europe would intrude on the ideal, egalitarian, socialist society that had been established. Living on this beautiful hill in the upper Galilee, I managed to remain unaware of the fact that, until 1948, this had been a Palestinian village, its original inhabitants driven out, their descendants now confined to squalid refugee camps in Lebanon. I ignored the remains of the pre-1948 Palestinian houses still in evidence on the kibbutz grounds and the ancient, now unharvested olive trees standing at the edges of its fields and roads. I was not able, however, to banish from my memory a meeting that took place that year with a Palestinian family living in a small town just down the road, a family displaced when their village, the remains of which lay in sight of my kibbutz, was turned into a pile of rubble. They told me how, following their expulsion by Jewish forces in 1948, they had returned again and again to their homes, despite being told by the Israeli army that their being there was a "security risk." Finally, the family told me, the village was dynamited. "Golda blew up our village!" was the way they put it. *Golda? My Golda Meir,* the hero of my people, along with David Ben-Gurion, the architect of the State of Israel and its first prime minister? *My Golda* was throwing people out of their homes, stealing their farms, dynamiting their villages?

Another seed had been planted.

Sacred Ground

Jerusalem is full of memorials. Not long after my confrontation with the Attali plaque, our delegation visited another, much larger memorial, one of the most famous in Israel if not the world. On a hilltop in the hills west of Jerusalem sits Yad Vashem, Israel's national memorial to the Jewish victims of the Nazi genocide and its museum of the Nazi Holocaust. Approaching the museum, I passed under a huge archway inscribed with the words of the prophet Ezekiel from the famous Vision of the Dry Bones: I WILL PUT MY BREATH INTO YOU AND YOU SHALL LIVE AGAIN AND I WILL SET YOU UPON YOUR OWN SOIL (Ezekiel 37:14). This inscription stopped me in my tracks. I had been in Jerusalem and the West Bank for four days. I was bursting with outrage at what I had seen. I was not feeling close to the redemptive Zionist dream. And there was more to come: since my last visit to Yad Vashem six years before, a new exhibit had been constructed, one that confronts you as soon as you enter.

I stood before a huge map of central and eastern Europe. Across this map was projected a photographic panorama of the lost world of the Jews of Europe: artisans, musicians, laborers, teachers, villages, houses of study, children. All gone. The movie ended with a photograph of a choir of Jewish children, somewhere in Europe, singing the Zionist hymn "Hatikvah" ("The Hope"), which now serves as the national anthem of the State of Israel.

I was shattered. A hand had reached into me, grabbed hold of my heart, and drawn me back into my past, into the collective memory of my people. Yes, I was upset with what I had seen going on in the West Bank, but how could I turn my back on my own history; from this incalculable, unfathomable loss; or, more so, from Israel, my deliverance? It had worked—I was hooked. What was I to do now? I had no choice. Emptied, numb, and confused, I turned and walked down the hall into the museum.

It's a brilliant exhibition. The space is subterranean—no windows, no light, no escape. One walks *down into it.* You are led along corridors and tunnels, with no way out but through. One traverses the whole familiar story: from the anti-Jewish laws enacted in the thirties; the walls of isolation, privation, and degradation closing in; to the Final Solution: the ovens, the stacked bodies, the faces of the starving, terrified children. Darkness closes your heart; you feel you will never escape from this place of evil and despair. And just when you feel overwhelmed by the horror, you turn a corner and find yourself in the final gallery, where the miracle is on display. There hang blown-up photos of the ships bringing the refugees to the shores of Israel, faces shining with hope and gratitude. There is pictured David Ben-Gurion reading from the Israeli Declaration of Independence as the State of Israel is born. Then, suddenly, ascending a wide flight of stairs, you emerge into the light and the open air, standing on a wide patio that looks out on the Jerusalem Hills. *It's the final exhibit.* And then it hit me—this was no mere museum. This was a lesson, this was indoctrination: from the biblical quote at the entrance, into the depths, and to this sight. Our Land. Our reward. Our destiny.

As we left the museum, my fellow delegate Diane turned to me. Had I seen what she had just seen, she asked? Had I realized that the policies of dispossession, marginalization, and humiliation we had witnessed in recent days were reminiscent of the ways that Jews were treated after the Nazi Party took power, in the years before the extermination camps and the ovens? Yes, I answered, I had seen. And at that moment something very deep inside me let go.

Treading, as I had so many times, the sacred ground of the Nazi Holocaust, I had for the first time broken *the Rule: Our* Holocaust, *the* Holocaust, must not be compared to any other disaster or genocide. It has to stand as the ultimate crime against humanity. I had also broken a rule not often articulated but nevertheless fully in force: One may never compare Israeli policy to Nazi crimes. The comparison has been called "obscene." I now know that what is obscene is to deny the comparison, to say, "This is *them*—this cannot be us."

I realized how dangerous this rule was to the Jewish psyche, and to any group or individual claiming an exceptional right to victimhood. I saw this mentality in the separation wall. I saw it in a Jerusalem being taken, stone by stone, neighborhood by neighborhood, by my own people seeking to establish their spiritual redemption and physical security at the expense of the Palestinians. To close one's eyes to this evil—that was the obscenity.

Leaving the museum that day, I now knew how to understand the calamity of the Nazi Holocaust in the context of contemporary Jewish experience. Even though I had been born three years after the defeat of the Third Reich, the murder of six million of my people would continue to be a formative historical event in my life. But now, finding the meaning of this tragedy for my people meant working for justice for Palestine. There were too many parallels, too many ways in which Israel was doing to the Palestinians what the Nazis had done to us. No, we had not built extermination camps. But we were turning into beasts, and we were killing a civilization.

The Charge

One Friday evening, on the last weekend of our tour, our interfaith delegation attended a Jewish worship service in West Jerusalem. The synagogue we visited caters to American Jews visiting or living in Israel. It was established by the United Synagogue of Conservative Judaism, an American Jewish denomination occupying a midpoint between Orthodox and Reform Judaism, the denomination in which I had grown up. Friday night is the traditional ushering in of the Sabbath, which, like all Jewish holy days, begins at sunset. It's a beautiful service, infused with a joyful, mystical spirit. The service opens with the singing of psalms and medieval hymns extolling the divine activities of renewal and contemplation that we imitate in observing the commandment to rest, as God did, on the seventh day. As the service began, I felt myself drawn into the singing and the spirit.

At that point, a large group entered; I didn't know them personally, but I knew who they were. It was a group of Jewish teenagers on a summer tour sponsored by this same American-Jewish denomination. They took up a section at the front of the room and began to sing enthusiastically, lifting up their voices and their arms to heaven, ecstatically welcoming the Sabbath in the style of the medieval Kabbalists. My heart froze. I was looking at myself, forty years earlier, a seventeen-year-old on the same synagogue-sponsored tour. I turned to Maia, one of our delegation leaders, a Quaker woman who had worked for peace in Palestine for many years, and whispered to her, "I know this group. They are in love with their Judaism and they are in love with Jerusalem. The Palestinians don't exist for them. They would see them dead for the pleasure of celebrating their Judaism in their Jerusalem." Maia simply looked at me and nodded her head; she understood.

It was an emotionally violent response; I had surprised myself. Several members of our delegation who had overheard my comment to Maia—the story had gotten around—were horrified by what I had said, and angry at me. To be sure, my characterization of these kids was unfair: I didn't know them. This was "my stuff" talking—my own anger and shame, my still-to-be-resolved feelings about how I had been programmed as a child. I was close to certain that the teenagers I was watching had not seen what I had seen and were not aware of what had happened and was still happening to the Palestinians of Jerusalem. But this was partly the point: they had been indoctrinated into the Zionist narrative, as I had been in my youth. Unaware of the cost paid for their "Jewish" Jerusalem by the Palestinian people, were they not complicit?

After the service, I sat with our Palestinian guide, Said. We had grown close over the two weeks we'd been together. I described to him what had happened in the synagogue, explaining to him how intense it had been to look in the mirror in this way, and I repeated my statement, but now making it very personal: "They would see you dead, Said, for the privilege of worshiping in their Jerusalem." He was silent, taking this in calmly. He, too, understood.

"These are my people," I said. "This is who I am returning to."

Said answered, "Then you know what you have to do."

I accepted the charge. But I had no idea what form that would take. I had nothing but questions about what to do with my newfound knowledge and strong feelings. But back home, the answers were waiting for me.

Chapter 4
WELCOME TO OUR SYNAGOGUE

Carrying out the charge from my Palestinian friend was to prove difficult. Returning to the United States, I encountered a state of affairs that was just as disturbing as what I had seen in the West Bank. I spoke to anyone from my Jewish community who would listen, explaining that our homeland project was deeply flawed, and that instead of redeeming ourselves from suffering and insecurity, we had put ourselves at enormous risk. There is another story of 1948, I explained, and it's the Palestinian story, and we had better learn that other story and do something about it before it was too late.

But the mainstream Jewish community was closed to my message. What I was saying about Israel was unacceptable, simply not to be countenanced. The most charitable characterization of my position was that I was "naïve," manipulated by people and forces who wished us ill. The arguments varied, but they were all based on a single assumption: defending the Jewish state had to be the paramount concern. Yes, it was unfortunate that innocent Palestinians had to suffer, but concern for Israel's security trumped all other considerations. The wall was regrettable, but it kept Israel safe from terrorism.[1] And finally: Israel was not perfect, but allowing criticism of Israel to surface would give aid and support to those who sought our destruction. Didn't I realize that anti-Semitism was everywhere, that we had to defend ourselves against the implacable hatred of our enemies? Besides, even if we were to acknowledge that the Palestinians had been dispossessed, how could we consider remedying their plight without destroying the Jewish character (i.e., the Jewish majority) of Israel?

Yes, a small number of rabbis were beginning to speak out, and organizations of Jewish activists were devoted to challenging Israel's human rights abuses and our government's policy of supporting this behavior. But the established Jewish community—the religious denominations, the philanthropic and social service agencies, the advocacy and watchdog groups, the political action committees—were arrayed to silence any word of dissent or questioning of the basic assumptions of political Zionism. They would fight, and fight hard, to protect the no-strings-attached financial and diplomatic support Israel enjoyed. Any person, especially a fellow Jew, who challenged the dominant narrative of a vulnerable Israel beset by powerful enemies faced a juggernaut of opposition, buttressed by accusations of anti-Semitism.

It was painful to be met with these reactions from my own community. But alongside the hurt and outrage I was feeling, I was becoming aware of something else: something stronger even than the glow of anger at the rejection by my own community, or the shame and horror over what I had seen. It was a yearning, but one very different from that expressed by

"Hatikvah." Was it possible, I wondered, that we Jews, who insisted on seeing the State of Israel as a prize awarded to us as a privileged, exclusive group, might open ourselves to a new vision? Could we learn to embrace an idea bigger and more sustainable than achieving our "redemption" through political power and military might? I wanted the society that had been created in Israel to retain its Jewish character, but also for it to lay claim to a vision that was bigger than the right granted by the Jews to themselves more than a hundred years ago to a national homeland in historic Palestine.

At Yad Vashem, I had begun to grasp what that vision might be. I realized that the meaning of the Holocaust was not to retreat behind ever higher walls of protection, but rather, to open our hearts to the universality of human suffering, and to our obligation, as part of humanity, to relieve it. I knew that being liberated from a history of oppression and suffering could not be achieved through the trampling of another people's dignity or the denial of their human rights. I could see that the nationalist project that was supposed to keep us safe wasn't working. As Israel continued to take Palestinian land and turn an indigenous people into a subject population, it was becoming increasingly isolated in the world. And Israeli society was suffering. I knew that Israelis could never build a healthy society based on the conviction that the world was a hostile place and that a second Holocaust was waiting around the next bend in the road. The more I understood the madness of this so-called solution to the problem of anti-Semitism, the more urgently I felt the need to do something about it. I had to act, both out of my concern for Israel and because of my personal outrage at the human rights abuses I had seen. It appeared, however, that I was not to be granted a hearing by the people I wanted most to reach.

The Church Opens Its Doors—and Its Heart

The Jewish establishment was dug in—stubbornly, blindly, and, in my view, tragically—refusing to acknowledge the catastrophic wrongness of Israel's course. I mourned this, and frankly, it scared me. But I was not to be given the opportunity to brood. As is often true, when one door closes, another opens. Even as I was encountering the resistance of the Jewish community, I made a discovery that changed my life.

The group I had traveled with in Israel and the West Bank was mostly Christian. We had made a covenant to speak about our experience when we returned to the United States. My new friends, therefore, began to set up speaking engagements for me at local churches. And an extraordinary thing happened: *the doors were flung open*. I found that Christians, like most Americans, were ignorant of what had happened to the Palestinians in 1948 and were equally unaware of the oppressive conditions under which Palestinians currently lived. When my audiences heard about the historic and present injustices visited upon the Palestinians, they responded as they would have to the story of any oppressed people. As I spoke in church after church, I sensed a deep passion for justice and a largely untapped store of commitment to this cause. I began to realize how important the church could be in breaking the political deadlock that was so disastrous, not only for the Palestinians, but also for the Jewish people.

But a huge barrier stood in the way of churches taking up this particular human rights cause. Everywhere I went I encountered Christians who gratefully received my message that something had to be done about Israel's mistreatment of the Palestinians, but who felt that because the church bore such a heavy responsibility for Jewish suffering, they could not say or do anything that might hurt the Jewish state, or that might even be perceived as critical of Israel. This was brought home to me in one of my very first presentations soon after returning to the United States.

I gave a talk in a historic church in downtown Washington, DC, a congregation well known for its commitment to human rights and social justice, both at home and abroad. I spoke openly about the horror I had experienced witnessing Israel's human rights violations, about my heartbreak and fear for my people. I charted my "conversion" from a Jew critical of some of Israel's policies but supportive of the Zionist vision to one who now was having serious doubts about the Zionist project itself. I said that I saw the dispossession of the Palestinians in 1948 and the ongoing colonization of Palestinian lands since 1967 as the root cause of the conflict, and that I was committed to seeking justice for the Palestinian people as the only path to peace.

The pastor of the church attended the presentation and listened intently. Afterward, he walked up to me and said that while he agreed that the human rights of Palestinians were being abridged, and that he admired me for speaking out, he felt that in talking about the situation, we had to be sensitive to the feelings of Jews. "What do you mean?" I asked. He answered, "As a pastor, I have studied church history, and I feel personally responsible for the Nazi Holocaust. I have been involved in social justice work for my entire career, including years working with an interfaith group of Christian, Muslim, and Jewish clergy. Until recently, Israel and the Palestinians simply didn't come up. But when the issue of the Presbyterian Church's divestment of its pension funds from companies involved in the Israeli occupation was raised in 2004, we decided not to push the issue, out of sensitivity for the rabbis in the group who were opposing divestment."

There are moments when you speak words you didn't know were in you. "Pastor," I said, "you need to do something else with your Christian guilt. We Jews are in big trouble with our national homeland project. Closing our eyes to it is the worst thing we can do. The rabbis who will not engage with you in an honest discussion about Israel and Zionism are not being friends of Israel. Israel is rapidly becoming isolated in the world and increasingly seen as a rogue state, pursuing racist and colonialist policies, and as a threat to peace in the region if not to the world at large.[2] If we Jews can't see this, then we are all the more in need of your help as a Christian leader and as a worker for justice and peace. And Christians, *especially* clergy, who are silencing themselves are not being friends to the Jewish people. We need you to speak up, not enable the muzzling!" He stared back at me, and even I was momentarily struck dumb. Where was this coming from? But it seemed I wasn't finished; my next words surprised me even more. "Pastor," I said, "as an American and as a clergyman, this must become your cause. Holding back is not what Jesus would want you to do."

It was my "Road to Damascus" moment. I might as well have been knocked to the ground by a voice from above. At that moment, I realized that I had been given a voice to speak, and an ear to hear. It was a voice that could speak to American Christians who were waking up to the plight of the

Palestinians, who were beginning to see the problems with the storybook narrative of the Jewish state they had been fed for so long. It was a voice to encourage these same Christians to examine the theology that had served to stifle the questions that inevitably arose about the God-given right of the Jews to rule over the other peoples of the land. It was an ear to hear their pained questions. "What should I do?" I hear from person after person who comes up to me after my lectures, "when my Jewish friends, family members, and business associates tell me that I must not question the actions of Israel?" Once, I was approached by a young woman at a church conference who tearfully described how her relationship with her best friend (who was Jewish) was coming apart because of her friend's angry reaction to any reference to Palestinian suffering. I hear from one pastor after another about how, after much hesitation and prayer, he approaches the rabbi he has been working with for years and is told, sometimes gently and sometimes not so gently, to back off: *This is our business, not yours.*

Welcome to Our Synagogue

My encounter with the pastor that day in Washington was the genesis of this book. Despite the audacity of my challenge to him—here was a Jewish psychologist lecturing a Presbyterian pastor about what Jesus expected of him!—the pastor didn't flinch; he neither backed off from his position nor dismissed my challenge. Our encounter that day was the beginning of an ongoing dialogue and a friendship I treasure. It was also a call—a moment that changed my life. To that point, my exposure to religion had been confined to the inside of my Jewish bubble. It was good to connect so powerfully with another faith tradition. I did not regard this as a rejection of Judaism or of my Jewish identity. It was just the opposite: by responding to this call, I have embraced the deepest part of me, the Jewishness I have always felt at my core, the Jew I have been in the process of becoming.

One evening, I found myself speaking to a group in a church sanctuary in New England. Someone asked me (as Christians tend to do; everyone wants to know where you worship) what synagogue I belonged to. The question was unexpected, and so was my immediate, spontaneous answer. I said, "You're sitting in it. This work and this witness is my place of worship. It's how I express my devotion to my faith tradition." We were in a Catholic church. A crucifix was suspended over the altar behind me. I continued: "And I know that the Galilean rabbi and visionary whose image hangs over my right shoulder would fully endorse that statement. So," and with this I opened my arms wide, "welcome to our synagogue!" I saw jaws drop—and then the group broke into applause. And I knew that this approbation was not for me. It was an acknowledgment of the significance of the moment.

Here is what was happening: a faith community was celebrating its devotion to social justice, a fundamental set of values that, although often out of sync with the prevailing political system or national culture, was finding its expression in the embrace of a just cause. I was learning that a fierce, focused commitment to justice was precisely the genesis and spirit of the early church: grassroots outposts of nonviolent resistance to tyranny. These early Christians pursued their faith in small, plucky communities. Gathered in their homes, living in constant fear of discovery and harassment or worse, they were making a stand for their way of life in the midst of the Roman Empire, a civilization and power structure that was attempting to undermine the values of compassion and equality that were the fundamentals of their beliefs and practices.

I have found this justice imperative operating on multiple levels in the American church. I have discovered small but determined pockets of activism in congregational mission committees, in denominational human rights task forces, and in local peace groups, which, if they had not yet taken up the plight of the Palestinians, were ready to place Israel and Palestine at the top of their agenda. This is emerging across a truly ecumenical landscape. It can be seen in progressive Catholic organizations and orders hosting speakers and sending nuns and priests to the Holy Land to defend Palestinian human rights, in the persistent and courageous actions of American Protestant denominations voting on resolutions to divest from companies involved in the occupation of Palestine, and in ecumenical conferences on the struggle for human rights in Palestine and in other places of conflict.

I have met evangelicals who, breaking the stereotype of religious extremists calling for Jewish domination of Jerusalem in order to hasten the End Times, express solidarity with the Palestinian call for justice and visit occupied Bethlehem to show support for Christian and Muslim Palestinians and to better understand their urgent situation. I realized that I was looking at a huge force: deep, wide, and passionate, and poised to take on this cause on a global scale. I recognized it as a movement that would change the politics of the conflict, a force equal in power and commitment to the movement of pastors and community leaders that led the American civil rights movement, and to the worldwide campaign, supported by the global church, to end South African apartheid. I have been inspired, encouraged, and deeply moved by the people I've met, struck by their hunger—there is no better word for it—to become educated about the situation and to find ways to become involved.

Two Questions

I had returned from the Holy Land with a single, burning question: Why are my people doing this? It was soon accompanied by a second, equally urgent question: Why are you, our Christian compatriots, helping us do it? Even though I was filled with hope by what I was seeing at the grassroots level, I was also discovering how powerful, deeply rooted, and widespread were the attitudes that underlay our government's policy of unconditional support for Israel and the general support this policy enjoyed from our society as a whole, including (and perhaps especially) the institutions of religion. I realized that Americans must fundamentally transform the way we understand Israel and Palestine in order to help bring the peace based on justice for Palestinians that is so desperately needed by Israelis and Palestinians alike. I had also begun to understand, beginning with that first interaction with my pastor friend, what a critical role the churches would play as we as a society questioned our support of Israel's policies and turned to action more in line with our cultural and political values and our national interests in the global arena.

As I began to look more deeply into our society's attitudes toward Israel and the Jewish people, I began to understand that these attitudes had become completely intertwined with the beliefs and doctrines we had developed as part of our shared experience. Confronted now with this urgent situation, we needed to ask ourselves about these beliefs: What does God expect of us? Are particular peoples chosen for special treatment, responsibilities, and privileges? Who really "owns" the land, and what does the Bible say about that? How is the Christian world supposed to relate to the Jews in the aftermath of the Nazi Holocaust? What had begun as an exploration of my own personal history in relation to the State of Israel was taking me into the deep waters of theology, church history, and the stories of some of the most powerful and inspiring social, political, and religious movements of our time.

Chapter 5

JESUS AND EMPIRE

P rophets state the obvious.

Sometimes they are sent by God on perplexing and seemingly impossible missions. Sometimes they speak in maddeningly confusing parables. But they always state the obvious, challenging us, as Jesus says in the Gospel of Luke (12:56), to see "the signs of the times," what is plainly before our eyes, as clear and indisputable as the weather.

Jesus often returned in his parables to the image of the widow. The figure of the widow appears in the well-known parable from the Gospel of Mark (12:41–44). It's the perfect Sunday school story, advertised in many Bibles under the heading "The Widow's Offering" or "The Widow's Mite." Jesus has positioned himself at the temple treasury, watching "the multitude putting money into the treasury. Many rich people put in large sums" (12:41). But it is a poor widow, Jesus tells his disciples, who has given the most by putting in her last penny, "everything she had, her whole living" (literally, "her whole life") (12:44).

Her whole life. This is not a pietistic homily on the humility of the widow, who out of her devotion to God gives her last penny to the temple. It is, rather, *a devastating critique of the system that takes the last penny,* the last crumb of resources from this person who has lost the support conferred by the patriarchal system, a society member who should be supported, not abandoned to grinding poverty. Where is the safety net for such as these? What kind of a society is this, where one of the most vulnerable, the most in need of support, is seen giving up her last crumb to the temple tribute system? Jesus declares that pouring money into the treasury has no value. The money is not going to feed the people. If it were, then where has this poor widow come from? She has come to reveal the truth about this tyrannous system.

Following his encounter with the widow, Jesus' confrontation with the tyranny of empire continues. Upset and outraged—notice how hanging around the temple tends to produce that reaction in Jesus—he walks out of the temple for the last time, and we find ourselves in this famous scene outside its walls:

The apostles—remember, these are simple Galilean country folk—are awestruck by the temple's grandeur, taken in by the scale and the majesty: "Look, teacher," they cry, "what wonderful buildings, what stones!"

"Do you see these great buildings?" Jesus replies. "Not one stone will be left here upon another, all will be thrown down" (Mark 13:1–2). *Jesus is making a political statement.* This is not my kingdom, he proclaims, not this world of greed and taxation, of grinding poverty alongside obscene wealth. My kingdom, he is saying, has nothing to do with invoking the divine covenant as a real estate contract, a license to steal, the making of my house into a marketplace. What Jesus is literally "deconstructing" is the very idea that God lives in a house or on a particular mountain (i.e., that any particular piece of territory is holy). Like the prophets, Jesus carried out his ministry in the tension between the brutal domination of kings and emperors and the enduring values of the Mosaic code—the law of God. Jesus was born into an imperial system, an occupation that represented the worst evil the world had ever known. The Gospels are the record of his ministry to the people groaning under that yoke. The story from Mark situates us in the very heart of that system. Jesus positions himself "opposite" the temple treasury (in the Greek, *kateante*, the position of judgment), where he can see everything that is going on, sitting in witness of the signs of the times.

Jesus Faces Down the Powers

Dr. Richard Horsley is professor of religion at the University of Massachusetts. He has devoted his career to understanding how the Gospels tell the story of a movement of nonviolent resistance to massive, systemic injustice. One day in 2012, we sat in the dining room of his home in Boston, the manuscript of his latest book spread out on the table. "The Bible tells a story, but not the one we learned in Sunday school!" Horsley said to me, as if he had just discovered this truth and couldn't wait to tell me more. "Read the Gospel of Mark start to finish. It comes to life! What's the main plot? It's not discipleship. The main plot is Jesus versus the rulers. Jeremiah, centuries earlier—same thing. He was telling the king not to throw in with the Babylonian Empire; it will ultimately destroy you!"[1]

Horsley understands the Gospels as the record of a grassroots movement responding to the catastrophic effects of Roman occupation on the culture and faith of the indigenous culture of first-century Palestine. He provides a vivid description of the systematic domination of Rome over Palestine in the centuries before and after Jesus' birth, showing how Jesus used his ministry to respond to the abuses of the Roman system. The Roman Empire extended its geographic reach and maintained its power by exploiting its subject populations through military occupation; economic control; and, in the case of revolt or noncooperation, brutal, terrorizing suppression. He points out that in the first century, the modern distinction between religion and politics did not exist. Over the centuries, however, in the process of transforming Christianity into an established religion and subsequently into the favored religion of the empire, the original thrust of Jesus' message was lost or distorted. In Horsley's terms, the Gospels have been *depoliticized*.

"I want to put religion and politics back together again," he told me. "Jesus faces down the rulers. This is what a prophet does. In the Gospel of Mark, it's one confrontation after another, and Jesus takes the initiative. He's the leader of a movement, making pronouncements and doing demonstrations, speaking truth to power—which the people didn't dare to do because of the threat of overwhelming violence. But when someone stands up to oppression, it inspires followers to resist also."[2]

Renewing Israel

In Horsley's view, the biblical Kingdom of God is a program for the renewal of Israel, the establishment of a social and political order that directly addressed the crushing economic and political injustices under which Jesus and his people were living. The Roman regime was, by design, destroying the original fabric of Jewish society, replacing it with a colonial society organized around the feeding of the increasingly hungry beast of a growing empire. In his 2003 book, *Jesus and Empire: The Kingdom of God and the New World Disorder,* Horsley points out that the farmers and villagers of the Palestine of Jesus' time "knew very well that many of their number were being transformed from freeholders farming their own ancestral land into tenants of the wealthy rulers and their officers who had taken effective control of those lands."[3] The driving force, therefore, behind Jesus' teachings was support for the peasants of Galilee against the damage to their families, health, psyches, and communities caused by the terrorizing oppression of Rome, with the active collaboration of Rome's client rulers in Judea and Galilee. In other words, Jesus was leading a popular resistance movement. Its purpose was to support the values and lifestyle of the agrarian, community-based society of first-century Palestine against the structure of control being imposed by Rome and its client government of king and temple. "My kingdom is not of this world," Jesus declares (John 18:36). The Greek word in that famous statement that is usually translated as "world" is *kosmos.* But *kosmos* translates more accurately as "system" or "order." Jesus was calling his suffering people to resist the oppressive *system* that had taken control of their lives by holding fast to their core beliefs and building community and political life in accordance with principles of love and compassion. Jesus was affirming that God calls us to a life centered on social justice.

"Recognition that Jesus' mission was primarily in opposition to Roman imperial rule poses a challenge to the standard, older construction of 'Jesus as opposed to Judaism,'" Horsley told me. Far from being about opposition to Judaism or an effort to "replace" Judaism with a new religion, Jesus' message was about a return to the core principles of the Mosaic covenant, which were dedicated to everything that Rome was not: equal distribution of resources, respect for human life and dignity, and compassion for the most vulnerable. "The Mosaic covenant," Horsley writes, "was, in effect, a constitution, a constituting set of principles for early Israel as an independent agrarian people. Economic and political relations were integral to the covenant and utterly inseparable from the religious dimension."[4]

The troubled history of the church in relation to Judaism and the Jewish people has tended to lead us away from this key truth: that Jesus was calling the people to a life of faithfulness to Judaism—not suggesting that the faith be "replaced" by another. In *The Shadow of the Empire: Reclaiming the Bible as a History of Faithful Resistance,* Horsley explains that the early Church's understanding of a Jesus opposed to Judaism was "simply unhistorical. It began with Christians' shameful early attempts to shield themselves from Roman persecution by distancing themselves from "the Jews" who had rebelled against and been defeated by the Romans in the years 6–70 CE. But at the time of Jesus, Christianity had not yet emerged as a religion separate from Judaism. In fact Jesus' opposition to Roman imperial rule belonged to the more general Judean and Galilean opposition that took the forms of protests, strikes, movements, and widespread revolts, by scribal groups and Jerusalemites as well as by peasants. As with those protests and movements, Jesus was deeply rooted in and drew upon a long Israelite tradition of opposition to foreign rule."[5]

This is what Horsley means by calling for the "repoliticization" of the Gospels. "I am pushing for replacement of the concepts of 'early Judaism' and 'early Christianity' with more precise historical references to the Judeans and Galileans living in village communities under the rule of the temple-state in Jerusalem, and Jewish rulers appointed by Rome," Horsley told me. "In this connection, one of the main factors then was the class division between the villagers and their rulers."[6] At the time that Jesus was growing up in the Galilee, these conditions gave rise to intense political unrest, resistance, and rebellion. Indeed, resistance to empire was a fundamental component of Jesus' message. Jesus was not the first leader to advocate resistance, but he was the first to say that it had to be *nonviolent.* This, in some measure, was a pragmatic move: armed resistance to Rome was suicidal. (Horsley and others speculate that Jesus would have witnessed the horrendous Roman suppression of the popular revolts in the early decades of the first century CE.) Rather, Jesus' message was about an alternative lifestyle that returned to God-given principles governing human relations. It was about supporting the growth of the *ecclesia,* the small gatherings of the faithful firmly based in the everyday life of the indigenous community. The model of *ecclesia* was, after all, the communal system instituted by Paul throughout the Mediterranean basin during the early years of Christianity. The references to food and to forgiveness in the Lord's Prayer, for example, are concerned not with duties to God, theological principles, or ritual observance. Rather, the prayer speaks directly to relationships between people: forgiving indebtedness (indebtedness having been the chief mechanism, along with taxes, of forced impoverishment and land-taking used by the Romans and their client rulers), feeding people, and social justice. "Thy will be done *on earth*" is the point of the prayer prescribed by Jesus to his followers. An understanding of the Gospels in which devotion to God is inseparable from direct action in the world also forms the basis of modern theories of nonviolent direct action, a topic that we will turn to in coming chapters.

The New Rome

Horsley also sees compelling and urgent parallels between the Roman Empire and modern U.S. policy. "Just as Rome put Herod in place in his palace and put the high priest in place in the temple, so the U.S. support and military aid for despotic regimes, and its own military and economic adventures throughout its history, are clearly doing the same thing,"[7] Horsley told me, not hesitating to draw the contemporary parallel. "In our early American history, America saw itself as the new Rome, and the church was the cheerleader for that. The Christian denominations in America's early history put that out very strongly. So supporting empire is in the church DNA! Even though the Mosaic covenant is counter to all that, the church is still finding ways to support the status quo rather than staying true to its legacy, its birth."[8]

Yes, Horsley judges America's record on the world stage harshly. And he is critical of the part played by the religious establishment in that history. But he is not out to bash the church. Look again at his words: he calls on the church to stay "true to its legacy, its birth." In this he stands in a proud tradition. Horsley is reading the same Bible as an American pastor jailed for civil disobedience in America's South in 1963—and is arriving at the same conclusions. In his "Letter from Birmingham Jail," the Rev. Martin Luther King Jr. laments the failure of the churches to stand up to the racist acts of government officials and to support the "bruised and weary Negro men and women" who were rising up in protest:

> In deep disappointment I have wept over the laxity of the church. But be assured that my tears have been tears of love. There can be no deep disappointment where there is not deep love. Yes, I love the church. How could I do otherwise? I am in the rather unique position of being the son, the grandson and the great-grandson of preachers. Yes, I see the church as the body of Christ. But, oh! How we have blemished and scarred that body through social neglect and through fear of being non-conformists...So often the contemporary church is a weak, ineffectual voice with an uncertain sound. So often it is an archdefender of the status quo. Far from being disturbed by the presence of the church, the power structure of the average community is consoled by the church's silent—and often even vocal—sanction of things as they are.[9]

King is reading the same Bible as Horsley, and it tells him the same story. Like Horsley, King is calling on the church to be the church in our time as it was in its earliest days: facing down the powers and invoking the timeless, God-given principles of compassion and social justice that are the bedrock of the tradition:

There was a time when the church was very powerful—in the time when the early Christians rejoiced at
being deemed worthy to suffer for what they believed.
In those days the church was not merely a thermometer
that recorded the ideas and principles of popular opinion; it was a thermostat that transformed the mores of
society.[10]

Plotting Goodness

A growing number of pastors and theologians today, who
contemplate, as Martin Luther King Jr. did in his day, the
church's "silent—and often even vocal—sanction of things as
they are," are opening up their Bibles and coming to the same
conclusions as historian and scholar Richard Horsley. And
they are calling on the church to reconnect with its roots.

Brian McLaren, a pastor, author, activist, and speaker, is
considered one of the most influential Christian leaders in
America today. The founder and pastor of Cedar Ridge Community Church in Spencerville, Maryland, McLaren now de-
votes himself full time to writing and speaking. As he told me
when we spoke in early 2013, he sees his work as "helping
churches to plan a better future." A prolific writer, McLaren
has authored more than twenty books in which he challenges
Christians, as the title of one of his books reads, to "find
our way again," and to question many of the assumptions,
attitudes, and behaviors that have long dominated the faith
across the ecumenical and political spectrum.

Like Horsley and, more to the point, an increasing number
of Christian clergy, churchgoers, and those who have left off
going to church, McLaren is troubled by the violence and op-

pression the church has supported, perpetrated, or enabled by its silent complicity over the two thousand years of its history. In his 2012 *Why Did Jesus, Moses, the Buddha, and Mohammed Cross the Road?: Christian Identity in a Multi-Faith World*, McLaren ponders the symbolism of the fateful event known as the "Conversion of Constantine." As the story goes, the fourth-century Roman emperor had a vision of a cross in the sky inscribed with the words CONQUER BY THIS.[11] Whatever veracity we grant this story, for McLaren there is a grim significance to this event that prefigured the elevation of Christianity to be the official religion of the Roman Empire. He invites us to

> imagine a different conversion, one that never happened but could have. Instead of a gold-plated, bejeweled spear-cross with the words "Threaten and kill by this," imagine that Constantine had seen a vision of a basin and a towel with the words, "Serve by this," or a vision of a simple table of bread and wine with "Reconcile around this," or a vision of Christ's outstretched arms with "Embrace like this," or a vision of the birds of the air and flowers of the field with "Trust like this," or a vision of a mother hen gathering her chicks with "Love like this," or a vision of a dove descending from heaven with the words, "Be as kind as this." But it was not so.[12]

It's critical that we in the United States consider our history as a civilization, McLaren told me. "We have to look back at all the times we have gotten it perfectly wrong. We were wrong in the way we used the Bible to justify land-taking and attempted genocide of the native peoples. We were wrong in the way we used the Bible to justify a slave-based economy. We were wrong in the way we used the Bible to justify segregation. And before, during, and after those episodes, we were wrong in the way we used the Bible to justify anti-Semitism. And so with all of those grave and long-standing mistakes in our past, I think we have to be especially vigilant not to repeat those errors again."[13] In the following passage, we find McLaren, like Horsley, standing beside Jesus, contemplating the temple built on the sweat and suffering of the people, and asking, "What has happened to my kingdom?" How do we bring our hearts and lives back to the core of our faith? How do we become good with God again?

> As with Columbus in 1492, so with Constantine in 312: the ways we retell our history form our identity. Our Christian histories, like our political ones, shield us from the full truth about how we became who we are, and in so doing, they keep us from seeing ourselves as others see us. Our standard histories support an oppositional identity where "we" are the virtuous ones, the victims, the defenders of truth, the peacemakers, and "they" are the aggressors, the invaders, the heretics, the evil ones...From Constantine to Columbus to the other Conquistadors to the Colonizers to the present, we have mixed authentically Christian elements of love, joy, peace, and reconciliation with strictly imperial elements of superiority, conquest, domination, and hostility. We have created a new religion with an identity far different from the one proclaimed and embodied by Jesus in Galilee, or by James and Peter in Jerusalem, or by Paul around the Mediterranean, or by the Christian scholars

of the second and third centuries. In other words, what we call Christianity today has a history, and this history reveals it as a Roman, imperial version of Christianity.[14]

Reading these words, I am profoundly moved by the understandable, and justified, anger and grief expressed by this pastor at the waste, the sin, and the betrayal of the true and original nature of the church. But I am struck even more by the yearning expressed in McLaren's words—a yearning for a Christianity evocative of what Martin Luther King Jr. was calling for and that, through King's powerful conviction in the truth and power of such a Christianity, created a movement that changed America and continues to inspire and guide struggles against tyranny. It is Horsley reminding us that Jesus' ministry was grounded in an unwavering commitment to the principles of the Mosaic covenant, the same blueprint for a just society that Jesus was spreading out before the congregation on that Sabbath in the synagogue in Nazareth, or, in McLaren's words, "a decentralized, grassroots, spiritual-social movement dedicated to plotting goodness and saving the world from human evil—both personal and systematic."[15] To build such a church today, McLaren says, would mean "proclaiming the same good news of the kingdom of God that Jesus proclaimed. It would mean seeking to do so in the manner Jesus proclaimed it—in word and deed, through art and teaching, in sign and wonder, with clarity and intrigue, with warning and hope."[16]

It is no surprise, therefore, that McLaren has been an advocate for Palestinian rights. When he led a pilgrimage in 2010 to Israel and the Palestinian territories, his blog posting titled "More from the West Bank" created some buzz: "Have you seen Brian McLaren's latest blog? He's an evangelical, and listen to what he's saying about Israel!"

Here is the entry for January 22, 2010:

What a day it was today. Halfway through, many in our group of twenty felt that we couldn't take much more. We've heard heart-shattering stories of Palestinians being arrested without cause, tortured, humiliated, re-arrested, re-tortured... But what is especially powerful—and what keeps us from being overwhelmed with cynicism or anger—is the lack of hatred among the Palestinians we are meeting with, both Christians and Muslims. Again and again we hear the word "nonviolent" and we see a desire not for revenge or even isolation... but for reconciliation... They want to live in peace with Israelis. They want Jews, Muslims, and Christians to learn to live together as neighbors. A fellow in a refugee camp said, "I want to have Jewish neighbors so we can relate as equals, as human beings, not as guards and prisoners... We have been victimized, but we never want to be victimizers."[17]

In their refusal to hate and in their desire for coexistence, even in the face of unrelenting oppression, McLaren saw these Palestinians living under occupation enacting the principles and values he had been espousing in his writing. These oppressed Palestinians—and McLaren's blog does not indicate whether they were Christians or Muslims, and it doesn't matter—these women and men, humiliated at every turn and facing dispossession at the hands of settler colonists, supported by a powerful government and claiming divine right for their actions, were carrying out Jesus' instruction to love your enemies. They were without question "plotting goodness" in their small but critically important corner of the globe. Perhaps inspired by these Palestinians, McLaren does not indulge in Israel-bashing, nor does he single out the Jewish people for censure. He was already painfully familiar from his own upbringing how religious doctrine can be used to justify one group's oppression of another. In his latest book, McLaren describes one "key Christian doctrine" that has been particularly destructive over the ages:

> [A] distorted doctrine of chosenness tells many sincere but misguided Christian Zionists that the Jews have been chosen by God to own certain land without concern for the well-being of their non-Jewish neighbors. As a result, these Christians fervently support Israel in a Domination Narrative, justifying the continued military occupation of the West Bank and Gaza. They may even support the Purification Narrative that inspires some Israeli settlers and political parties to drive Palestinian Muslims and Christians from their homes, whether through sudden expulsion or gradual colonization and appropriation. These well-meaning Christians, often seeking to redress the horrible legacy of Christian Anti-Semitism, seem to have forgotten that the Domination script is not the way of Jesus. They forget how sincere Christians in South Africa abused the same doctrine of chosenness to justify Apartheid, or how Christians in the U.S. used the same doctrine of chosenness to justify unnumbered crimes against Native Americans and African Americans, or how Christian anti-Semites

through the centuries used this doctrine to justify their unconscionable treatment of their Jewish neighbors in the first place.[18]

As one who had grown up in the Jewish version of this "chosenness doctrine," I found McLaren's powerful statement resonating strongly for me. And I had to agree with him that we Jews could not have succeeded in our modern pursuit of "domination" and "purification" without the support of the Christian world. Christian Zionists maintain that the Jewish possession of the Holy Land presages the End Times. The establishment of the State of Israel was, in this view, the next step toward the fulfillment of God's plan as is foretold in the Bible. I had to agree with McLaren that Christians needed to answer for how this "chosenness doctrine" was being applied in our day. How ironic it was that, in their attempt to atone for millennia of Christian triumphalism that had led to, among other sins, the demonization and persecution of the Jews, Christians were reverting to very same fundamental doctrinal error—and hurting the Jews again in the process, this time by not confronting us in *our* sin. "Today, Palestine is the place," McLaren told me, "where we are most culpable for perpetuating this same dysfunctional and discredited way of using the Bible." As he wrote in another blog post from Palestine, "I believe it's time for Christians of good will to speak out more directly against the kind of Christian Zionism that treats the Palestinians with the same disregard that Jesus refused to be part of in his day regarding Samaritans. That kind of theology of divine favoritism needs to be abandoned as a moral embarrassment."[19]

A New Theology of Land

How McLaren grapples with the doctrines of chosenness and divine favoritism that were part of his own religious legacy is a powerful example of "doing theology." Theology is not fixed; we *do theology* when the times require us to act with compassion and courage. As Martin Luther King Jr. discovered during the difficult early days of the Montgomery bus boycott, besieged by hatred and violent opposition in his fight for racial equality, the initiative to "do theology" often comes on suddenly, even traumatically, and it is always followed by clarity about the action that is required. It is Moses summoned by God to deliver his people from the misery of bondage in Egypt; Jonah sent to the people of Nineveh to rescue them from their own self-destruction; Paul on the road to Damascus thrown to the earth by the blinding light of God's truth; the apostles visited by tongues of fire that burned out of them the conviction that, speaking the language of only one nation, they would rule over an earthly kingdom in Jerusalem. In all cases (and often accompanied by protest on the part of a reluctant prophet or disciple) the scales of denial fall from their eyes and they come to know God, not through study or passive "belief" but through action in the world. A theology that favors one people over another is one that must give way to this process of awakening and doing. And, to McLaren's point, when it is the case that the deed to a piece of real estate is part of the bargain, the stakes become that much higher, the failure to wrestle with such a theology that much costlier. In the next chapter, we will look more closely at how our theology of the land has changed over history as part of our growth as a civilization. We'll see how it remains a crucial area for doing theology as we work to bring about a world of justice and compassion.

TO THE ENDS OF THE EARTH: THE MEANING OF THE LAND

The Book of Acts gives us a world where politics and faith converge. It is a world in which men and women set out to heal a broken, hurting world. Those first followers of Jesus were driven by values, beliefs, and life-changing experiences. Acts describes a world in which the power of the Spirit, an authority greater than earthly powers, directed human actions. It is a primer in first-century geopolitics, a guide for community organizers, a playbook for a campaign to change the world.

It is forty days past Easter. Jesus, having now appeared to his disciples on a number of occasions, has instructed them not to leave Jerusalem. They must wait for the fulfillment of the promise of the Father, when, in Jesus' words, "you will be baptized with the Holy Spirit." In typical fashion, Jesus doesn't waste words explaining the why or how of this; and the disciples, as usual, are clueless. More than clueless—they get it completely wrong. As they have so many times before, the eleven remaining disciples proceed to ask the wrong question, a question that reveals that they still do not understand what Jesus has been talking about for the three and a half years of his ministry, even now, even after Easter. "Is this the time," they ask him, "is it now, Lord, that you will restore the kingdom to Israel?" Even now, they do not comprehend what Jesus meant by "the Kingdom of God." They think it is about an earthly kingdom. When, they are asking Jesus, are we going to get our country back?

In his response, Jesus provides a strong hint, and it is the very last thing he says before he ascends to heaven: "You will receive power when the Holy Spirit has come upon you; and you will be my witnesses in Jerusalem, in all Judea, and Samaria"—but he doesn't stop there—"and to the ends of the earth" (Acts 1:8). Of course, the answer leaves them guessing. It is through experience that they will learn what this baptism by the Spirit is about—and how long, difficult, even dangerous it will be is, of course, still unknown to them. So, at the close of this first chapter of Acts, we, like the disciples, are waiting to find out what it means to receive power.

After a brief piece of business involving the replacement of the now-missing twelfth apostle, we find ourselves in chapter 2, on the day of Pentecost. The power from the Holy Spirit does indeed arrive as promised, but probably not in the way expected. It comes not as a gentle bird of peace, not as a voice from heaven saying, "This is my beloved son," but as violent winds and tongues—tongues!—of fire that confer the ability to speak in all the languages of the known world. *This* is the power that came to the disciples. *It was not about restoring the earthly kingdom to Israel.* It was not a restoration at all, not a return to a former state of glory or stability. *It was not that kind of power.* It is something completely new. The power of God's presence has extended beyond the kingdom of Israel to the ends of the earth: all places, all peoples, all humanity, all the earth. Jesus' followers were speaking in the native language of each nation; in other words, in a universal language.

Pentecost tells a story, and the story is clear: if humankind is to survive, if we are to be with God, we must move away from possession of territory and toward the honoring of the entire earth, away from the particular to embrace the universal. It is about what land means, to what use it is to be put. In the rushing wind and the fiery tongues of Pentecost, the transition was now complete. Pentecost is the story of contrasts between the kind of power imagined by the apostles when they ask, "When will you restore the Kingdom of Israel?" and a very different power: the power, bestowed by the Holy Spirit, to be God's witnesses to the ends of the earth.

The apostles had to be set straight about what it was they were supposed to do. They were faulty, erring human beings susceptible to the influence of the culture that surrounded them, men and women who had grown to adulthood in an imperial society that sought to remove them from the true source of their power: community, compassion, and loving kindness. Jesus recruited them in those early days of his ministry to reconnect them to this true source of power, so they could take this message—the meaning of his life and of his sacrifice—to the ends of the earth. Like us, the apostles required the power of prophecy, sometimes accompanied by special effects, to remind them to look around and read the signs of the times.

Ancient Debate, Modern Crisis

Dr. Gary Burge is a professor of the New Testament at Wheaton College, on the outskirts of Chicago. Wheaton is one of the country's foremost Christian colleges, attracting top-notch students and faculty. It counts Rev. Billy Graham as one of its most famous alumni. Considered a bastion of conservative Christianity, Wheaton prides itself on holding to its legacy while still taking on the challenging issues of modern life: science versus religion, sexuality, and interfaith relations. Perhaps no one personifies this process of Christianity meeting the challenges of the modern world better than Gary Burge. And nothing exemplifies his journey more powerfully or dramatically than his confrontation with the question of the meaning of the Promised Land.

As an exchange student in Lebanon in the early 1970s, Burge witnessed the suffering of the Palestinians who had been made refugees between 1948 and 1949, when the Galilee was cleansed of hundreds of thousands of Palestinian villagers and city dwellers. Caught between Israeli invaders and Lebanese military factions, these defenseless civilians, who had been confined to squalid camps since being driven from their homeland decades before, saw the destruction of even these poor temporary communities and suffered terrible loss of life, including children. Claimed by no one, stateless and vulnerable, they continued to be, in Burge's description, "the refuse of Middle Eastern history."[1] In 1990, by then a professor visiting the Holy Land with students, Burge found himself in Ramallah, in the West Bank, witnessing the roundup of Palestinian children by Israeli soldiers following a stone-throwing episode. He was shocked by the brutal treatment, and in one case the death, of innocent children at the hands of these Israeli troops. Soon after, traveling to occupied East Jerusalem, he witnessed young Israeli men and women in uniform physically abusing and teargassing Palestinian civilians demonstrating in the Old City. Although he was sensitive to the historic suffering of the Jewish people, Burge was outraged and horrified by the violence now being exhibited by the Israelis. There, in the ancient heart of Jerusalem, he could not help but draw the analogy to the suffering of the Palestinians of Jesus' time at the hands of Rome. Sitting in the remains of an ancient Roman fortress in the heart of the Old City, "among the ruins of the Roman army that terrorized and battered this land during Jesus' day—an army that Jesus knew all too well, an army that had slapped him, mocked him, and crucified him," Burge, deeply shaken, asked himself, "were the Israelis now behaving like the Romans once had?"[2] The experience convinced him of the urgent need for a new theology of land to guide the Christian response to a just resolution of the conflict.

In 2003, Burge published *Whose Land? Whose Promise? What Christians Are Not Being Told about Israel and the Palestinians,* in which he chronicles these early experiences. In the book, he questions the use of the land promise as justification for Israel's domination and mistreatment of the Palestinians, and suggests that the New Testament extends the promise beyond the tribal and national boundaries of the Jewish people. In his 2010 *Jesus and the Land: The New Testament Challenge to "Holy Land" Theology,* Burge goes further, asserting that, in its view of the land, the New Testament clearly departs from any kind of territoriality, for any people—even the New Israel of the Church. Reading *Jesus and the Land,* I could barely contain my excitement. Here was a Bible scholar and an evangelical Christian confirming what my own reading of the New Testament had been saying to me loud and clear: Jesus, leading a movement to free his people from the political domination of Rome and the spiritual peril represented by that tyranny, had definite things to say about the meaning of land. It was a departure even from some of the most radical statements of the Old Testament prophets. "Christian theology," Burge writes in *Jesus and the Land,* "asked withering questions about territorial religion, especially of the sort found in Judea."

> The New Testament shows no interest in building a Christian Holy Land, no passion for constructing a kingdom in the name of Christ that might be centered at Jerusalem. We hear no calls in the New Testament that would soon become familiar to Byzantine and European armies. Neither is there any interest in the New Testament to look at the Hebrew Scriptures and Judaism and validate their territorial claims. The New Testament community did not share in the growing momentum within the first century to make the Holy Land exclusively Jewish once more. Throughout the entire century including the great war of AD 66 the followers of Jesus separated themselves from Jewish territorialism.[3]

Burge was drawing conclusions that were frankly political: "The great temptation is for God's people to treat the Holy Land as space, as something to be possessed...as something owned... *to grasp the land and to commoditize it as a political holding*" (emphasis added).[4] Working from New Testament texts, Burge was directly and unapologetically challenging a theology that would grant the Jews the right to dispossess an indigenous population. Clinging to the land as possession, as a divine right, and as territory was *spiritually* wrong, according to Burge, and the Gospels and Pauline theology were the basis of his position! What was so refreshing and encouraging to me was that Burge was not holding back out of concern that his words might be perceived as a claim that Christianity had come to replace or displace Judaism. The issue of replacement theology was not the point here; this was about a different debate, one of critical importance to the Judeans and Galileans of that time and that, in fact, has emerged as just as critical an issue in our time. I read on: "The church was born into a Jewish world saturated with debates about territorial faith, and it chose—deliberately—not to compete as yet one more territorial religion...Throughout the entire century including the great war of AD 66 the followers of Jesus separated themselves from Jewish territorialism...The Gospels show us with keen subtlety how Jesus navigated these debates and how he dislodged his own followers from the passions that inflamed territorial movements of his day."[5]

All the Languages of the World

In December of 2012, I spoke with Burge and asked him to elaborate on this debate. It wasn't long before we landed back in the first century, in fact in that very same room in Jerusalem in the days just before Pentecost. "Restoring the Kingdom to Israel" was an issue that was being hotly debated at the time, Burge told me. "You had strong factions within the Jewish community who were interested in gathering the Jews in from the Diaspora, speaking not Greek, or Arabic, or any of the dozens of languages of the empire, but Hebrew, and establishing Jewish political and military hegemony over Palestine," he explained. And Jesus was wading directly into this debate. "God's interest is not in the particular but the universal, in all of humanity, not a particular people, nation, or tribe—in unity, not exclusivity. Jesus was asking them: Is it going to be about strengthening the center, or going to the margins?"[6]

These are not simply questions of biblical scholarship or historical accuracy for Burge. They matter deeply to him, as issues that lie at the core of his faith as a Christian. In *Jesus and the Land,* he writes, "Paul's view of the land is that Jerusalem and its Temple are places that enjoy historic respect but cannot claim a universal or lasting *theological* significance... The new identification of the church as the Temple springs from Paul's thinking about the new place where God will dwell... The historic devotion reserved for Judea, Jerusalem, and even the Temple has undergone change. What God has done in the Spirit and what has been realized in the church has irretrievably altered Paul's understanding of a holy location, even holy land."[7]

I asked Burge if he could expand on this point: what did he believe were the implications for how we relate to land possession today? His answer was bold and unequivocal: "Looking at the New Testament, I realized we are not meant to live tribally, we are not supposed to live according to this territorial agenda. Instead, as Paul says in Galatians Three, 'In Christ there is no Jew or Gentile, slave or free, male or female.' What he is saying is that God's project in the world is to create a community of men and women in whom there is genuine blessing for one another. For me, this is a core conviction of my Christian faith."

Burge renounces without question the church's shameful history of persecuting the Jews. But he does not confuse the *un-Christian* denigration of the Jews with the *very Christian* departure from the territoriality that was maintained by the Jewish establishment and by some of the counter-establishment sectors of the Jewish community in the Palestine of Jesus' time. Burge's willingness to articulate the anti-territoriality that was an integral part of early Christianity—and in so doing, I believe, to call for this message to be clearly sounded by the church *in our own time*—is of utmost importance not only for the church but for society as a whole. It needs to become an important part of our conversation today, a conversation that to this point has been dominated by assumptions that support the opposite. Territoriality and exclusive privilege were what Jesus was challenging in his ministry and what Paul continued to deconstruct in articulating his vision for the church as the new Israel. In a very real sense, we are living now in the reality of the Book of Acts—it is political! The problem is not anti-Semitism; the problem is territoriality, grasping power, dispossession, us and them, particularity versus universalism, exclusivity versus inclusiveness. The very same debate that raged then, played out in the dramatic events recorded in the New Testament, needs to rage again today.

The Real Deal

For Gary Burge, there is no difference, no dividing line between the spiritual and the political. As he told me when we spoke, "We need to see our work to change the world as the core of our spiritual lives. The early Christians saw personal transformation as the gateway to political change. So, then, the question for me, as a transformed person, as a Christ follower, is: How do I live in the world? Do I go to a monastery, or have a private religious huddle? No—I go into the world and announce kingdom values."[8]

Going into the world is what Bob Roberts, the pastor of NorthWood Church in Keller, Texas, is all about. Bob, as he will be the first to tell you, is "the real deal": an East Texas Baptist pastor who wants to spread the good news of Jesus far and wide, and who has planted more than two hundred churches throughout the United States. But he is also an East Texas Baptist pastor who has built schools in Vietnam and Afghanistan, maintains ongoing relationships with Buddhist monks and Muslim imams across central and western Asia, and has close connections with Palestinians, both Christian and Muslim. Like Gary Burge, Roberts has been profoundly changed by his travels, which have set him on a theological journey.

What happened to Bob Roberts is what has happened to so many American Christians, including and especially clergy, when they make contact with these so-called "others" who, depending on your vocation, have to be "converted" religiously or "won over" to our American way of life. Once real contact is made, one's assumptions about these "others" are challenged. "It's funny how things change," Roberts wrote in his 2010 book, *Real-Time Connections.* "Those I feared most in my youth have now become those I love the most...As I began to visit Islamic nations and to get to know Muslims on a personal basis, for the first time in my life I felt conflicted

over my attitudes and prejudices toward these people. My eschatology was directly conflicting with my love for them and
my desire to tell them the good news of Jesus. Why didn't my
understanding about the Great Commission harmonize with
my end-time theology, which favored Israel over other Middle
Eastern nations? I realized that something was wrong. And
it wasn't just me. *It was affecting our nation and our foreign
policy*" (emphasis added).[9]

Many of the theological convictions I had been raised
with gave the Jewish people a privileged position in the
purposes of God; as a result I had been taught to be sympathetic toward our religious forerunners, the Jews. In
many areas of the American church today, support for
the nation of Israel is strong and is driven by theological
convictions about God's purposes in the end times...As
a predominantly Christian nation, some of those *theological* convictions have also spilled over into our *governmental* support of the Israeli nation. (emphases in
original)[10]

And Roberts struggled with this. It's not an easy transition:

My expanding vision of the kingdom of God was undermining all my previous understandings and creating
some real conflict for me. Often, when your thinking
begins to change, you begin to rationalize things in order to look for something that can rescue your former
beliefs. I thought, "Who knows for sure what God's intent is for the Jews and Palestinians in Israel? Since
the Jews and Muslims are both there, both wanting the

same land, maybe it's better to side with the Jews and not upset the applecart."[11]

Roberts was up against a lifetime of training in a particular understanding of the Bible and of history. Like most of us, he wanted to hold on to the beliefs, assumptions, and perceptions that had guided his life to that point. But for him, this desire to remain in his "comfort zone" was not as strong as the voice inside that was asking to be heard. The truth he thought he had known simply couldn't prevail against the power of what he was seeing and the testimony of the people he had been meeting. His vision of the Kingdom of God was indeed expanding, and with that came questions. And rather than suppress those questions, Roberts did the difficult thing: he pursued them, in the very place that was most likely to challenge his old ways of thinking.

Roberts sought out Bishara Awad, a Palestinian evangelical pastor living in the West Bank town of Bethlehem. Bishara was born in Jerusalem, in a neighborhood where Jews, Muslims, and Christians had lived side by side in harmony for hundreds of years. During the battle for Jerusalem in the 1948 Arab-Israeli conflict, Bishara's father was killed by a sniper's bullet. The family became refugees when Jewish forces took their neighborhood and all Palestinian residents were evicted from their homes.

When my new friend Bishara shared his personal story with me, my eyes were fully opened to the falsehood of my former prejudices and understanding of the Middle East. When Bishara told me his story I was heartbroken. Keep in mind that his family had lived on that land for *centuries.* I wondered, was it right for the Jews to take over their nation and control it? By supporting Israel, was I saying that I supported actions like this? Don't mistake what I am saying here. I have always been disturbed by what the Jews suffered in the Holocaust, and I continue to recognize this as a great evil. But does the evil of their suffering justify their present treatment of the Palestinians—confining them with walls, requiring special identification, restricting access to jobs, and pushing innocent people out of their ancestral homes? Is it ever right to respond to one injustice with another? As a Texan, I know that we Texans would fight like Crockett at the Alamo if another nation tried to take away our land. What justified the actions of Israel? Was it somehow acceptable for them to do this because they were God's "chosen" people?[12]

"At this point," writes Bob, "I again recognized that there was something wrong with my theology. The Great Commission teaches that God has no longer confined his redemptive work to a single nation—he loves people from every nation, tongue and tribe. If that is true, then any end-time theory or doctrine that excludes specific people from the reach of God's love is necessarily flawed."[13] He continues:

The New Testament affirms that the gospel is for every tongue, tribe, and nation. Practically speaking, that means that the gospel is for the Afghani Muslim, and it is for both the Jew and the Palestinian...the kingdom of God is no longer defined by the borders of a single nation or the real estate of a specific place. It crossed the geographic boundaries of nations, establishing its rule in the real estate of every heart committed to God.

The identity of "God's people" had shifted for Bob. "No longer are we citizens of a literal nation state," he wrote; "now we are kingdom disciples. It's about more than just my eternal destiny; it's about God's larger work in history and creation."[14]

Bob Roberts's story is not unique. It is the story of so many pastors, missionaries, humanitarian workers, and pilgrims who have allowed their hearts to follow what their eyes have seen and their ears have heard. And what those hearts find is love and awakening and confusion and conflict and, finally, certitude about what is, after all, the message conveyed by the Holy Spirit on the day of Pentecost, a Spirit that, clearly, is still at work in the world.

Kingdom of God 2.0

A theology of land is important not only because of its relevance to the political situation in the Holy Land of today but also because it focuses on the most urgent theological issue of our time: the particular versus the universal. The question of the land has begun to capture the attention of the church globally and ecumenically. In 2008, in Bern, Switzerland, the Palestine Israel Ecumenical Forum of the World Council of Churches convened a conference on the topic "Promised Land." American theologian Harvey Cox challenged those assembled with this question:

What do we really mean by "promised land"? How has the term been hijacked and used for various political reasons, when maybe that is not the significance of the texts at all? Ancient Israel is often confused with modern Israel. They are not the same. We can talk about an integral relationship which must be there theologically between Christians and the Jewish people. Jesus was Jewish; the whole background of Christianity comes from the Jewish people, but the Jewish people and the modern State of Israel, though they overlap in certain ways, are not the same, and therefore we have to be thoughtful and self-critical about how that theme is dealt with.[15]

The story of the land is the story of God's relationship to humankind through history. It begins in Genesis and continues through Revelation. The meaning assigned to the land, the role it plays in the story, reflects the response of people to changing historical contexts and experiences. The original promise of the land sets in motion a dramatic story: the transition from the tribal to the universal, from territory possessed and conquered to the establishment of a global order of equality, peace, and social justice. The Old Testament gives us the essential ingredients for the ultimate achievement of the Kingdom of God, but the Bible does not serve up this feast all at once. God gives the people a land, just as he gives them kings. And it is for us, with the help of the prophets and Jesus, to work out what this means.

In the Old Testament narrative, God begins by choosing one family, the family of Israel, to play a crucial role in establishing the divine plan for a human society based on compassion and loving kindness. The land plays a central role in the unfolding drama of this covenantal relationship. The people are special, or *kadosh*, set apart from the other peoples, and they are given the land in tenancy as a part of this covenant. The drama continues when the people demand a king. God tells Samuel to warn the people that a king will subvert the primary covenantal goal of establishing a just world: he will see the land as his possession, distribute resources unfairly, destroy community and family life, and ultimately bring down the wrath of God (1 Samuel 8:11–17). Of course, this is precisely what happens: ultimately, in the biblical narrative, the "kingdom" falls and the people are expelled from the land and sent into exile.

But even through these changes, the promise to the people of Israel is itself never withdrawn. They retain their special relationship with God and the special connection to the land. Although the Israelites are enjoined to treat the non-Israelites among them justly, and even as equals, the non-Israelites are nevertheless called "strangers" or "resident aliens," as the Hebrew word *ger* is sometimes translated. All through the vicissitudes of the divided kingdom—the destruction of the northern kingdom and subsequently of Jerusalem, the exile, and the return—this fundamental three-way interlacing of people, God, and land is maintained. Yes, living on the land is conditional to following God's law—the covenant goes both ways, of course—but the promise of restoration is always there. The land is for the people of Israel as their inheritance, and even with the ups and downs of the relationship, including exile itself, it's never taken off the table.

Even with the prophets' protestations against the abuses of king and priest, this core connection, the promise itself, persists. The return recorded in Jeremiah and the time of Ezra and Nehemiah can be seen as a *restoration*. The temple is to be rebuilt; this is never in question.

In its original proclamation, therefore, the Kingdom of God was *specific.* It was tied to the fortunes and narrative of a particular people or tribe. Fast-forward to first-century Palestine: The historical frame is the Roman Empire, the ultimate expression of tyranny and greed. The temple is still standing. Jerusalem is ruled by a client government installed by that empire. This is the context of Jesus' ministry, which is a direct response to the evil of that arrangement, and the frame for his revolutionary concept of a Kingdom of God. Like the prophet Samuel, Jesus knew that kings by their nature become part of systems that favor the few and the privileged. So it is in every historical era, at every point in which a particular society confronts a challenge to the social justice imperative. Jesus was reaching into the great storehouse of his tradition, a tradition that established righteousness above adherence to cultic observance, kindness and compassion above territoriality and the accumulation of possessions, devotion to the one God above nationalistic or tribalistic strivings. Jesus' vision of the Kingdom of God dispenses, finally, with the concept of God's indwelling in the land, of a particular location as the place where God is to be worshiped. In the Christian vision of the Kingdom of God, both the land and the people lose their specificity and exclusivity. Temple—gone. God dwelling in one place—over. The notion of territory as a clause in the covenant disappears. And, significantly, Jesus' kingdom takes the next step: it jettisons the *am kadosh,* or "special people," concept. The special privilege of one family/tribe/nation separated from the rest of humanity is eclipsed.

We've arrived at Kingdom of God, version 2.0.

The Battle for Jerusalem

Israel's national anthem "Hatikvah" ("The Hope") embodies the Zionist dream and ethos: "The hope of two thousand years, to be a free nation in our land, the land of Zion and Jerusalem." This yearning is understandable and it is powerful. Zionism presented a kind of desperate logic for the Jews of nineteenth-century Europe, and was very much in line with the ethnic nationalist sensibilities and movements of the time. But we have to question how sustainable it is as a political and national project today, when the direction of history is away from nationalism (and especially ethnic nationalism). Nation-states based on the dominance of one group and on adherence to one particular religious tradition are frowned upon at best. In light of modern events, it is clear that the dream expressed in "Hatikvah" of a haven for Jews has resulted in the territorial grasping, tribal exclusivism, and depredations of rulers warned about in Scripture. Despite the protestations of some progressive Jews who argue that the dream of a democratic Israel can overcome the reality of an ethnic nationalist state, and the fervent belief held by Christian Zionists that the State of Israel presages the Second Coming, commitment to political Zionism has, tragically but unavoidably, subverted the principles of equality and human dignity in which the early Zionist settlers believed so fiercely. Israel's systematic and mounting violations of fundamental human rights, and of international law protecting those rights, has led to the political logjam in which we find ourselves today. It is the fundamental barrier to peace.

In pursuit of the goal of living as a free people in Zion, the State of Israel has pursued policies that doom the project to failure. Since 1967, Israel has pursued a relentless program to make Jerusalem entirely Jewish, allowing only for isolated pockets of non-Jewish neighborhoods within this vision of a "greater Jerusalem." "Jerusalem will never be divided" is the political rallying cry. But an "undivided" Jewish Jerusalem ends the possibility of Jerusalem as the capital of a Palestinian state in the two-state scenario. An expanded, all-Jewish Jerusalem also effectively cuts the remaining Palestinian areas of the West Bank into two, similarly foreclosing the possibility of the partition of the territory into two viable states.

The world has taken notice of the importance of Jerusalem in the political sphere. In early 2012, the Arab League convened an international conference on Jerusalem in Qatar. Politicians, academics, clergy, activists, and journalists from around the world attended. The large number of clergy present was an acknowledgment that what is being played out is not just a national or political conflict. Understanding the root causes and finding the solutions would require asking questions about deeply held beliefs. The Rev. Stephen Sizer was among the speakers. The title of his paper was "Jerusalem: The City of God in Christian Tradition."

Stephen Sizer is a pastor in the town of Virginia Water, in the south of England. He is acknowledged to be one of the world's foremost experts on Christian Zionism. He has had a big impact in the United States, due in part to a ninety-minute video in which his work is featured, entitled *With God on Our Side*.[16] The video is an exploration and searching critique of Christian Zionism that includes interviews with Palestinian Christians lamenting how Christians are leaving the Holy Land because of the Israeli occupation. He presents the testimony of evangelical Christians who, having visited the region and seen what is transpiring under Israeli rule, are now asking hard questions about a theology that sees the State of Israel as God's plan. Sizer is a devout Christian, grounded in the Bible and espousing an eschatology that does not depart from that held by most religiously conservative Christians. At the same time, he challenges firmly held beliefs and assumptions with respect to Israel, the Jewish people, and the role of the land. Some Jewish organizations in the United Kingdom have accused Sizer of anti-Semitism, a charge he vigorously denies. He is, however, a fervent defender of the human rights of Palestinians and an advocate for the Arabic-speaking churches in the Middle East.

In his speech in Qatar, Sizer firmly opposed Israel's claim on Jerusalem, challenging the way in which Israel's annexation of the city and expulsion of its Palestinian residents has been theologically justified and in some cases vigorously promoted by Christian Zionist organizations. He began his address by laying out how powerful Christian Zionism has become as a political force, especially in the aftermath of the capture of East Jerusalem in 1967, an event portrayed by many evangelicals as "confirmation that Jews and Israel still had a role to play in God's ordering of history" and that the return of Jesus was imminent.[17] Sizer reported on the Third International Christian Zionist Congress in 1996, sponsored by the International Christian Embassy Jerusalem (ICEJ). There, some 1,500 participants signed a declaration that stated "[b]ecause of the sovereign purposes of God for the City, Jerusalem must remain undivided, under Israeli sovereignty, open to all peoples, the capital of Israel only, and all nations should so concur and place their embassies here...the truths of God are sovereign and it is written that the Land which He promised to His People is not to be partitioned."[18] In 1997 the ICEJ sponsored a full-page ad in the *New York Times* signed by prominent American evangelicals such as Jerry Falwell, Oral Roberts, and Pat Robertson entitled "Christians Call for a United Jerusalem." The declaration urged fellow Christians to "[j]oin us in our holy mission to ensure that Jerusalem will remain the undivided, eternal capital of Israel. The battle for Jerusalem has begun, and it is time for believers in Christ to support our Jewish brethren and the State of Israel."[19]

In his address, Sizer argued that this Christian Zionist picture of the role of Jerusalem is inconsistent with the Bible. Christian Zionism, he maintained, is being used to promote a political agenda that is not only wrong with respect to human rights and international law, but also violates fundamental biblical principles. The message of the prophets, he pointed out, is that pride, arrogance, and nationalistic claims will be punished by God. "The prophetic message is clear," pronounced Sizer. "God holds his people morally accountable and will tolerate neither arrogance or complacency.[20] Like the prophets, Jesus was challenging narrow, arrogant, and nationalistic attitudes. But, as Sizer points out, Jesus takes one giant step further. This is expressed in the startling exchange with the Samaritan woman in the Gospel of John. The woman, surprised that Jesus, a Jew, would even speak to her, displays the prevailing assumptions of even the common people in first-century Palestine: "You say that the place where people must worship is Jerusalem!" To which Jesus replies, "Believe me, woman, a time is coming when you will worship the Father neither on this mountain nor in Jerusalem!" (John 4:20–21).

Thinking Like Christians

The conversation about the role and meaning of the land has persisted throughout history. As we've seen, it played an important role in the birth of the church. The "debate" about territoriality was of crucial concern to the Judean and Galilean farmers and tradespeople in Jesus' time. It was a critical issue in that context because land-taking was one form of Roman oppression; in fact, it was one of the key ways in which the empire undermined family and community ties, in order to weaken resistance to imperial power. Territoriality and nationalism were not, of course, the sole province of the superpower. The apostles in the Pentecost story displayed the nationalistic strivings and assumptions that were commonly held by the subject people themselves. The apostles believed that resistance to Rome required the return of political sovereignty to Israel, with all that this implied with respect to territoriality, centralization of power, and reliance on military force. Enter Jesus: he unfurls the scroll in his inaugural public appearance, spreading the good news that adherence to God's law is the key to the Jews' release from captivity. Then, in the final set of instructions before his ascension, having equipped the disciples with the ability to speak in all the world's languages, Jesus sends them out into the far reaches of the world. To use Burge's words, he is leading the people away from centralization and toward the margins, away from the nationalistic, the tribal, the "us and them," and toward a vision of unity and universal compassion.

This is why the theological debate, the one to which we are summoned today, is so important. It's a critical conversation, beginning as an internal, personal process, continuing inside our communities, then within our societies or nations, and finally on a global basis. The internal debate began for pastor Bob Roberts meeting Buddhists in Vietnam and Muslims in Afghanistan. It began for pastor Stephen Sizer witnessing the dispossession of Palestinians in the Holy Land, just as it did for Bible scholar Gary Burge on the streets of Ramallah and Jerusalem. Sitting among the remains of a previous occupier that day in Jerusalem, Burge began his own questioning of the theology in which he had been reared: "Reformed theologians like me," writes Burge, "actually stand with Christian Zionists committed to a longing for Christ's return. The chief difference is that reformed theologians make profound investments in the world. We are not sectarian. We devote ourselves to promoting Christ's commitments here. And we do not despair about the course of the world. We have not abandoned it...This is my ultimate complaint perhaps: Christian Zionists believe in Jesus, but I wonder if they are always thinking like Christians in this matter."[21]

"Thinking like Christians in this matter" is precisely what is needed now, and—here is the beauty and the paradox of it—this means seeing the world around us in terms that transcend national, religious, and ethnic identities and labels. Sectarian, tribal, and nationalistic thinking, whether expressed religiously or politically—and in the first century, this distinction did not exist—is what Jesus was confronting in his time, and it is what we confront today. This is the power and the importance of the issue of the land. The time has come to set out from Jerusalem, speaking in all the languages of humankind, bringing the message of love and compassion to the ends of the earth.

Chapter 7

MY LEGS WERE PRAYING: THE BLACK CHURCH AND THE CIVIL RIGHTS STRUGGLE

On December 1, 1955, Rosa Parks was arrested in Montgomery, Alabama, for refusing to give up her seat on a bus to a white man. Three days later, the newly formed Montgomery Improvement Association decided to stage a one-day boycott of the city's bus system. The boycott that had been planned to last one day continued for over a year, culminating in the December 26, 1956, Supreme Court decision declaring segregated buses to be unconstitutional. At the time of Rosa Parks's arrest, Rev. Martin Luther King Jr. was the pastor of the Dexter Avenue Baptist Church, a small but prosperous congregation. King was a young preacher with solid credentials who had come to Montgomery a year earlier. He was interested in building a church, not becoming involved in a movement that would eventually transform a nation. But on the Monday following the declaration of the boycott, King relented to fellow pastor and organizer Ralph Abernathy's entreaties to become president of the Montgomery Improvement Association, thinking that the dispute would be

resolved quickly. By mid-January 1956, as the situation esca-
lated, besieged by daily threatening phone calls, King realized
that his life had changed irrevocably. On a sleepless night
following a particularly vicious and frightening phone call,
he experienced what theologian and historian Charles Marsh
called "the kitchen visit." Thinking of the threats to his family and of the potential violence that might be brewing in
the fight he had taken on, King wrote, "I felt myself falter-
ing...growing in fear." Bowing over the kitchen table, he
prayed a fervent, desperate prayer: "Lord, I am here taking
a stand for what I believe is right. But Lord, I must confess
that...I am afraid...The people are looking to me for leadership, and if I stand before them without strength and
courage, they too will falter. I am at the end of my powers. I
have nothing left."[1]

Marsh continues his description of what happened next,
quoting from King's autobiography:

As he prayed alone in the silent kitchen, King heard
a voice saying, "Martin Luther, stand up for righteousness. Stand up for justice. Stand up for truth. And lo, I
will be with you. Even until the end of the world." Then
King heard the voice of Jesus. "I heard the voice of Jesus saying still to fight on. He promised never to leave
me alone. No never alone. No never alone. He promised
never to leave me, never to leave me alone."[2]

This was the moment of truth for King—when the moral
imperative knocked him to the ground in what can only be
described as a transforming "Road to Damascus" experience.
There would be no turning back. "My uncertainty disap-

peared," he wrote later about this experience. "I was ready to face anything."[3] This was a theme that King would return to again and again in his public utterances and his writing with respect to his personal safety: that this cause was bigger than he was, and bigger than the personal aspirations that he had brought with him to Montgomery.

Another event of profound significance happened in those early days of the boycott. On January 30, King's house was bombed. Rushing to the scene from a nearby church where he had been speaking, he encountered a large group of supporters on his front lawn and on the street in front of the parsonage. The mood was angry, and King feared that the boycott would turn violent. He addressed the crowd:

> We cannot solve this problem through retaliatory violence. We must meet violence with non-violence. Remember the words of Jesus: "He who lives by the sword will perish by the sword." We must love our white brothers, no matter what they do to us. Jesus cried out in words that echo across the centuries: "Love your enemies, bless them that curse you; pray for those that despitefully use you." This is what we must live by. We must meet hate with love.[4]

Something had been clarified for King, and the implications would be huge for the movement that was being born. King realized that adherence to nonviolence was crucial for the cause of justice, not only because God abhors violence, but because, as Jesus was pointing out, *violence doesn't work.* It only increases the suffering, brings on more violence at the hands of the oppressor, and reinforces societal reliance on physical force. But there was something else King realized, something equally, if not more, important: by practicing nonviolence, you lead the oppressor toward his own liberation and healing. Marsh continues: "King emerged from the Montgomery bombing with a single-minded theme, the transformative power of love. He began to speak forthrightly of the 'weapon of love,' of 'compassion and understanding for those who hate us,' of 'the truth of the real God.'"[5]

The Way of Nonviolence

An additional realization accompanied King's embrace of nonviolence: the rejection, in Marsh's words, "of piecemeal and gradual reform." Not only had King experienced the blindingly clear realization of the moral imperative driving his work. He had also reached a turning point that would define the movement and increasingly determine its direction. Up to that point, King's approach to the segregation standoff had been characterized by the "gradualism" that was in line with theories of societal change he had brought with him from his theological education. King had grown increasingly doubtful about this approach for bringing about racial equality in the heated atmosphere of the American South.[6] In the first days of the boycott, King's demands to the bus company consisted of cautious steps toward a compromise that, although seeking to ease the indignities, did not challenge segregation itself on a principled basis. But on January 30, three days after the "kitchen visit," King's position made a sharp turn. "Segregation," he said, "is evil, and I cannot, as a minister, condone evil."[7] He authorized the boycott committee's attorney to begin the process of challenging the segregation laws themselves.

This is the theme that King was to articulate more fully in the "Letter from Birmingham Jail." The writers of "A Call for Unity," eight white Alabama clergymen (five bishops, two pastors, and a rabbi), had published an open letter to King, jailed for his participation in a demonstration against segregation in the city's retail stores. Citing "evidence of increased forbearance and a willingness to…work on various problems that cause racial friction and unrest," the authors of the letter entreated King to end the "extreme measures" of public demonstrations, calling instead for "honest and open negotiation in the courts and…among local leaders, and not in the streets."[8] To which King responded: *we cannot wait.* Nonviolent direct action, King maintained in his response, is the right course for our churches, for our society, and for our leaders—*and it is what our Christian faith requires.* The Montgomery experience had shown him that "this was a spiritual movement depending on moral and spiritual forces."[9] This was the Martin Luther King Jr. who, writing from the jail cell in April 1963, observed that "I have almost reached the regrettable conclusion that the Negro's great stumbling block in his stride toward freedom is not the White Citizen's Councilor or the Ku Klux Klanner, but the white moderate, who is more devoted to 'order' than to justice; who prefers a negative peace which is the absence of tension to a positive peace which is the presence of justice." King explained, "I am not afraid of the word 'tension.'…We who engage in nonviolent direct action are not the creators of tension. We merely bring to the surface the hidden tension that is already alive. We bring it out in the open, where it can be seen and dealt with."[10]

The Power of Faith

The story of Martin Luther King Jr. and the movement that coalesced around his leadership is about the power of faith. It demonstrates what the church can achieve as an organizing framework and as a spiritual force in the struggle against injustice. It is no accident that the civil rights movement was born in the church, and that the founders and leaders were people deeply rooted in their religious heritage. The songs and rallying cries that buoyed their spirits and kept them focused on their goal were hymns and spirituals about freedom, liberation, community, and fortitude in the face of adversity. With the advent of black liberation theology in the United States in the 1960s, many of these themes were given theological expression within the specific context of the African American liberation struggle. In fact, black liberation theology was developed in part as an answer to those in the movement who were ready to jettison Christianity as the oppressive "white man's religion." Even though it was indisputable that Christianity had been an instrument of oppression, proponents of black liberation theology asserted that this was the result of human imperfection, not the fault of Christianity. Indeed, the core of Christianity, born in a political context of domination and cruelty, was opposition to tyranny and commitment to human dignity and equality.

Theologian, educator, and civil rights leader Howard Thurman (1899–1991) was one of the earliest proponents of what came to be called black liberation theology. As early as 1949, Thurman articulated the potential of Christianity to provide the road map and the spiritual power for the lib-

eration of black people, if only its adherents would follow
Jesus:

> The striking similarity between the social position of
> Jesus in Palestine and that of the vast majority of Amer-
> ican Negroes is obvious to anyone who tarries long over
> the facts. We are dealing here with conditions that pro-
> duce essentially the same psychology. Living in a climate
> of deep insecurity, Jesus, faced with so narrow a margin
> of civil guarantees, had to find some other basis upon
> which to establish a sense of well-being. *He knew that*
> *the goals of religion as he understood them could never*
> *be worked out within the then-established order.* (em-
> phasis added)[11]

Christianity transcends historical eras in its commitment
to universal principles of equality and justice. Although it
sprang from the particular experience of one oppressed
group, its implications are universal. Theologian and South
African antiapartheid activist Allan Boesak was deeply influenced by black liberation theology and by the Black Power
movement in the United States. Boesak provides a stirring
definition of black theology, placing it squarely within the liberation theology frame:

> Black theology is a theology of liberation. By that we
> mean the following. Black theology means that libera-
> tion is not only "part" of the gospel, or "consistent with"
> the gospel; it is the content and framework of the gospel
> of Jesus Christ... In its focus on the poor and the op-
> pressed, the theology of liberation is not a new theology;

it is simply the proclamation of the age-old gospel, but now liberated from the deadly hold of the mighty and the powerful and made relevant to the situation of the oppressed and the poor...[12]

As Martin Luther King Jr. famously wrote, "[i]njustice anywhere is a threat to justice everywhere. We are caught in an inescapable network of mutuality."[13] This was key to his concept of "the beloved community"—people united across national, racial, and religious lines in commitment to the work of compassion and equality. It may remain "broken, scattered, an eschatological hope," in Charles Marsh's words,[14] but it is a hope that drives oppressed groups and communities acquainted with oppression to oppose injustice. It is the drive to establish connections wherever the heart of the church is to be found. "The end," wrote King, "is reconciliation; the end is redemption; the end is the creation of the beloved community."[15] Today, the encounter of the African American community with the struggle of the Palestinians is the most recent example of the power, timelessness, and inescapability of this network of mutuality.

Why Should I Care?

"You know, Lucas, I don't think that you're going to be exhausted when you go to Palestine by seeing something that's different, something that you're going to have to wrap your head around. You're going to be exhausted because when you get there you're going to see something that's so familiar."

In October 2012, a historic delegation visited the West Bank. The group included veterans of the civil rights movement of the 1950s and '60s, younger human rights leaders, social justice activists, peace builders, and educators. The Israeli Nonviolence Project of the Dorothy Cotton Institute sponsored the delegation.[16] Rev. Lucas Johnson of the Fellowship of Reconciliation was one of the twelve African Americans who, together with eight Jewish Americans, comprised the delegation. When I spoke with him a few months after their return, Reverend Johnson told me that he often thought back to those words from his fellow delegate and mentor, Rev. Osagyefo Uhuru Sekou. It was to be Johnson's first visit, and his colleague was giving him fair warning in describing his own experience as an African American first witnessing the Israeli occupation. For Johnson, the decision to join the delegation had not been easy. Yes, he was aware of the human rights issues in Palestine, but with all that he had to be concerned about in the United States, why should he care? Why take this on? "To go to Palestine was a whole other level of commitment," Johnson told me. [17]

Reverend Sekou's words to him were a big part of the answer to Johnson's question. This delegation and others like it are evidence of the African American community's growing realization of the importance of active involvement in the Palestinian cause. For that reason, more and more organizations have been sponsoring visits to the region by African American clergy, community and peace activists, and political leaders. The visits have had an enormous impact. They have raised difficult questions for the participants, the key issue perhaps being the very one raised in the conversation between Reverends Johnson and Sekou: Why care?

Johnson continued: "The struggle against racism has never been a struggle that's confined to the United States. And we do ourselves a disservice if we think that it is. We can't defeat it at home if we don't also work on defeating it abroad. For me to have gone and for me to have cared is to move more fully into the type of freedom fighter that I hope to become. It's about living up to that legacy and to that tradition that is so meaningful and important to me—so I'm really glad that I went."

For Johnson, encountering Israel and Palestine raised core issues for his human rights work at home. "Israel is unfortunately a significant part of the global economic and political system that is affecting our own communities. And so to some extent I'm still fighting the same battle when I'm in Palestine. If we sit back and allow it to happen, we find ourselves complicit. I'm reminded of the criticisms that were leveled against Martin Luther King Jr. when he began to engage against the Vietnam War: 'You pay attention to civil rights in this country. Don't go concerning yourselves with other contexts and other places.'"[18]

Here are King's words addressing those challenges in his historic speech "A Time to Break Silence," delivered at the Riverside Church in New York City on April 4, 1967:

"Why are you speaking about the war, Dr. King? Why are you joining the voices of dissent?" "Peace and civil rights don't mix," they say. "Aren't you hurting the cause of your people?" they ask. And when I hear them, though I often understand the source of their concern, I am nevertheless greatly saddened, for such questions mean that the inquirers have not really known me, my commitment, or my calling. Indeed, their questions suggest that they do not know the world in which they live. In the light of such tragic misunderstanding, I deem it of

signal importance to try to state clearly, and I trust con-
cisely, why I believe that the path from Dexter Avenue
Baptist Church—the church in Montgomery, Alabama,
where I began my pastorate—leads clearly to this sanctuary tonight.[19]

The connections to the present day are almost startling.
The Riverside Church speech was drafted by theologian, historian, and nonviolent activist Vincent Harding, one of King's
close associates throughout the civil rights movement. Now
professor of religion and social transformation at Iliff School
of Theology in Denver, Colorado, Harding was also on the
Palestine delegation with Lucas Johnson. Like Johnson and
Sekou, he was painfully reminded not only of his own experience of racial segregation at home in the United States, but
also of what he had witnessed in South Africa.

"There are great difficulties in their simply being able to
have homes in the area where the Israeli government decided
they want Jewish Israeli settlers to be," Harding said in a
news report after the delegation's return. "There are places
where Palestinians are not allowed to go in this country,
where their ancestors have lived for generations. So there is
essentially a system of apartheid."[20] African Americans understand all too well what they are seeing. And the Palestinian
call is bringing an increasing number of African Americans
to Palestine to see for themselves.

A Rallying Cry for the Black Church

In 2011, Interfaith Peace-Builders, the organization that sponsored my first visit to the West Bank in 2006,[21] organized its

first African Heritage Delegation. The goals of the delegation were to "exchange lessons learned from Black Power, Civil Rights, and anti-apartheid struggles in the US with those waging similar campaigns in Palestine/Israel, to strengthen African-American leaders to work for change upon return home, and to further link African American delegation participants with work being done in other anti-war, peace and justice communities in the United States."[22] Rev. Carolyn Boyd of Plymouth Congregational United Church of Christ in Washington, DC, was on that delegation. Reverend Carolyn, as she is known, speaks passionately and powerfully about her faith and her commitment to human rights. I knew she wouldn't hold back when I asked her to talk about her visit to the West Bank.

When you are sitting in a bus at a checkpoint, when you are watching human rights being violated in all kinds of ways, you understand because it's in your blood, it's part of the DNA, of your experience as an African American. It was so clear to me. It shook me at my core. *I could feel it.* Seeing the segregated roads reminded me of my own story. So how could my story, which is so linked to the suffering of many people, not be linked to the Palestinian struggle? After all, didn't we learn ourselves, and didn't we teach the world, that "injustice anywhere is a threat to justice everywhere"? So this story of a people who because of the color of their skin have been forgotten by the world, and on top of that, this having been justified by *theology,* that to me is a rallying cry for the black church. I'm longing for my church, the black church, to again claim its big, proud, prophetic voice—and speak loudly against this injustice. If more and more African Americans could understand what I now understand, and brought this into the light, we would be a mighty army.[23]

Reverend Carolyn envisions an army energized by this connection, a church reinvigorated by the "inescapable network of mutuality."

I feel that our church has lost its way. We have so many issues in the black community: crime, domestic violence, broken homes, and broken marriages, our prison industrial complex that continues to take our men and our women. The black church is confronted with all these things, and increasingly has less resources to tackle these issues. But the fact that we have weathered the storms of oppression and the storms of racism and the storms of injustice has shaped who we are. It gives us this incredible inner strength and wisdom that we can't keep to ourselves. The web of life is interconnected.[24]

Soon after her return from her first pilgrimage, Reverend Carolyn made a remarkable statement during a private discussion with me. "The Palestinian cause," she told me, "is a redemptive cause for the African American church." It was for her, not for me, to make this declaration, but I told her that I agreed wholeheartedly. I added that I saw this cause as redemptive for the church in all its variety and diversity, but that this was a case where the African American church could lead, as it did in the civil rights struggle. I also told her, perhaps in the nature of a confession, that as a Jew, I had a particularly strong investment in the involvement of the African American community in this struggle.

My Legs Were Praying

There is a profound history of connection between the Jewish and African American communities in the United States, and this resonates strongly for me personally. My father was active in the Anti-Defamation League (ADL) of B'nai B'rith, a Jewish advocacy organization founded early in the twentieth century initially to defend Jews against anti-Semitism. By midcentury, the ADL had taken on as part of its mission opposition to other forms of prejudice and racism in American society. My father began my education early. I recall one day saying in his presence a word I had heard from some extended family members, a Yiddish word for black people used by Jews of my parents' generation. *Schvartze* may not equal the viciousness of the N-word, but it comes close. My father's reaction was immediate and clear, and I never used that word again.

Some of my earliest memories are of accompanying my father to countless appearances at Philadelphia synagogues where he gave talks about what we then called "prejudice"—white-on-black racism. For my father, as for so many Jews during that era, being Jewish could only mean actively working for human rights as a member of the society in which we lived. According to some estimates, 25 percent of the Freedom Riders to the South in 1961 were Jewish, and approximately 50 percent of the white student Freedom Riders. In the 1960s, Jews comprised nearly half of the lawyers working on civil rights cases in the South. It is similarly estimated that Jews made up anywhere from one- to two-thirds of the white volunteers who participated in the voter registration drive during the Freedom Summer in 1964.[25]

My friend Hannah Schwarzschild, a lawyer and longtime human rights activist, is the daughter of Henry Schwarzschild, who, at the age of thirteen, fled with his parents from Nazi Germany, settling in the United States where he became well known as a courageous and tireless proponent of civil liberties and human rights. For Henry and his daughter Hannah, as for so many other survivors of Hitler's terror and their children, the lesson of the Nazi Holocaust is "never again"—*for anyone.* In 2011, Hannah, working with a coalition of Jewish groups exerting international pressure on Israel to lift the siege of the Gaza Strip, published a short essay remembering her father's activities in the summer of 1961:

> Fifty years ago next month, my father, then a 35-year-old refugee from Hitler's Germany with a young wife and two small children at home, boarded a Trailways bus headed for Jackson, Mississippi. Like the 427 other freedom riders who rode voluntarily into the terror that was the segregated South in May and June of 1961, my father set out to violate the illegal state laws that barred white-skinned people from sitting together with black-skinned people on public transit—laws that were vigorously enforced not only by police but also by the Ku Klux Klan and the White Citizens' Council. Only weeks before, a mob of angry segregationists in Anniston, Alabama had attacked and set fire to a bus with dozens of black and white freedom riders trapped inside...My father was

not naïve. He knew the dangers. He also knew that the goal of ending segregation was remote. He went, as he wrote many years later, not because he believed that his mission would succeed, but "as an act of faith in the validity of a moral act. I went because I needed to go."[26]

Fifty years after her father's experience, Schwarzschild went on to explain in the essay, she was helping to organize, in her words, "a modern-day Freedom Ride" to focus international attention on another urgent injustice: Israel's siege of the Gaza Strip, "the world's largest open-air prison." It consists of 1.6 million people, mostly refugees and the children and grandchildren of Palestinians made refugees in 1948 when Israeli Army forces drove them out of their villages and cities to make way for the Jewish state. "All movement of people and goods in and out of Gaza by land, air and sea is still controlled—mostly prohibited—by the Israeli military," wrote Schwarzschild. "That is why I have been working, along with so many other Americans who care about equality and freedom, to send a U.S.-flagged ship, named The Audacity of Hope, to break the siege of Gaza...[O]ur ship will carry a brave band of unarmed human rights activists as well as the audacious hopes of thousands who have committed their money and time to this nonviolent mission of resistance to enduring racism and injustice. Israeli government officials have vowed to send snipers and attack dogs to stop the flotilla's supposed 'terrorists' and 'provocateurs' from entering Gaza. Anyone who doubts their seriousness is simply not paying attention."[27]

Schwarzschild does not fail to point out the historical parallels:

[T]here were leaders who similarly tried to block the Freedom Riders from "provoking confrontation" with the State of Mississippi in 1961. There will always be voices urging complacency and "patience" in the face of injustice. The organizers of the U.S. Boat to Gaza have read and re-read Dr. King's Letter from a Birmingham Jail many times over these last months, and we are guided by its deep wisdom as the campaign to denounce our non-violent direct action as "extremism" and "provocation" escalates from both inside and outside the halls of Congress. When The Audacity of Hope heads for Occupied Palestine and Gaza in June, its passengers will not be guaranteed safe passage by any government. They will have no more assurance of success than did my father when he stepped onto that Trailways bus a half century ago. They will be armed only with a legacy of the courage of their activist forebears, the moral outrage of a growing worldwide movement for freedom and justice in Palestine, and the steadfast hopes of an illegally occupied people. They will be reasserting their faith in the validity—indeed the necessity—of a moral act. They will be going because they need to go.[28]

Schwarzschild's moving tribute to her father, and her own commitment to the present-day liberation struggle that calls to her as a Jew grounded in the values of her tradition, echo clearly the moral imperative that propelled American Jews into the thick of the civil rights movement. Reinforcing this shared history is a profound theological connection between the African American freedom struggle and the biblical narrative of liberation from slavery. The life of civil rights leader

Fannie Lou Hamer exemplifies this in the most moving and powerful way. Charles Marsh describes Hamer's appearance at Sunday worship in a Mississippi church during the 1964 Freedom Summer drive to register black voters. Invited by the pastor to speak after the Scripture reading—it was from the Book of Exodus—Hamer "rose majestically to her feet. Her magnificent voice rolled through the chapel":

> "Pharoah was in Sunflower County! Israel's children were building bricks without straw—at three dollars a day!" Her voice broke, and tears stood in her eyes. "They're tired! And they're tired of being tired!...And you, Reverend Tyler, must be Moses! Leadin' your flock out of the chains and fetters of Egypt—takin' them yourself to register—*tomorra*—in Indianola!"[29]

According to Marsh, it was Hamer who combined the Christmas spiritual "Go Tell It on the Mountain" with "Go Down Moses" to transform the final line from "Go tell it on the mountain / That Jesus Christ is born!" to "Go tell it on the mountain / To let my people go!" Perhaps unique in American Christianity, African American Christians place the Old Testament Exodus narrative alongside the crucifixion and resurrection of Jesus, and in this there is a powerful spiritual connection between Jews and African Americans. It is therefore no accident that this was expressed in the active participation of Jews in the civil rights movement. There is an iconic photograph of Abraham Joshua Heschel, perhaps the greatest Jewish scholar and teacher of the twentieth century, locking arms with Martin Luther King Jr., Ralph Abernathy, Fred Shuttlesworth, and Ralph Bunche in the Selma-to-Montgomery March in

March 1965. Heschel wrote of the experience, "When I marched in Selma my legs were praying."

A Big, Proud, Prophetic Voice

It has been particularly difficult, therefore, for African Americans, confronted with the human rights issues faced by Palestinians, to deal with the fact that their solidarity with the Palestinian struggle places them at odds with the Jewish establishment. Vincent Harding weighed in on this issue: "There is a long history of anti-Semitism in the Western world," he said. "I know what my Jewish brothers and sisters had to go through for centuries, and to have it focus in such a horrific way in the Holocaust. Then to see what is now developing in a land where they settled to escape from the Holocaust is painful."[30]

Lucas Johnson spoke to me about this candidly: "I certainly felt betrayed by my Jewish friends who were not speaking out enough. I had even tempered my own speaking out because of my relationships with Jewish colleagues and friends." *Isn't it painful and ironic,* I thought, listening to Johnson's words, *that where once there was common cause, a powerful alliance for justice represented so dramatically in the photograph of Heschel marching with King, there is now this uneasiness, even wariness?* Reflecting on the powerful, inspiring responses to the Palestinian cause from the African Americans I was meeting, and considering the incalculable contribution of the civil rights struggle to the nonviolent movement for Palestine that is now under way, I felt a sharp sense of loss. At the same time, I feel hope, and an even stronger sense of inevitability that this new alliance will come to be.

When Vincent Harding saw what Israel was doing, his heart hurt for my people. The pain that he feels is an act of love. The same is true for Lucas Johnson. Now that he has seen what he has seen and knows what he knows, he is clear about the implications for his relationships with Jewish friends: "I may not owe it to them, but they matter enough to me to have gone just for them," he said to me. "Does that make sense?" Yes, it does make sense. Going to see and to then be willing to speak out is an act of love. In choosing "a positive peace which is the presence of justice" rather than a "negative peace which is the absence of tension," Johnson, Harding, Reverend Carolyn, and the growing numbers of African Americans who have traveled to the Holy Land to witness the signs of our times are demonstrating a key principle of nonviolence. As Martin Luther King Jr. wrote, "Injustice must be exposed, with all the tension its exposure creates, to the light of human conscience and the air of national opinion before it can be cured."[31] Johnson may not feel that this is something he owes his Jewish friends, but this Jew is grateful for his witness and for his voice. There is an invitation here waiting to be accepted, an opportunity for Jews to remember the gift of our connection with the African American community and the values and the shared experience that link us. It is Abraham Heschel praying with his legs; it is Henry Schwarzschild jumping on that bus. This was spirit that joined us then; this is the spirit that calls to us now.

The Palestinians are reminding us. And they are calling us to account—not only the Jewish community, but all Americans; not only the black church, but all churches. Indeed, it's a redemptive cause for the church, and for the African American church in particular, with its deep roots in the Bible as a narrative of liberation that gave hope to an oppressed people and its record of translating that faith into a real-world struggle. The black church can lead, as it has done before. It is Lucas Johnson's "living up to that legacy and to that tradition that is so meaningful and important to me," as he opens his eyes and his heart to the Palestinian struggle. It is Carolyn Boyd's appeal to "the black church to again claim its big, proud, prophetic voice."

Chapter 8

HOW THE CHURCH SAVED SOUTH AFRICA

The story is told that Archbishop Desmond Tutu, having passed from this world, presented himself at the pearly gates. St. Peter, peering over his large book at this diminutive man with the twinkling eyes, asked him who he was. "Well, I'm Desmond Tutu, former Archbishop of Cape Town and a leader of the antiapartheid movement in South Africa." St. Peter flipped through a number of pages and finally said, "Sorry, we have no record of you here. I'm going to have to send you to the other place." Thus dismissed, the archbishop did as instructed. About a week later, St. Peter had another visitor. It was the devil himself, demanding to be seen. "What are you doing here!" exclaimed the dumbfounded St. Peter. "That Tutu you sent us," replied the devil, obviously upset and desperate, "you've got to take him. He's giving us hell!"

This story was told to me by Rev. Edwin Arrison, an Anglican priest from Cape Town, South Africa, and general secretary of Kairos Southern Africa, as I sat with him in late 2012 in Washington, DC. As a student in the 1980s, Arrison was active in the antiapartheid movement. As president of a church student group, he was detained and imprisoned by the South African government in 1985 and again in 1986 for months at a time. Arrison is one of the moving forces behind the organization Kairos Southern Africa—more on that in a bit.

I first met Arrison in Bethlehem in 2009, at the launch of the Kairos Palestine document, "A Moment of Truth: A Word of Faith, Hope and Love from the Heart of Palestinian Suffering."[1] He was one of a delegation of South African clergy, academics, and activists invited to an international meeting called by the World Council of Churches to celebrate the release of this historic document. Written by a broadly ecumenical group of Palestinian Christians, the document calls on the world to witness the suffering of the Palestinian people and to stand with them in their nonviolent resistance to oppression. *Kairos* is Greek, one of the words for "time" in the New Testament, but unlike *kronos,* which denotes linear or chronological time, *kairos* is God's time—in the words of the South African Kairos document, "A moment of grace and opportunity, in which God issues a challenge for decisive action."[2] It is the time when, in American theologian Robert McAfee Brown's words, "Opportunity demands a response. God offers us a new set of possibilities and we have to accept or decline."[3]

All those assembled in this ecumenical gathering from every continent were strongly supportive of the Palestinian cause. Yet many, especially the Americans and Europeans, had worries about bringing the Palestinian call back to their church constituencies. Would this appear "too political" for the church institutions back home? Would we be suspected of embracing "liberation theology"?[a] Or, most frightening, what about the section at the end of the Kairos document that called for boycotts? There were some who claimed that this would be a deal breaker. How could we bring this home to our churches?

The South Africans, I soon discovered, were among the most prophetic people attending gathering. "Hang on," they told us, displaying the brand of grim wisdom that comes only from experience. "This is just the beginning. It took us forty years to bring about the end of apartheid in our country, and the sanctions were a major part of it. It's a long struggle, and this is what it's going to take. If you are not up for this, best to bail out now. But know this, and we can tell you from our experience, if you persist in the face of the opposition that you will face, you will succeed."

Indeed, the South Africans knew all about giving hell hell.

Of all the delegations in the room, the South Africans had earned their seats at the table. South African Christian leaders, clergy, theologians, and lay activists inaugurated twentieth-century Kairos theology in 1985 with their "Challenge to the Church: A Theological Comment on the Political Crisis in South Africa."[4] It was a document that began a global movement. Between 1985 and 1993, a number of Kairos documents appeared, from Latin America, Asia, and the United States, each taking on the cause of the oppressed

---

a. Liberation theology interprets the Gospels in relation to unjust economic, political, or social conditions. Originating in the Catholic Church in Latin America in the 1950s and '60s, it has been applied in the context of liberation struggles on every continent. It is controversial, having been opposed by the Roman Catholic Church as heretical, and rejected on a political basis by some Christians as being associated with left-wing politics or as a "Christianized Marxism."

and dispossessed in the spirit of the Gospel of Matthew, chapter 25. Then there was a hiatus—until 2009. When the Palestinians set about to write their document early that year, they turned to the South Africans. "It is time for us to write our own Kairos," said the group of Palestinian clergy, theologians, and peace activists who had realized that their Kairos time had come. "Can you help us?" A group of South Africans, including authors of the 1985 document (from many denominations and traditions, white and black), traveled to Palestine to meet with the Palestinians. They provided encouragement, shared their experience of writing their own document, and offered comments on the developing draft; but they also made it very clear that this was the Palestinians' statement. It had to speak with their voice and speak to their issues, both political and theological. And this is as it should be: each Kairos document, each Kairos movement, stands in its own context. To quote the Palestinian document: "to speak the Word of God courageously, honestly and lovingly in the local context and in the midst of daily events."[5] But it is precisely in this way that each Kairos document is connected to all the others, and all stand on the shoulders of the groundbreaking work of the South Africans.

It was therefore entirely in keeping with this close connection that in April 2011, the newly formed Kairos Southern Africa organization invited a delegation from Kairos Palestine to Johannesburg for a conference in which Kairos Palestine would be formally endorsed. I was honored to have been invited as one of several non-Palestinian and non–South African internationals. It was my first visit to South Africa, and I was not prepared for what I saw there, or for the impact of meeting the people who had lived through and fought apartheid. The experience, perhaps second only to the experience of seeing the occupation of the West Bank, has set the course for my life ever since.

Seventeen years had passed since the election of Nelson Mandela as the leader of the new South Africa. Apartheid was gone—the cruel racist laws; the machinery of a brutal, repressive police state—but the fruits of centuries of colonization and virtual enslavement of an indigenous population by a white colonial minority remained. The townships were still there: sprawling enclaves and cities within cities of shocking poverty and 70 percent unemployment. The economic disparities along racial lines, the unemployment, and the violence were all worse than they had been in the apartheid years. And so, as awed as I was to be in the presence of the women and men who had gone to jail and seen half their friends killed or exiled, but who had never faltered in their commitment to justice over those years, I was also overwhelmed by the depth and scope of the suffering and injustice that I saw in the South Africa of today.

Why? I asked my hosts, the men and women who only decades ago had risked their lives and fortunes in the struggle to end institutionalized racism in their country and in their church institutions. Why are you so wholeheartedly and passionately committed to this cause? Why little Palestine? You have massive problems here. The postapartheid era is proving more challenging in some ways than the struggle to end apartheid, as you endeavor to find a way out of the deep structural inequality that still exists.

The answers came without hesitation. First, the world was here for us during our struggle. Second, we know what apartheid is. We cannot stand by. This must be our struggle as well. But the deeper answer became clearer as I got to know these church people, theologians, and lay activists. *We need this struggle,* they told me. Reverend Arrison sat with us that day in Washington and told us in complete frankness what I had heard from those fighters against apartheid on that visit to Johannesburg two years earlier. "After we had our elections in 1994, having 'won the battle' and gained our democratic government, we lost our prophetic bearings. We forgot how to be in solidarity with ourselves as well as with others. So that when the Palestinians came to us, and we decided to be in solidarity with them, it has helped us recover our own soul. It has allowed us to rededicate ourselves to our own mission here in South Africa and to be in solidarity with human rights struggles throughout the world. Rather than taking energy away from our mission here, it has given us the energy to focus on," in Arrison's words, "the Palestinian in our backyard."[6]

This same point was driven home repeatedly in conversations with people and in my encounters across South African society. As Arrison told me, "Kairos Palestine is a blessing for us." Solidarity with the Palestinian struggle, he was saying, has put the South African church in touch with its prophetic, faithful heart. It set the South African church leaders more surely on the ground on which they live spiritually, ground they had been in danger of losing since the end of apartheid in their country. "The energy we put into Palestine," he said, "does not diminish our energy to deal with our own issues. It adds to it."[7]

South African theologian Tinyiko Maluleke, lamenting the loss of moral focus on the part of postapartheid South African leadership, described to me how a moral and ultimately spiritual focus is easily lost when the bureaucracy of government takes over. "Justice," he said, becomes instead "'Who is your chief justice, what is your criminal justice system, are you able to deal with crime, is everybody equal before the law'—a very technicist understanding of equality before the law. This is what has occupied us now, not justice in the broader, theological biblical notion of justice for people as creatures made in the image of God." Maluleke maintained that, from biblical times, throughout history, and up to the present day, it is the mission of theology to hold the powers accountable; but the institution of religion more often than not is cautious and timid rather than prophetic. "Say something scandalous!" Maluleke urges. "Propose something theologically radical! Because you can't have a theological revolution that's just rational. If you are going to be rational, you cannot go far."[8] Like Arrison, Maluleke credits the exposure of South African clergy, theologians, and activists to the injustices committed against the Palestinians for sending South Africans back to their own country inspired and ready to confront the urgent issues at home. "No wonder the Palestinian issue has so captured us here in South Africa," he remarked to me. "In our postindependence situation, justice has become a legal term!"

A pastor from Swaziland (a nation bordering South Africa and one of the member countries of the organization Kairos Southern Africa) told me that knowing about someone else's troubles and struggle helps you understand your own, because you don't feel so isolated. For a southern African, I learned, solidarity with the Palestinian struggle is not about taking on another burden or cause on top of the issues at home. It is not a net gain in responsibility. Rather, especially in the context of the monumental challenges facing southern Africa today, it makes the load lighter. So this meeting in

2011 was more than a simple expression of solidarity with the Palestinian struggling for freedom and self-determination. It was an affirmation of the overall mission of the church in southern Africa. As one of the several non-African and non-Palestinians, and the only North American in attendance, I realized that this extraordinary gathering carried a critically important message for the church globally, and the church in the United States in particular.

Church Confession, Church Struggle

In order to understand that message, we need to know a bit about the history of the church's struggle with South African apartheid.

As early as the late 1950s, statements began to emerge from South African church bodies expressing the fundamental conflict between apartheid and Christian principles. The church was beginning to confront not only its silence in the face of the racist laws, but also the fact that it was practicing racial separation and discrimination within its own walls. Most important, the church was calling into question ways in which Christian doctrine had been employed and was continuing to be used to justify policies of separation and discrimination. By the 1980s, as uprisings in the townships and the government's brutal suppression of all forms of resistance, both violent and nonviolent, brought the country to a boiling point, some South African church leaders were openly expressing support for and solidarity with the resistance movements and the political parties that were in direct opposition to the apartheid regime. Anglican bishop Desmond Tutu had assumed leadership of the South

African Council of Churches and was taking an increasingly vocal stance against apartheid.

Then came Ottawa.

In 1982 the leaders of the World Alliance of Reformed Churches (WARC) met in Ottawa, Canada, for the General Council meeting of the world body. Nine black pastors from South Africa refused to partake of the Lord's Supper with their white colleagues because they could not do so at home in apartheid South Africa. The World Alliance got the message: WARC declared the church to be in *status confessionis.* Nothing moves, they declared, all other church business takes a backseat until this betrayal of the core values of our faith is addressed. They then suspended the white South African Dutch Reformed Church member churches from the worldwide church body. The WARC leaders knew that the South African church bore responsibility for having helped create the very structures of separation and discrimination upon which the current state had been founded, and for having provided theological support for the racist policies of the regime when it took power in 1948. Furthermore, they realized that the church on a global level had been complicit in its silence and in its tacit acceptance of the situation in South Africa, and as such was in violation of the fundamental Christian principles of equality under God, the unity of all creation, and the dignity of all living things. Taking the lead in responding to this action by the world denomination, the Dutch Reformed Mission Church (the "colored" church within the Dutch Reformed Church family in South Africa) that same year declared itself in a confessional state and issued a statement that "apartheid is a sin, that the moral and theological justification of it makes a mockery of the Gospel, and its consistent disobedience to the Word of God is a theological heresy."[9] In this "Confession of Faith," thereafter known as the Belhar Confession, written in 1982 and officially adopted by the Dutch Reformed Mission Church in 1986, the church officially rejected "any doctrine which absolutizes either natural diversity or the sinful separation of people...or breaks the visible and active unity of the church..."[10] From 1990 onward, the white Dutch Reformed Church started to confess that the theological justification for apartheid was a sin. But it was not until 1998 that it was readmitted into the World Alliance of Reformed Churches on the basis of its renunciation of apartheid, even though to this date it has still not fully adopted the Belhar Confession.

The Belhar Confession was followed in 1985 by a towering statement of theological courage, titled "Challenge to the Church: A Theological Comment on the Political Crisis in South Africa," signed by 150 South African theologians. Also known as the Kairos document, it was soon seen, in the words of John Allen, a South African journalist and the biographer of Desmond Tutu, "as one of the most important theological documents of its time."[11] The 1985 Kairos document signaled the final stage of the struggle that culminated in the end of apartheid in 1994. South African theologian and church historian John de Gruchy, the author, with his son Steve de Gruchy, of *The Church Struggle in South Africa*,[12] has pointed out that *church struggle* has two meanings: the struggle was of the church not only with apartheid, but *with itself*. This recognition of church struggle is one of the keys to understanding what the story of the church in South Africa has to teach us.

Charles Villa-Vicencio, a renowned theologian who held the

key position of national research director of the Truth and Reconciliation Commission (TRC), was one of the authors of the
Kairos South Africa document. In the spring of 2011 I sat with
him in his home in Cape Town, and he answered in words
that echoed what I had heard from every South African church
leader when I posed the question "Tell us how you did it!"

"It was messy," he told me, "it was long, and as a church *we
were never united.* But those of us who took a stand prevailed
because our cause was just, and because, eventually, we had
the support of the global church. That's why Ottawa was so
important. The South African church would not have gotten
to the point where it was such a significant force of resistance without solidarity from the global church," he continued. "You must not think that the entire institutional church
in South Africa was against apartheid. The English-speaking
or so-called 'nonracial' churches talked about opposition to
apartheid, there were huge resolutions and so forth, but they
were not standing up and looking the beast in the eye and
saying, 'No more.' It was a small coterie—don't let anyone tell
you that we were united. It was messy and it was long. And
we hung in."[13]

"We realized," Villa-Vicencio told me, "that this was not
only or simply a struggle against the political order. We had
to take on not only those in the government, but those in
our own church institutions who wanted to hold on to the
existing order. Many in the institutional church regarded
us as heretics! It was the church in confrontation with the
church." This is the meaning of what John and Steve de
Gruchy called "the church struggle," and it's a key lesson
for the church in the United States. As Villa-Vicencio also
pointed out, it was in the context of this *church struggle* that

the Kairos document was born. "It's where we distinguished between the theology of the church and the theology of resistance."

The South African Kairos document articulated a moral imperative to recognize the evil of apartheid and to take direct and clear action to address it. But true to its title ("Challenge to the Church"), this historic document spoke directly to the institution of the church itself, presenting a *theological* imperative—challenging the faithful, in Villa-Vicencio's words, to "wrench the church from its slumbers."[14] "A church, he wrote several years after the publication of the Kairos South Africa document, "trapped in the dominant structures of oppression, controlled by entrenched bureaucracy, [and] conditioned by a history of compromise" ignores the voices of the oppressed at its peril."[15] Addressing the South African church's history of complicity with apartheid, the Kairos South Africa document described the "church theology" that had supported the racist policies of the government. It announced that a profound crisis for the church had arrived, a "moment of truth." "*At this moment in South Africa the Church is about to be shown up for what it really is and no cover-up will be possible*" (emphasis added).[16]

This is what I brought home with me from South Africa: Whereas the Palestinian document was the cry of the oppressed, the South African document was the *confession of the complicit.* I realized that the struggle of these South African theologians, priests, and pastors was the model for the present and coming church struggle in the United States. No, the oppression of the Palestinians was not happening literally in our midst, in our cities, or by legislative authority within our own country (the story of how we dealt with the

U.S. version of legalized racism has its own lessons to teach), but the complicity of the United States in what is happening in occupied Palestine could not be clearer. Reading the confession of the South African church over its role in supporting apartheid, I read the story of our own theological and political support for *the building of apartheid in our time.* If the Palestinian call was reviving the Kairos movement in South Africa—if in response to this urgent situation, Kairos movements were springing up across the globe—what would it mean if the church in the United States failed to join the struggle?

Kairos South Africa: A Challenge to the Church

In the South Africa Kairos document, South African Christians, black and white, address not the perpetrators of the evil in the Pretoria government, but rather their own church, and what they name the "church theology" that was complicit in both creating and maintaining the vast system of apartheid. It is a theology, the document asserts, that "tends to make use of absolute principles such as reconciliation and nonviolence and applies them indiscriminately and uncritically to all situations. Very little attempt is made to analyze what is actually happening in our society...Closely linked to this is the lack of an adequate understanding of politics and political strategy."[17] Church theology is as powerful as it is pernicious because it flies under the false flag of defending human rights and opposing oppression. "In a limited, guarded and cautious way this theology is critical of apartheid," explain the authors. "Its criticism, however, is superficial and counter-productive because instead of engaging in an in-depth analysis of the signs of our times, it relies upon a few stock ideas derived from Christian tradition and then uncritically and repeatedly applies them to our situation."[18]

The brilliance of the South Africa Kairos document is that in their analysis of three "stock ideas" (reconciliation, justice, and nonviolence) the authors go straight to the heart of the faith—to the heart of the Gospel, in fact. As we read the South Africa Kairos document today, the parallels to the apartheid system now in place in Palestine jump from the page.

Reconciliation

"Church Theology" often describes the Christian stance in the following way: "We must be fair. We must listen to both sides of the story. If the two sides can only meet to talk and negotiate they will sort out their differences and misunderstandings, and the conflict will be resolved." The fallacy here is that "Reconciliation" has been made into an absolute principle. But there are conflicts where one side is a fully armed and violent oppressor while the other side is defenseless and oppressed. To speak of reconciling these two is not only a mistaken application of the Christian idea of reconciliation, it is a total betrayal of all that Christian faith has ever meant. In our situation in South Africa today it would be totally unchristian to plead for reconciliation and peace before the present injustices have been removed...No reconciliation is possible in South Africa without justice.[19]

This analysis goes to the heart of the problem when applied to the situation in Israel and occupied Palestine today.

One of the most striking features of the discourse in the United States is the preoccupation with the need for a "balanced" perspective. Here is how this typically plays out: you may not talk about house demolitions, checkpoints, restrictions on movement, the death of innocent civilians, targeted assassinations, or any other examples of Palestinian suffering, without presenting what is usually termed the "other side." The "other side" is the recognition of the suffering of the Israelis, who have endured five wars, terrorist attacks, and the sense that they are surrounded by implacable enemies.[20] You may not talk about the dispossession of the Palestinians to make way for the Jewish state without noting historic Jewish suffering or the displacement of Jews from Arab countries after the establishment of the State of Israel.[21] On its face, this seems fair. But in the current discourse, the demand for "balance" is not about being fair. Rather, it is used to blunt scrutiny of those actions of Israel that are the root cause of the conflict. As the South African document so effectively sets out, appeals here to principles of "reconciliation," "dialogue" and "balance" often serve not to advance but to obscure the issue of justice. The example of South Africa demonstrates that it is only when the *structures of inequality and discrimination* have been removed that activities devoted to reconciliation between the parties can be undertaken. "True justice, God's justice," the South Africa document states, "*demands a radical change of structures*" (emphasis added).

Justice

The very serious theological question is: What kind of justice? An examination of Church statements and pronouncements gives the distinct impression that the justice that is envisaged is the justice of reform, that is to say, a justice that is determined by the oppressor, by the white minority and that is offered to the people as a kind of concession. It does not appear to be the more radical justice that comes from below and is determined by the people of South Africa. There have been reforms and, no doubt, there will be further reforms in the near future...But can such reforms ever be regarded as real change, as the introduction of a true and lasting justice?[22]

By 1985, the Pretoria government was on the ropes: isolated in the world, facing economic sanctions, and brutally suppressing the rapidly spreading protests in the cities and townships. In desperation, it offered reforms: blacks in the national parliament (but with less voting power than whites) and "homelands" for blacks, which were political enclaves surrounded by a white-ruled South Africa, the so-called Bantustans. It was, in effect, a "two-state solution" in which the subject race was politically and economically subordinate to the white ruling class. Reform, therefore, had become a key issue in the antiapartheid struggle. The Kairos authors were particularly concerned about the implications for the struggle against racism, because these offers by the government mirrored for them the attempts of some of the churches to enact superficial changes that did not address the underlying racial inequalities built into church practice and through which the churches continued to support the racist government policies. Let us remember that the central focus of Belhar—really, the whole point of the confession—was that *any* distinctions based on race were violations of the most fundamental values of Christianity.

Jesus was clear about the uncompromising stance required of those who would bring the alternative order he called the Kingdom of God. "Do you suppose," he asks his disciples, "that I came to give peace on earth? I tell you, not at all, but rather division" (Luke 12:51). It was not that Jesus wanted people to fight with one another, or that he was advocating conflict. The Greek word typically translated as "division" is *diamerismon*: to make a clear distinction between right and wrong; *to know the difference*. This is how we can understand the statement by Jesus in Matthew 10:34: "I have not come to bring peace, but a sword." This is the sword that cleanly and clearly separates truth from words that obscure and blunt the truth. It is knowing the difference between a theology that supports the policies and institutional structures of oppression and a theology that, in response to history and human affairs, stands boldly with the widow, the orphan, the poor, and the dispossessed.

Those who have witnessed the inexorable construction of illegal settlements and the all-but-completed infrastructure of barriers, checkpoints, permits, and separate roads in occupied Palestine have come to understand that without fundamental modification, the "two-state solution" on the table today will in effect legitimize an apartheid system worse in some ways than the one that held South Africa in its grip. And yet, this is the solution, in effect the "reform" to "end" the Israeli occupation, to which politicians and media continue to pay lip service. To continue to call for "negotiations" while this process of colonization and economic control is allowed to progress unabated is to accede to a structure of inequality that is both unacceptable and unsustainable. "Progressive" thinkers among Jews disturbed by Israel's behavior attempt to find ways to remove or remediate the most egregious aspects of Israeli policy without addressing the root cause of the abuses, which arise inevitably from Israel's attempt to maintain Jewish rule over a diverse population. Martin Luther King Jr.'s "Letter from Birmingham Jail" was his answer to the southern clergymen who sought to soothe the sting of segregation without disturbing the power structure that kept the racist system in place. *"What kind of justice?"* ask the authors of the South Africa Kairos document. Apartheid, they declared, cannot be reformed—any effort to modify or remediate the system without addressing the fundamental structures of inequality would be a betrayal both of the struggle and of their beliefs as Christians.

Nonviolence

The problem for the Church here is the way the word violence is being used in the propaganda of the State. The State and the media have chosen to call violence what some people do in the townships as they struggle for their liberation, i.e. throwing stones, burning cars and buildings and sometimes killing collaborators. But this excludes the structural, institutional and unrepentant violence of the State and especially the oppressive and naked violence of the police and the army. *These things are not counted as violence*...Thus the phrase "violence in the townships" comes to mean what the young people are doing and not what the police are doing or what apartheid in general is doing to people. (emphasis added)[23]

The parallels are obvious. Israeli state violence, not only in its overt forms, but as structural violence in the form of imprisonment, restrictions of all kinds, and unequal access to services and distribution of resources, is contextualized as self-defense. Palestinian resistance is framed as terrorism. The document continues:

> In practice what one calls "violence" and what one calls "self-defense" seems to depend upon which side one is on. To call all physical force "violence" is to try to be neutral and to refuse to make a judgment about who is right and who is wrong. The attempt to remain neutral in this kind of conflict is futile. Neutrality enables the status quo of oppression (and therefore violence) to continue. It is a way of giving tacit support to the oppressor.[24]

The Challenge to the American Church

The South Africa Kairos document was the result of a decades-long church struggle to claim the church's prophetic heart. It arose from a context of the church—comprising black and white, theologians, pastors and lay leaders—acknowledging its complicity with a political system that violated the fundamental values upon which Christianity was founded. This is where the U.S. church finds itself as it witnesses Israel's ongoing dispossession and oppression of the Palestinians. The time has come to make a choice. It is the choice between theologies that cling to exceptionalist doctrines that pervert the words of Scripture into supporting oppression and land-taking, and a movement of renewal and a return to core values of universalism, social justice, and human dignity—the building of the Kingdom of God here on earth. The challenge to the U.S. church is as clear as that faced by the South African church three decades ago. Theologian Walter Wink reminds us that the pursuit of justice requires active involvement and often discomfort:

> Most Christians desire nonviolence, yes; but they are not talking about a non-violent struggle for justice. They mean simply the absence of conflict. They would like the system to change without having to be involved in changing it...When a church that has not lived out a costly identification with the oppressed offers to mediate between hostile parties, it merely adds to the total impression that it wants to stay above the conflict and not take sides. The church says to the lion and the lamb, "Here, let me negotiate a truce," to which the lion replies, "Fine, after I finish my lunch."[25]

Wink's admonition speaks directly to us as we witness the continued dispossession of the Palestinian people while the endless and so-called peace process continues. *One has to take sides.* Wink drives the point home when he says, "When church leaders preach reconciliation without having unequivocally committed themselves to struggle on the side of the oppressed for justice, they are caught straddling a pseudo-neutrality made of nothing but thin air...Likewise, blanket denunciations of violence by churches place the counterviolence of the oppressed on the same level as the violence of the system that has driven the oppressed to such desperation. Are stones thrown by youth really commensurate with buckshot and real bullets fired by police?"[26]

Like the South African clergy and church leaders of the antiapartheid struggle, increasing numbers of Christians in the United States, confronted with the ethical and religious imperatives presented by the human rights issues in Israel and Palestine, have been turning to the options of nonviolent direct action that are available to them. These include divesting church investments from companies profiting from the occupation of Palestinian lands, participating in boycotts of goods produced in the occupied West Bank land, or advocating for the U.S. government to cease funding Israeli government actions recognized as illegal under international law. In this they are often challenged, on institutional and personal levels, by voices in the Jewish community and in the churches, who say that boycotts of Israeli goods or sanctions directed at the Israeli government are acts of anti-Semitism or threaten the security and well-being of the State of Israel.

When challenged in this way, remember South Africa. The sanctions and boycotts that finally brought the South African government to the table were not motivated by hatred of the South African people. The international antiapartheid movement did not destroy South Africa—*it saved South Africa,* by bringing about the end of the political system that had poisoned the society and made it a pariah among the nations of the world. The sanctions, together with the resistance movements, gave the citizens of South Africa hope for the future by ending the racist system and bringing about a true democracy. *It was a loving act.* And it was the churches of South Africa, with the overwhelming support of the global church, that played a key role in liberating South Africans, both black and white, from the evils of apartheid. Can we see the growing church activism for justice for Palestinians in the same way, as the vanguard of love for the people of the Holy Land—Jews, Christians and Muslims, Israelis and Palestinians—all in desperate need of liberation?

An Apartheid Ambush

In December 2012, a group of twelve South African Christian leaders visited the West Bank. Their visit was undertaken, in the words of the South Africans' report, "in direct response to the Palestinian Christians' invitation to come and see for ourselves."[27] The delegation included Southern Africa heads of the Methodist and Presbyterian Churches, the secretary-general of the Evangelical Alliance of South Africa, a senior member of the Dutch Reformed Church, and a representative of South African youth. Their experience resembled that of many South Africans who have seen the occupation: "Our exposure to East Jerusalem and the West Bank was overwhelming," they reported, "one which traumatised us."[28]

It is not easy to be confronted with injustice and suffering that is so close to your own. We're reminded of the reports of African Americans in the previous chapter, finding themselves suddenly reinserted into a scenario that was shockingly and painfully familiar. Not long ago, South African theologian Charles Villa-Vicencio shared with me an experience from the apartheid years: "I remember the first time I went to Palestine, in the late 1980s. I was with a black South African and I remember him saying to me at the time, 'This is worse than what we've got in South Africa.'"[29] It is an observation that many South African visitors have echoed upon witnessing the situation in Palestine today. The members of this recent delegation did not mince words:

Being South African, it felt like walking into another apartheid ambush. We witnessed violations of the international human rights law and the international humanitarian law on so many levels—the multiple house demolitions, the discriminatory legal system, the daily intimidation, the Apartheid Wall and its associated regime of restrictions on movement and access, the damage to olive groves, the imprisonment of a large percentage of Palestinians including children, the confiscation of water and land, the closure of previously bustling streets and businesses, separate pavements and a system whereby the colour of Palestinian vehicles' number plates restrict them to certain roads.[30]

Because this was a church delegation, special attention was paid to the experience of the Palestinian Christians: "We heard from Christians how they have experienced a political and an identity catastrophe (the *Nakba*) since 1948, when the State of Israel was declared and 750,000 Palestinians became refugees. Moreover, they experience a theological catastrophe as Christianity is being used to justify the oppression of the indigenous Palestinian people."[31]

A theological catastrophe. For these South African pilgrims, the plight of the Palestinian people was not only about the human rights of an oppressed group. It was about the church, it was about the Gospels, it was about the core of their own faith and the stirring in them of a powerful sense of mission:

What we have discerned is in alignment with what the Palestinian Christians propose in their kairos document, "A Moment of Truth: A word of faith, hope, and love from the heart of the Palestinian suffering." This urgent appeal to the international community proposes resistance to Israel's occupation as an act of love. We also come with the understanding that all humans— Jews, Muslims, Christians and all others—are created in the image of God, and that, as phrased by the Palestinian Christians, *"this dignity is one and the same in each and all of us. This means for us, here and now, in this land in particular, that God created us not so that we might engage in strife and conflict but rather that we might come and know and love one another, and together build up the land in love and mutual respect."*[32] As Africans we in turn bring our understanding of the spiritual concept of "ubuntu" whereby a person is a person through others, thus recognising the interconnectivity between all which expresses the value and meaning of life and of relationships. As such we recognise the humanity and the dignity of both the oppressed and the oppressor. We resist fundamentalist, exclusivist theologies and ideologies, but we do not do so from a perspective of hatred, violence or separateness. (emphasis in original)[33]

Indeed, what had "ambushed" these church leaders was not only the shock of recognizing the same injustice they had suffered in their own country, but their own vivid memory of what they had accomplished in their struggle, a reminder of what the church can do, a reminder of the power of faith and of the interconnectivity of all human beings. When people of the church come together around issues of human rights and oppression, there is a common language and clear understanding. It is the church within the church. The Kairos challenge is the same that confronts seekers of justice in every age and every place, the same appeal to those spiritual values that must form the heart and become the driver for the struggle. The church is taking this on—in South Africa, in the United States, and in a growing number of centers in Europe, Asia, and South America. And it is the church, globally, that will be crucial in ending the system that is destroying Israeli society from within, a system that represents one of the most longstanding and shameful violations of human rights in the world today. What I experienced in South Africa convinced me that an energized South African church will play a leading role in the global movement to end apartheid in our time.

Chapter 9

VOICES FROM PALESTINE

I sat in the tent, and it was full of light.

Fawzieh al-Kurd is the matriarch of one of the three families who were expelled from their homes in the Sheikh Jarrah neighborhood of Jerusalem between November 2008 and October 2009. Close to sixty people, 1948-era refugees from West Jerusalem and other parts of what is now Israel, had been resettled in this neighborhood in the 1950s by international agreement. Now they had been evicted by the Israeli government, their homes turned over to fundamentalist Jewish settlers. Fawzieh's family was the first—ejected forcibly in the middle of the night by Israeli military on November 9, 2008. Fawzieh's husband, Muhammad, confined to a wheelchair and in fragile health, died eleven days after the eviction.

The evicted Palestinian families have erected temporary shelters on the streets and on adjacent properties in protest: they are not leaving.

When you visit Sheikh Jarrah, you are in the heart of the

occupation. Yes, one can say the same thing about Hebron, a city in the West Bank, south of Bethlehem, where six hundred Israeli settlers, protected by a garrison of Israeli soldiers, hold sixteen thousand Palestinians prisoners in their own city; or Jayyous, a village in the northern West Bank where farmers are barred from their fields by the separation barrier; or at the Bethlehem checkpoint, where thousands of men and women trying to reach their places of work, visit family, or get to hospitals by daybreak begin to line up at 2:00 A.M. in narrow lanes that resemble cattle chutes. But there was something about this latest outrage that drew me, on my way out of the country in December 2009, after attending the World Council of Churches' launch of the Kairos Palestine document, to pay a visit to these families. What is happening in Sheikh Jarrah is part of the project, plain for all to see, to create a wholly Jewish Jerusalem. "Greater Jerusalem" is a microcosm of Israel's all-but-completed colonization of the West Bank: it has become a city maintained for Jews, the remaining Palestinians confined to shrinking enclaves. Along with existing and planned Jewish neighborhoods, a Sheikh Jarrah with its Palestinian residents replaced by Jews will help complete a ring of Jewish settlements that will enclose the entire city. As the displaced families continue their protest, lawyers for each side continue to make their cases about who owns the houses. But the source of this suffering is not a dispute between two parties claiming the same piece of property. This is something else: a dispute between a party that is willing to share and one that is not.

I sat in the tent with Fawzieh, who seemed at peace despite the trauma, indignity, and loss she had suffered. Not that she did not have questions or a lot to say: How, she asked, can they accuse me of wanting to make war when one of the names I use for God in my daily prayers is *salaam*—peace? Why, she continued, are they doing this to us when we believe in the unity of all peoples? She then recited, at length and from memory, the sura from the Koran that asserts the holiness and value of all the prophets that came before Muhammad, including Moses and Jesus, and the duty of all Muslims to honor them.

I walked across the front yard, garbage strewn and littered with the ruined kitchen appliances and furniture that had been the al-Kurds' property, and approached a group of black-suited, black-hatted young men—religious Jews, the current occupiers of the al-Kurd home. I spoke with them in Hebrew, proffering my Jewish credentials: "My grandfather was born less than a mile from here, a fifth-generation Jew in the Holy Land." The men—some seemed more like boys—regarded me with suspicion. Having observed me sitting with Fawzieh, they knew where my sympathies lay. As we talked, I realized that their facing me from the other side of a very clear dividing line was fine with them. They didn't expect to change my views, and they were clear about theirs. In fact, as I attempted to engage them, I understood that a sense of being embattled was an essential element of their identity. In their minds, they were the present-day Jewish pioneers, God's warriors. Covering the front door of the house were stickers reading THE PEOPLE OF ISRAEL WILL BE VICTORIOUS!, using the Hebrew word for military victory. It was a source of pride for them that their actions (robbing families of their homes) were engendering rage and indignation and even organized protests. This was part of the hard work of reclaiming the land for God. They dismissed my suggestion that they consider the suffering and the human rights of the people they had displaced. God, they said, has given this to us. We are supposed to be here.

I had heard that claim so many times before that it didn't affect me to hear it again. But on that day, I found myself particularly upset by their assertion that the people they had displaced deserved to be supplanted by God's Chosen because they were teaching their children to hate the Jews. This, too, I had heard before, along with the other racist beliefs that many Israelis hold about the Palestinians (dirty; thieves; bad parents). But I had just been listening to Fawzieh's pain—not about losing her home, but about what was happening to her grandson. This is a boy, she told me, who had been earning high grades in school and had demonstrated a gift for writing, but whose only wish now was to grow up to be a pilot "so that he could kill Jews." This was her pain: that her future, the future for her family and her community that she had planned and had wished for, that indeed her faith had directed her toward, was being stolen. A house could be rebuilt, but a future generation could not so easily be redeemed. It hurt her heart.

The battle is joined. It is the conflict between those who plan a future based on dispossession, grasping, and fear, and those who desire to live in a community committed to welcoming and inclusiveness. Here, in this little neighborhood, the Jews barricade themselves behind gates and doors and declare victory. The Palestinians sit in their tents, like Abraham of old and, indeed, like Palestinians in any West Bank or Gaza village or city, they open their homes to all comers. They serve coffee. They offer their hope and they share their pain. They appeal to the international community to witness their situation and not to sit idly by.

Armageddon, Straight Ahead

On that day, the street was quiet except for the families and a smattering of other internationals like me, in the company of my friend Nora Carmi from the Sabeel Ecumenical Liberation Theology Center. Two days earlier there had been a large demonstration on this very street. Whereas the displaced Sheikh Jarrah families protested through their steadfast and quiet presence, the demonstrations in support of the families organized by internationals, Israelis, and Palestinians, though nonviolent, grew large and did sometimes produce physical confrontations with supporters of the "other side" and with Israeli police. At this and previous demonstrations on this street, the atmosphere was often tense, voices were raised in anger and outrage, and there were arrests of protesters who had crossed police lines. The previous month, Rabbi Arik Ascherman of Rabbis for Human Rights had posted a piece on the organization's website entitled "Armageddon, Straight Ahead." Rabbis for Human Rights is an Israeli organization devoted to protecting human rights in Israel on a wide range of issues. You will find Rabbi Ascherman and his colleagues confronting Jewish settlers and Israeli soldiers in the West Bank when Palestinian farmers are being harassed or when Palestinian homes are threatened with demolition. Now he has taken on the cause of the Palestinians of East Jerusalem. Ascherman's language in the piece is telling. Arriving at Sheikh Jarrah on the day of one of the protests and clearly shaken, Ascherman wrote, "I see a Palestinian anger burning so strong that, unlike what usually happens, neither the threat of arrest or the use of overwhelming force is a deterrent.

"In similar situations," he continued, "I have urged Palestinians to calm down, but here I felt that I had no right and that it would do no good...Israel's democracy has failed up until now. International pressure has failed up until now. The activist community has failed up until now...I see Jerusalem in flames—I see Armageddon straight ahead."[1]

Arik Ascherman has committed his life to nonviolent opposition to the occupation. Witnessing the settlers moving into the homes under the noses of the dispossessed families, he could only stand by silently, witnessing the outrage and feeling, perhaps, the violence stirring in his own heart. As I read his words and as I identify with his feelings, I find myself wondering: Is there a wish here that the seething violence at this outrage will finally break out in what he terms "Intifada 3"?[2] I will not second-guess what might have been going on in his mind or heart as he wrote his words, but I will confess to what was going on in mine when I read them: the wish that something would happen to break the deadlock, to put an end to the suffering of the Palestinians and slam the brakes on Israel's headlong rush into disaster. I imagined that Rabbi Ascherman at that moment was thinking that no one, certainly not he, had the right to deny these people their right to resist the crimes being committed against them, even when that resistance might take violent forms.

A Cry of Pain, a Cry of Hope

I was in the country, along with more than sixty Palestinian and international religious leaders, theologians, and peace activists, to attend the conference organized by the World Council of Churches' Palestine Israel Ecumenical Forum to launch the Kairos Palestine document, "A Moment of Truth: A Cry of Faith, Hope, and Love from the Heart of Palestinian Suffering." In this powerful, courageous document issued in 2009 from Bethlehem, the Palestinian Christians speak on behalf of their entire people in occupied Palestine and in exile. Kairos Palestine was written, in the words of its preamble,

> because today we have reached a dead end in the tragedy of the Palestinian people. The decision-makers content themselves with managing the crisis rather than committing themselves to the serious task of finding a way to resolve it. The hearts of the faithful are filled with pain and with questioning: What is the international community doing? What are the political leaders in Palestine, in Israel and in the Arab world doing? What is the Church doing?[3]

The authors of the Kairos document were confronting the same reality that prompted Rabbi Ascherman's cry of pain and frustration. Ascherman's biblical reference was fitting: Armageddon is the symbol for the final battle between good and evil. But in their urgent cry, the authors of the Kairos Palestine document were concerned not with the end of days or the clash of opposing armies but with the present-day struggle between hope and despair, between compassion and human connection versus the imposition of power over the powerless. The document expresses the redemptive vision that was articulated so long ago in these very hills, in this very city. I had heard Fawzieh express that same vision. Sitting with her, I found myself telling her that I had come to her tent to support her, but that it was *my* bruised heart that was being healed by her loving spirit. I sat in the tent and it was full of light.

The light in that tent is the same light that emanates from the Kairos document. The document is a cry of pain that points to hope. This hope is grounded in community and in a fierce commitment to nonviolence. It reaches out to the forces that continue the attempt to thwart that hope and that spirit of dignity. It recognizes that to fail to resist the injustice would be to compound the sin by failing to honor the humanity of the oppressor. Resistance, the authors of the document point out, is not only about saying "no" to evil. It must also involve active, compassionate engagement with the other: in the words of the document, "[s]eeing the image of God in the face of the enemy."[4]

Amid the din of protesters and counterprotesters and the arguments between litigants about who are the rightful owners of parcels of land, Jerusalem today is the site of a struggle between the occupiers and the dispossessed. It is not in the courts, the arguments of lawyers, or the declarations of politicians that this conflict will be resolved. It is in the higher court of immutable principles of human rights and universal justice.

The same month that I visited Sheikh Jarrah, Palestinian human rights attorney and activist Jonathan Kuttab proposed in the *Los Angeles Times* that peace would be found not in separation, but in coexistence. What is this "two-state" future, he wonders, as Israel continues to take more and more control of the entire territory? "As the options keep narrowing for all participants," he writes, "we need to start thinking of how we can live together, rather than insist on dying apart."[5] That day I contemplated the front yard of the al-Kurd home.

It looked like a garbage dump, strewn with the family furniture that had been tossed out by the occupying Israeli settlers. *This is the future of this land if Israel's project of dispossession continues,* I thought to myself. You can see the similar evidence of the destruction of a society in the cities, in the countryside, at the checkpoints, in the refugee camps, all along the obscene separation wall, and in the deepening horror of Gaza. Disaster, chaos, loss, ruin—for both peoples.

Or it can be the light in the tent: Fawzieh's vision of peaceful coexistence—her smile, in spite of it all. The open tents of the families sitting opposite their homes, now occupied by Jewish families and festooned indecently with Israeli flags. The growing realization that, as Kuttab suggests, if we cannot live together we will die together. Palestinian human rights activist Ali Abunimah recently characterized Israel as resembling a failed state. He, too, pointed to a "shared future" for Israelis and Palestinians as the only path to peace, writing that "despite the failed peace process industry's efforts to ridicule, suppress and marginalise it, there is a growing debate among Palestinians and even among Israelis about a shared future in Palestine/Israel based on equality and decolonisation, rather than ethno-national segregation and forced repartition."[6]

This is how it will be won, whatever the ultimate political solution will be: through the spirit of people who believe in community and in shared hope; through the resistance of women such as Fawzieh, sitting in their tents in the shadow of the occupiers. It will be won through the resistance of the women, men, and children who awaken every day in their occupied land and go on with their lives, fully claiming their identity as Palestinians. It will be won through the witness of the authors of the Kairos Palestine document, who, like the men and women of the South African church decades before, saw clearly what their faith as Christians required of them, if they were truly to see themselves as the church:

> The mission of the Church is prophetic, to speak the Word of God courageously, honestly and lovingly in the local context and in the midst of daily events. If she does take sides, it is with the oppressed, to stand alongside them, just as Christ our Lord stood by the side of each poor person and each sinner, calling them to repentance, life, and the restoration of the dignity bestowed on them by God and that no one has the right to strip away.[7]

In an act of witness and resistance, they have thrown down this challenge to their oppressors:

> Even though we have fought one another in the recent past and still struggle today, we are able to love and live together. We can organize our political life, with all its complexity, according to the logic of this love and its power, after ending the occupation and establishing justice. Our future and their future are one: either the cycle of violence that destroys both of us or a peace that will benefit both.[8]

Reading the Signs of the Times

By the end of the first decade of the twenty-first century, it was becoming clear to Palestinians that not only had the Oslo Accords failed to bring about a Palestinian state, but that the annexation and control of the West Bank by Israel was intensifying: settlements were growing, the separation wall and network of Jewish-only roads nearing completion, Jewish "Greater Jerusalem" expanding at the expense of what few Palestinian neighborhoods still remained, the noose of occupation tightening. Accordingly, in 2009, in the words of Rifat Odeh Kassis, coordinator of Kairos Palestine, "at a particularly dark moment of Palestinian reality"

> the Kairos Document has emerged—a moment that has itself emerged from many dark decades of Palestinian history. The Palestinian people have experienced dispossession, dispersion, manipulation, and control at the hands of foreign regimes for the past six decades; they have suffered direct military occupation for more than four decades. They have, over time, attempted many means of resistance, all of which were ultimately in vain. The endless political negotiations have reached a dead-end; there is no indication that this so-called "peace process" will advance, and certainly not with an outcome that is remotely just.[9]

Kassis goes on to explain the genesis of the document. "We—ultimately a group of 15 interdenominational Palestinian Christian leaders—decided to name our document 'kairos,' in order to evoke the South African document issued in 1985." This was done, writes Kassis, "in order to honor the legacy of their call for justice," but also "to show that religion can and should play an active and positive role…in the conflict and its resolution."[10] The Palestinian document honors the legacy of the South African document in articulating a powerful theological imperative. It begins, as does the Kairos South Africa document, with a summons to the church to fulfill its historic and sacred duty.

> This document is the Christian Palestinians' word to the world about what is happening in Palestine...The document requests the international community to stand by the Palestinian people who have faced oppression, displacement, suffering and clear apartheid for more than six decades...Our word is a cry of hope, with love, prayer and faith in God. We address it first of all to ourselves and then to all the churches and Christians in the world, asking them to stand against injustice and apartheid, urging them to work for a just peace in our region.

Having issued this call, the authors go on to identify the "signs of the times" that require a response. They set out the oppression itself in theological terms, as "a sin against God and humanity because it deprives the Palestinians of their basic human rights, bestowed by God." "Our reality," they write, "is one of Israeli occupation," beginning with a description of the separation wall erected on Palestinian territory that "has turned our towns and villages into prisons...making them dispersed and divided cantons." The accounting of the reality of occupation continues with the prison of blockaded Gaza, the ever-increasing settlements "that steal and ravage our land," daily humiliation and delay at the military checkpoints, home demolitions, the emptying of Jerusalem of its Palestinian inhabitants, and the tragic fate of millions of refugees, "waiting for their right of return, generation after generation. What will be their fate?"[11]

Like the South African document, Kairos Palestine bases its call to the world and to the churches in particular on the message of the Gospels. The authors are quite clear, as were their South African predecessors, about the key role played by theology in perpetuating the injustice. The document demonstrates its strong, prophetic voice in directly stating the destructive effect of the misuse of text: "We know that certain theologians in the West try to attach a biblical and theological legitimacy to the infringement of our rights...The 'good news' in the Gospel itself has become 'a harbinger of death' for us...Any use of the Bible to legitimize or support political options based on injustice...strip[s] the Word of God of its holiness, universality, and truth."

In the tradition of the South African document, the Palestinian "Moment of Truth" boldly puts forward a theology that requires Christians to work actively to carry out the mission of the Church of Jesus Christ:

Our Church points to the Kingdom, which cannot be tied to any earthly kingdom. Jesus said before Pilate that he was indeed a king, but "my kingdom is not from this world" (John 18:36). Saint Paul says: "The Kingdom of God is not food and drink but righteousness and peace and joy in the Holy Spirit" (Romans 14:17). Therefore, religion cannot favour or support any unjust political regime, but must rather promote justice, truth and human dignity. It must exert every effort to purify regimes where human beings suffer injustice and human dignity is violated.[12]

"Why Am I Being Silenced?"

Since the publication of the Kairos document, the Christian Palestinian voice invoking this call for kingdom building has been growing stronger. In 2010 a historic conference took place in Bethlehem, organized by the Bethlehem Bible College. As an evangelical institution, the Bible College, as it is called, was addressing itself in particular to American evangelicals, most of whom by default subscribe to some form of Christian Zionism. The first conference exceeded expectations, with hundreds of attendees from around the world, but predominantly from the United States. In 2012 the second Christ at the Checkpoint conference drew double the attendance of the first. The majority of those present were evangelical Christians from the United States, in Palestine for a week of lectures, workshops, prayer, and exposure to occupied Palestine through daily excursions. I was privileged to attend, and for me one of high points was an address by Munther Isaac, a Palestinian theologian who, in the most personal and passionate way, drove home the message of Kairos Palestine. Vice academic dean of the Bible College, Isaac had served as the conference director. Young, handsome, with piercing eyes and a calm but intense demeanor, Isaac held us spellbound as he delivered his address.[13] Surveying the large audience, he thanked those assembled for "coming here to listen to us, to listen to the story of the Palestinian church." He made it clear that his talk would be "a reflection on my personal journey and theology of the land.

"For us Palestinians," he pointed out, "it is not an academic study, the theology of the land. It is very personal. And that is why I will start with my context. And when I speak about my theology of the land, I will speak in the first person. Because it is about my life." He also prefaced with a warning: "If you sense any anger in my talk—we've been through a lot." He continued: "I am a Palestinian Christian, not invented.[b] I was born in Bethlehem to an Arab Palestinian family. I can trace my family to at least ten generations that we have been living here in Bethlehem. I am an evangelical Christian, a follower of Jesus, a sinner saved by grace."[14] After these prefatory remarks, Isaac, as promised, demonstrated how the doing of theology for a Palestinian is an intensely personal matter. He wasted no time getting to the point: "I do not hate the Jewish people. It is against my new nature in Christ to hate." But, he continued, "it seems that I can no longer speak about my suffering without suffering the consequences of being labeled either anti-Semitic or a replacement theologian."[15]

Replacement theology is one of the names given to the church doctrine that has accounted for so much Jewish suffering. A doctrine that has been used to demonize Jews and denigrate Judaism, it has been repudiated by theologians and church bodies, and is a major focus of Christian penitence for sins against the Jewish people. But on this point, Isaac invites us to enter into a nuanced discussion. He points out how the Christian renunciation of anti-Judaism has been used as a weapon to silence critics of Israel and has rendered him and his fellow Palestinians invisible. "I believe that *replacement theology*...has become a dirty word," he said. "It's even considered by many a heresy. And I am more convinced that

---

b. This reference to Republican presidential candidate Newt Gingrich's 2011 statement that the Palestinians are "an invented people" drew appreciative laughter and applause from the audience.

most who use the term define it as any theology that is different from Christian Zionism."

Isaac is doing serious theology here. Recall that he is addressing an audience made up chiefly of non-Arab Christians who were raised in various versions of a theology that holds that the land of Israel belongs to the Jews by divine promise, historical right, or some combination of the two. (It is important to note that in this theology there is little to no distinction made between the biblical Promised Land and the modern State of Israel.) In this theology there is no room for Palestinians; they are discounted, or simply disappear. Pastor John Hagee of Christians United for Israel, a prominent U.S. Christian Zionist ministry, certainly discounts them, and in racist tones that would likely be rejected by everyone Isaac was addressing that day.[16] However—and this is Isaac's point—a wide range of Christians, while rejecting the dispensationalist eschatology advanced by Hagee and others, still feel that in order to renounce anti-Semitism, they must ignore the Palestinians or at the very least place their rights as secondary to the existence of a secure (and majority) Jewish state.

"Our mere presence and voice presents [sic] a dilemma for many Christian Zionists, who still prefer the traditional simple picture: the axis of good and axis of evil picture," he told the audience. "It keeps them safe when they speak and talk about the Middle East. We were at best ignored." Look at your theology, Isaac challenged us that day. "It is one thing to have a theological position. It's another to ignore the question about the ethical ramifications of that theological position."[17]

Of course, Isaac said, Jewish suffering is real, and the church has to answer for it. But, he continued, *replacement theology is not the problem; anti-Semitism is.* I understand that some forms of replacement theology might be anti-Jewish, and we must stop this and we must realize this. The rejection and persecution of Jews in Europe is tragic and shameful. But let us get our priorities and values in order. Who is suffering now, and what are we called to do?" And here his promised anger emerged, as he spoke directly and prophetically:

> Every time we speak, we Palestinians must bring the other side of the story or we are considered as biased or untrustworthy... We are always criticized because we only blame Israel and mention Israel's wrongdoing without criticizing other nations and forces that destabilize the Middle East, like Hamas and Iran and Hezbollah. Only after we Palestinian Christians speak about all the wrongdoings in the world, then we have the right to talk about our own suffering. To me this is insulting. It is basically saying to me that my perspective is invalid and that my suffering is not real, but invented and imagined.
>
> How many times have I been humiliated in my life at a checkpoint? Yet please tell me how I can share about this in a balanced way, and I will do it. We have lost land. We have documents. How can I speak about this in a balanced way? I'm open to suggestions. I have an aunt and an uncle who were born here but no longer are able to enter here because Israel simply will not allow them to. At the same time, any Jew who was not born here can easily move here and take the land that was taken from us. Please tell me how to say this story in a fair and bal-

anced way. If we say that the occupation is the core of the problem for us, then please respect this. This is how we see things. We are not inventing our suffering. The checkpoint is our reality. You cannot dictate the way in which we cry about our suffering.

The question here is this: Why am I being silenced? Why are you attacking me, not my message? Why are you not responding to my theology, to my message, to my pain? You ignore the message and attack the messenger. *Why am I being silenced?*[18]

Then, answering the charge of promoting anti-Jewish theology or, by extension, taking an anti-Israel political position, Isaac spoke the word of God as he understands it. A Palestinian Christian defending his rights to live in his own country, he speaks simply and unapologetically from the core of his faith:

I read my Bible literally. And in my literal reading, the offspring of Abraham is Jesus. And then I continue to read my Bible literally, and it tells me that if I am in Christ, then I am Abraham's offspring, I am heir according to the promise. Again I choose to read this literally. In other words, the land, the blessing, and indeed the whole world are mine in Christ, who inherited all things. The sphere of the kingdom is not limited. We must go from Jerusalem to Judea to Samaria to the ends of the earth.

Now am I teaching replacement theology here? I am not claiming that I replace the Jewish nation. I believe I join biblical Israel. Regardless, notice that such a possible revival does not need a gathering of ethnic Israel in the land.

Isaac then reassures his audience: "By challenging any theological claim [that] ethnic Israel has to date to the land, I am by no means calling for the destruction of the modern state of Israel. The Jewish people suffered a lot throughout history, and they have the right to a state where they live safe and secure, and it is only natural that they seek the state in this land…What I'm saying is I recognize Israel today and want to move forward. But please do not force me to accept a theological claim for Israel today as a test for my orthodoxy or as a proof I am not anti-Semitic or as a precondition to reconciliation."[19]

Concluding his address with a stirring call to world Christians, Isaac makes a bold claim: We Palestinians, he declares, are the conscience of the world—and you are in need of us! But is this any bolder than Jesus' injunction to his followers in the Gospel of Matthew that "what you do for the least of these, you do for me"? To evangelicals in particular Isaac addresses this question:

You want the proof that the Bible is right? You don't do this by pointing to self-fulfilling prophecy. Or by pointing to world events as prophecy fulfillment. This is not how you prove that the Bible is right. *We prove that the Bible is right by radical obedience to the teachings of Jesus,* proving that the teachings of Jesus actually work and that they can make the world a better place. Let us love our enemies, forgive those who sin against us, let us feed the poor, care for the oppressed, walk the extra mile, be inclusive not exclusive, turn the other cheek, and maybe then the world will start taking us seriously and believing in our Bible.

My call for the Church today is: be prophetic! In other words, *be the Church*. The world is in desperate need of a conscience. The world needs us. We are the light, the salt. The Palestinian church must survive in Palestine. We must continue to be a light and provide hope in this part of the world. For this we need each other. Will you hold my hand? Will you help me stand? Will you listen to me cry? Will you walk next to me? Pray with me? Will you help me shine the hope of Jesus in this dark world?[20]

The Logic of Love

In Munther Isaac we hear the voice of the Kairos Palestine document, a document that declares, "Religion cannot favour or support any unjust political regime, but must rather promote justice, truth and human dignity."[21] This is the call, sounding louder and clearer and more urgent with every year that the injustice grows before the eyes of the world. The global church is waking up, paying attention, and asking, what is to be done?

Again, the answer, indeed the road map, is found in the Bible. The Palestinians, like the South Africans and the leaders of the American civil rights movement before them, draw water from the same well. Having named and described the problem in specific, contextual terms, the Kairos document presents a powerful and inspiring exposition about the duty of nonviolent resistance to tyranny. "Love is seeing the face of God in every human being. Every person is my brother or my sister. However, seeing the face of God in everyone does not mean accepting evil or aggression on their part. Rather, this love seeks to correct the evil and stop the aggression."[22] "Christ our Lord has left us an example we must imitate," the document declares. "We must resist evil but he taught us that we cannot resist evil with evil. This is a difficult commandment, particularly when the enemy is determined to impose himself and deny our right to remain here in our land."[23]

Difficult, indeed. And so, having laid out that which is so obvious to any Palestinian living under occupation, Kairos quotes what is perhaps the most difficult commandment of all: "You have heard that it was said, 'You shall love your neighbour and hate your enemy.' But I say to you, Love your enemies and pray for those who persecute you, so that you may be children of your Father in heaven" (Matthew 5:45–47).[24]

How, then, is this to be accomplished? In Kairos Palestine, the authors address this question directly:

We say that our option as Christians in the face of the Israeli occupation is to resist. Resistance is a right and a duty for the Christian. But it is resistance with love as its logic. It is thus a creative resistance for it must find human ways that engage the humanity of the enemy. Seeing the image of God in the face of the enemy means taking up positions in the light of this vision of active resistance to stop the injustice and oblige the perpetrator to end his aggression and thus achieve the desired goal, which is getting back the land, freedom, dignity and independence.[25]

Resistance with love as its logic. Resistance is required, state the authors of the document—yet only resistance grounded in the most fundamental principles of our faith "can stand firm in the face of the clear declarations of the occupation authorities that refuse our existence and the many excuses these authorities use to continue imposing occupation upon us."[26] The Kairos document affirms that the very ability of Palestinians to continue as a presence in their land will be accomplished only through the active practice of these principles. The section on resistance concludes with a call to the world to support Palestinians in their struggle:

Palestinian civil organizations, as well as international organizations, NGOs and certain religious institutions call on individuals, companies and states to engage in divestment and in an economic and commercial boycott of everything produced by the occupation. We understand this to integrate the logic of peaceful resistance. These advocacy campaigns must be carried out with courage, openly and sincerely proclaiming that their object is not revenge but rather to put an end to the existing evil, liberating both the perpetrators and the victims of injustice. The aim is to *free both peoples* from extremist positions of the different Israeli governments, bringing both to justice and reconciliation. In this spirit and with this dedication we will eventually reach the longed-for resolution to our problems, as indeed happened in South Africa and with many other liberation movements in the world. (emphasis added)[27]

The reference to South Africa is pointed and apt. This is a clear endorsement of a civil-society call to nonviolent direct action *on theological grounds*. In referencing explicitly the successful global-level campaign that liberated South Africans from apartheid, and implicitly the movement that ended legalized racism in the United States, the authors of Kairos Palestine are invoking, once again, the power of the church to fulfill its responsibility and its call, in Munther Isaac's words, "to make the world a better place through radical obedience to the teachings of Jesus." This call is being heard. The Kairos Palestine document is being studied in churches throughout the world, including the United States. More and more Christians are heeding the document's call to "come and see" by going off the "tourist trail" to actually visit the Palestinians in Israel and the West Bank, and in particular to connect with Palestinians in their homes, churches, hospitals, and schools, where they are working to keep their community alive and vibrant. In their congregations, their local church-based task forces, and their denominational mission committees, U.S. Christians are inviting Palestinian speakers to their congregations and conferences. They are giving serious consideration to church-based initiatives to boycott goods from illegal settlements, to divest from companies profiting from the occupation, and to press the U.S. government to examine the destructive nature of its unconditional and massive support for Israel's expansionist and oppressive policies. Despite the predictable efforts to silence or muffle the call of the oppressed, the call is being heard, the faithful are responding, and the movement is growing.

We Refuse to Be Enemies

Palestinian nonviolent resistance takes many forms. It has been said that simply getting up in the morning in occupied Palestine, sending your kids to school, and going about your day is an act of resistance. Faced with a military and civil presence that at every turn and in countless ways says, "You don't belong here," Palestinians find ways to fulfill Jesus' instruction to love your enemy, and to follow the Kairos document in developing means of creative resistance that "engage the humanity of the enemy"—and in so doing, preserve their own humanity.

On a hilltop in the fertile valley just south of Bethlehem, on the ancient Road of the Patriarchs leading to Hebron sits the Nassar farm. On this hundred-acre plot of land, earmarked for annexation by the Jewish state, the story of the Israeli occupation of Palestine is unfolding. What ultimately happens to this farm and this family will tell the tale of whether this region is destined to be a place of continued suffering and conflict or of reconciliation and hope. In 2012 alone, more than eight thousand international pilgrims visited this farm, named Tent of Nations. At the entrance, visitors are greeted by a large stone on which is inscribed, in Arabic, English, Hebrew, and German, WE REFUSE TO BE ENEMIES.

Daoud Nassar is the grandson of Daher Nassar, a Palestinian Christian who purchased the land in 1916. Daher Nassar, like his fellow Palestinians, paid taxes to the Ottoman sultan. And like those other farmers and villagers, he saw control of the land pass to the British Crown at the close of the First World War. His sons, Bishara and Naif, who took over stewardship of the farm, saw British troops replaced by Jordanian regulars in 1948, and then the blue Star of David hoisted over the territory in 1967, when the State of Israel took control of the West Bank. Only this last ruler has tried to take their land from them. In 1991, using one of its chief methods of colonizing the occupied territories, Israel declared the Nassar property "state land." The burden was then on the family to prove ownership. Faced with legal hurdles that Israel has set very high, few Palestinians have been able to successfully demonstrate land title in the West Bank, a territory that has changed hands many times in the last two hundred years and where traditional methods of assigning ownership and boundaries, methods that do not conform to modern legal practice, have prevailed. Israel's campaign of displacement is working. Farm by farm, village by village, Palestinian farmers and shepherds in the 60 percent of the West Bank under direct Israeli civil and military control are retreating to the Bantustans,[28] the teeming urban enclaves intended for those Palestinians who will not or cannot emigrate, which are accessible only through the network of restricted roads controlled by Israel. Daoud Nassar, however, who now manages the farm along with several of his siblings, has pursued the case to the Israeli Supreme Court, spending close to $200,000 in legal fees and land surveys over an eighteen-year period, and the court has upheld his claim. Frustrated by this, occupation authorities and settler groups have attempted to gain the land by private means—that is, buying it through questionable third-party arrangements, another common method of land acquisition. Daoud has been asked to name his price, but he remains steadfast. "We are not permitted to give up," he says. "This land is our mother. Our mother is not for sale."

"My father grew up on this farm," Daoud writes in his memoir, *Daher's Vineyard—Tent of Nations: My Father's Dream*.[29] "From his birth to his death, this land was in one way or another a troubled land. His Christian conviction led him to say that this should not be so. It is not an exaggeration to say that he has fashioned his life on the Beatitudes in the Gospel of Matthew: 'Blessed are the peacemakers, for theirs is the kingdom of heaven.' Daoud is convinced that Christians are called to be peacemakers, and his dream was to make the farm a place where children and young people could learn the art of peacemaking. For the last twenty years, Daoud and his family have been working to realize his father's dream. The crucial question, asks Daoud, is "how can I bring about a situation in which someone who has decided that I am his enemy can become my friend?" The farm is Daoud's answer to this question:

> On the farm, we have made certain changes which can help us take forward the vision. Under the conditions imposed by living as Palestinians in Area C, I cannot get water or electricity. So we have dug cisterns that catch and store rainwater. We have no electricity supply, but through donors we have electricity generated by solar panels. Not only have these solutions overcome an injustice, but they preserve our environment. Both the Israelis and we Palestinians claim to love this land, but neither community, in fact, treats it with a great deal of love. For example, the Israelis degrade the environment by abusing its water supply. They plant the settle-

ments—often ugly and aggressive looking—on the tops of beautiful hills. They pour vast amounts of concrete for their new roads, often spoiling the natural contours and creating ugly scars. The separation barrier itself is perhaps the ugliest wall in the world, and it is very greedy of the land—often Palestinian land—that it consumes. At the Tent of Nations we want to set an example of respect for the environment. The very fact that we are working our land and making it productive is a way of helping us and others reconnect with the land, which we Palestinians call "our mother."

On February 14, 2012, the Civil Administration of Judea and Samaria (a.k.a. the government of Israel) issued an order declaring one third of the existing hundred-acre farm to be state land, and giving the family forty-five days to appeal or the land would be taken. The family immediately appealed, and at this writing (in January 2013), no decision has been rendered on the appeal. Meanwhile, the peacemaking work continues at the Tent of Nations. The constant stream of international visitors continues to grow, and Daoud's wife, Jihan (with the assistance of international volunteers), conducts English-language and health classes for women in the women's center they have established in the nearby village. Planning continues for the summer camps for local children and the annual international women's week of seminars and meetings. And, always, there is the planting of trees, new orchards added every month bearing the names of churches, peace groups (including a Jewish group from the United Kingdom that planted 250 olive trees to replace trees uprooted by settlers), and communities throughout the world who share the vision of the Nassar family and their faith in the power of love. "Peace can only grow from the grassroots," says Daoud; "it can never be imposed from above."

The Power of Forgiveness

Rev. Naim Ateek is a Palestinian Anglican priest. He was eight years old in 1948 when his family was expelled from their village in the southern Galilee. Reverend Ateek is the founder and director of Sabeel Ecumenical Liberation Theology Center in Jerusalem. He is a man of deep faith who has articulated a theology that responds directly to the historic and present suffering of the Palestinian people. Like Daoud Nassar, Ateek believes that it is critical for Palestinians to maintain a nonviolent stance, in practice as well as in their hearts. In his first book, *Justice and Only Justice: A Palestinian Theology of Liberation,* Ateek makes the case for a justice-based approach to bringing peace to his native Palestine. He acknowledges the challenge to maintain nonviolence in the face of the structural violence of a powerful, militarized state, pointing out that "any resistance to the state, even nonviolent resistance, is interpreted as undermining the security of the state." A state that places itself psychologically on a perpetual war footing, Ateek argues, and that feels vulnerable (regardless of the reality of its vastly superior military power), will respond violently to resistance even of the most nonviolent kind. This, Ateek explains, accounts for Israel's brutal suppression of Palestinian resistance, since Israel sees the "intifada as an act of war in order to legitimate the killings and beatings of so many innocent civilians."[30]

Ateek compares the Palestinians to the South Africans,

who also confronted a condition "in which it was difficult to be nonviolent in a situation that brings so much state violence every day and brings dehumanization, deportation and all kinds of injustice."[31] He argues that Christians can bring a true and deep understanding of creative resistance that can break the cycle of violence that oppresses both people, charging Palestinian Christians to pick up this mantle and provide the spiritual guidance their people desperately need. "[T]he challenge to the Palestinian Christians, and indeed to all Christians faced with bitterness and hate, is to keep up the struggle and not succumb to despair and hate," he explains. "Keep struggling against hate and resentment…Never stop trying to live the commandment of love and forgiveness…Remember that so often it is those who have suffered most at the hands of others who are capable of offering forgiveness and love."[32]

Bringing the Kingdom

Palestinian Christian peace worker Sami Awad perhaps best exemplifies Naim Ateek's prescription for nonviolent action. We were introduced to Sami Awad in the story of his father, Bishara, told by Pastor Bob Roberts a few chapters back. The Awads of Bethlehem (as we know, originally from Jerusalem) are a remarkable family. Bishara's brother Alex is a Methodist missionary who visits churches in the United States regularly and teaches at the Bethlehem Bible College. Awad's other uncle, Mubarak, is a nonviolent activist who was deported by Israel for his activities. As a young man, Awad was deeply influenced by his elders, and early on he committed himself to nonviolence as a way of life. After completing his studies in the United States, he returned to Bethlehem to found Holy Land Trust, an institute for the study and practice of nonviolence. Its mission is to transform individuals and communities through the "healing of historic wounds...[to] build a future that makes the Holy Land a global model for understanding, respect, justice, equality and peace."[33]

I spoke to Awad in early 2013 at his office in Bethlehem. I asked him what he thought the role of the church should be in bringing about peace for Palestinians and Israelis:

> I think that we Christians—I prefer to say followers of Jesus—have tended to ignore our faith in determining what peace looks like in this land. Christians assume that this is a Jewish-Muslim conflict, and that we Christians stand with the Jews in the Judeo-Christian tradition against the Muslims.[c] I don't see it this way at all. We are as much a party in determining the outcome in what happens in the peace process as much as the Jews and the Muslims. The role of Christians in this particular conflict is to stand with those who are committed to peacemaking on both sides, standing with those who are committed to human rights and with those who are committed to bringing the Christian values of love and compassion and care that Jesus taught us into this community.[34]

For Awad, the core of nonviolence is transformation, on both a personal and community level. We make a mistake,

---

c. This is a common misconception. Christians and Muslims have coexisted peacefully in the Holy Land for hundreds of years.

he says, if we think of nonviolence solely in terms of political goals or organizing strategy. Of course these are crucial, but we must begin with ourselves. This is what Jesus teaches us, what he means by "love your enemy." "Nonviolence," Awad points out, "is not just about standing up against the oppressor, because in many cases we end up demonizing the oppressor. We dehumanize them and then label this as nonviolence. The teachings of Jesus are not about that." Nonviolence, he explains, is as much concerned with transforming the oppressor as liberating the oppressed. The tools for carrying out this mutual transformation are practical. It begins at the interpersonal level, and from there translates directly into political solutions that can bring about a just, sustainable peace.

> Personal transformation means raising my level of awareness and mindfulness in order to know what prevents me from achieving my goals. It means listening to my fears and my doubts, to know where they come from and to honor them, but to create alternatives. For example, in working with Palestinian leaders, we ask them, "Can there ever be peace with Israelis?" The immediate answer of course is "No, we cannot make peace with them; they don't want peace." So we ask, "Where does your assumption that peace is impossible come from?" And the answer is "From our experiences with them!" So we see that it is the past that has been determining the decisions we make for the future. Once we realize this, we can explore what it would mean for the decisions that we make today to be led not by the past but by the future that we create for ourselves.[35]

When I heard Awad ask this question, something moved within me. This is the transformation I craved for my own people: to be free of the captivity of the past, a past that was destroying both the present and any hope for a future. In the next chapter, we will listen to the voices of some of my fellow Jews who join me in that wish and who, in their work, give ample reason for hope.

Chapter 10

HEALING AND HOPE: VOICES FROM THE JEWISH COMMUNITY

On December 27, 2008, Israel launched a devastating air and land attack on the Gaza Strip, which it had blockaded by air, sea, and land since the removal of its own illegal settlements in 2005. Rockets fired over the border by militant resistance groups in Gaza had been answered by air attacks from Israel over those years, but when Israel launched its attack, a cease-fire had been in effect. Over three weeks between December 27 and January 18, defenseless civilians had nowhere to flee as bombs from Israeli fighter jets rained down on them and Israeli troops advanced through the narrow streets. Over the course of three weeks more than 1,400 Gazans died, 400 of them children. Gaza is the most populated 140 square miles on earth. Eighty percent of the approximately 1.7 million inhabitants of Gaza are the descendants of Palestinians who were expelled from their villages and cities in what is now Israel by Israeli troops between April 1948 and early 1949.

The morning of December 28, as reports of the attack

became known, Rabbi Brant Rosen of the Jewish Reconstructionist Congregation in Evanston, Illinois, sat down at his computer and typed a short posting into his blog. It began with these words: "The news out of Israel and Gaza today makes me just sick to my stomach." Yes, Rosen granted, Israel has the responsibility to protect its citizens, but how, he wrote, "will squeezing the life out of Gaza, not to mention bombing the living hell out of it, ensure the safety of Israeli citizens?... So no more rationalizations. What Israel has been doing to the people of Gaza is an outrage. It has brought neither safety nor security to the people of Israel, and it wrought nothing but misery and tragedy upon the people of Gaza."[1]

Rosen took a deep breath, typed a few more words—"There, I've said it. Now what do I do?"—and pressed the Publish button.

Posting that blog entry was not a small step for a congregational rabbi with an employment contract. He didn't know what the consequences of this act would be or, as he had written, what, if anything, he would do next. Four months later, Rabbi Rosen was given the opportunity to answer that question. Every spring, Jews the world over join the State of Israel in celebrating the anniversary of the declaration of the state, or Independence Day. We Jews call it by its Hebrew name, Yom Ha'atzmaut. On April 29, 2009, Rosen posted the following blog, entitled "Why I Didn't Celebrate Yom Ha'atzmaut."

"I can no longer view this milestone as a day for unabashed celebration," he wrote. "I've come to believe that for me, Yom Ha'atzmaut is more appropriate observed as an occasion for reckoning and honest soul-searching."[2] And so on May 14, instead of "celebrating" Israel's founding on its sixty-first anniversary, Rosen welcomed nine Jews and four Palestinians into his home in suburban Chicago for a gathering sponsored by "Rabbis Remembering the Nakba." Similar gatherings were held in Berkeley, Philadelphia, and New York. They opened their gathering with this statement of purpose and belief:

We are united in our common conviction that we cannot view Yom Ha'atzma'ut—or what is for the Palestinians the Nakba—as an occasion for celebration. Guided by the values of Jewish tradition, we believe that this day is more appropriately an occasion for *zikaron* (memory), *cheshbon nefesh* (soul searching), and *teshuvah* (repentance). These spiritual values compel us to acknowledge the following: that Israel's founding is inextricably bound up with the dispossession of hundreds of thousands of indigenous inhabitants of the land, that a moment so many Jews consider to be a moment of national liberation is the occasion of tragedy and exile for another people, and that the violence begun in 1948 continues to this day. This is the truth of our common history—it cannot be denied, ignored, or wished away.[3]

In Rosen's words, "this powerful, sacred experience," based on core Jewish principles and accompanied by rituals from Jewish tradition, represented a turning point for him, as well as for the grateful and, in some cases, judging by comments to his blog, "awestruck" Jews who participated in person or at a distance from other parts of the country. It was groundbreaking, paradigm-shattering, game-changing stuff. I wonder if Rabbi Rosen and those with him on that evening were aware of the resonance of this event with a gathering of faithful Jews long ago, Jews also responding to the evil of dispossession and tyranny. They were people who, like Rosen and those who joined him, had turned to their faith tradition for guidance. It was a tradition that required, above all, commitment to justice and to compassion for the vulnerable and oppressed. The Gospel recounts the following statement by a young rabbi at a gathering in the Galilee long ago:

When he came to Nazareth, where he had been brought up, he went to the synagogue on the Sabbath day, as was his custom. He stood up to read, and the scroll of the prophet Isaiah was given to him. He unfurled the scroll and found the place where it was written:

> *"The Spirit of the Lord is upon me,*
> *because he has anointed me*
> *to bring good news to the poor.*
> *He has sent me to proclaim release to the captives*
> *and recovery of sight to the blind,*
> *to let the oppressed go free,*
> *to proclaim the year of the Lord's favor."*

(Luke 4:19)

Witnessing the movement for Palestinian rights that is growing within the Jewish community, we might ask whether courageous statements like the one read in four small meetings across the United States on that spring evening in 2009 were evidence that, on that day, "this scripture has been fulfilled in your hearing."

Becoming Jewish

The more we look at Jesus in his context, the more we see that we cannot—must not—separate him from the historical and political context of his ministry. Speaking truth to the difficult circumstances of a particular time and place is what calls out the faithfulness of followers; this is how movements get started. In reading from Isaiah, Jesus was not preaching from an ancient, dead text. On that Sabbath day in Nazareth, proclaiming good news for the poor and the freeing of captives, he was speaking to the reality of his listeners, people who were confronting, to use the words of Martin Luther King Jr., "the fierce urgency of now."[4] We all start in our hometowns: Jesus in occupied, suffering Galilee; Martin Luther King Jr. in the basement of a church in Montgomery, Alabama; Rabbi Rosen in his living room in Evanston, Illinois.

Theologian, educator, minister, and civil rights leader Howard Thurman unfurled his own scroll with the publication in 1949 of *Jesus and the Disinherited*. In this slim volume (it's said that Martin Luther King Jr. carried it with him, like a Bible), Thurman challenged the Christianity of his time, which he characterized as "sterile...muffled, confused and vague," unconnected to "what the teachings and life of Jesus have to say to those who stand, at a moment in human history, with their backs against the wall."[5]

Living in the context of Jim Crow America, Thurman was very clear about his calling as a theologian and a minister: "It is necessary to examine the religion of Jesus against the background of his own age and people, and to inquire into the content of his teaching with reference to the disinherited and the underprivileged."[6]

And so today we have Brant Rosen, a rabbi whose life and vocation have been profoundly affected by the oppression of the Palestinians, a people with their backs—literally—against a wall, as well as by his acute awareness of the peril faced by his own people as the builders of that wall. Rosen was responding to the urgent requirement to do something about it. It was a very Jewish thing for Rosen to do. Let's listen again to Thurman:

> We begin with the simple historical fact that Jesus was a Jew... It is impossible for Jesus to be understood outside of the sense of community which Israel held with God... Here is one who... became a instrument for the embodiment of a set of ideals—ideals of such dramatic potency that they were capable of changing the calendar, rechanneling the thought of the world, and placing a new sense of the rhythm of life in a weary, nerve-snapped civilization.[7]

Rosen and Jews like him—rabbis, scholars, activists, the list is long and growing longer—are acting in the finest tradition of our people. I read on—and came to a passage that took my breath away:

> How different might have been the story of the last two thousand years on this planet grown old from suffering if the link between Jesus and Israel had never been severed! What might have happened if Jesus, so perfect a flower from the brooding spirit of God in the soul of Israel, had been permitted to remain where his roots would have been fed by the distilled elements accumu-

lating from Israel's wrestling with God! The thought is staggering. The Christian Church has tended to overlook its Judaic origins, but the fact is that Jesus of Nazareth was a Jew of Palestine when he went about his Father's business, announcing the acceptable year of the Lord.[8]

What an astonishing, daring statement! Daring for his Christian readers, because it asserts Jesus' specialness, not as Messiah or one who creates a New Israel, but in his "perfect" connection to his Jewish roots. Daring for Jewish readers, because it is in Jesus' very Jesus-ness that he demonstrates his *Jewishness*. When Jesus put those core Jewish values into action, he became, in Thurman's words, "an instrument for the embodiment of…ideals of such dramatic potency that they were capable of changing the calendar, rechanneling the thought of the world."[9]

It's a theme that won't let go of me. One Sunday afternoon soon after my visit to the West Bank, I returned home following a presentation at a church, one of many that I had recently delivered to Christian groups about my experiences in Palestine. My wife turned to me, and, only half joking (after twenty-five years of marriage she had learned to expect the unexpected), asked, "Are you becoming Christian?" I had not been prepared for the question, but the answer was right there. I said, "No, I'm becoming Jewish."

It's a new opportunity; it's a second chance. It doesn't mean changing our stripes or our identities or "converting." There is something wrong with our language and with our cultural and religious heritage that require us to adopt labels that denote an identity or identification with a religious or national group but that may say little about the values that define who we are. One can identify as a Jew, Christian, Muslim, Buddhist, or secular. We call ourselves American, South African, German, Korean, Indian, Czech. But what membership, in what community, nation or faith community, expresses who one truly is?

Empire or Community?

Dr. Marc Ellis is one of the foremost Jewish theologians of our time, a scholar who has fearlessly challenged conventional assumptions about Jewish identity. His groundbreaking 1987 *Toward a Jewish Theology of Liberation* asked Jews—indeed, all people concerned with questions of faith and how it is expressed in modern history—to confront how the Nazi Holocaust and the creation of the State of Israel have defined Jewish self-perception. Identity can become "frozen" by the power of huge, formative events such as these, argues Ellis, leading to the failure of individuals and collectives to "ask the right questions for their time."[10] The key issue facing the Jewish people, Ellis maintains, is "the continual struggle over our direction as individuals and as a people—toward the isolation of empire or toward the solidarity of community."[11] Ellis takes the Jewish community to task for its embrace of political Zionism as the answer to anti-Semitism and as an essential element of Jewish identity. "Mainstream Jewish life," he writes, has "evolved into a new form of Judaism, one that seeks and maintains empire, not unlike Constantinian Christianity."[12]

For Ellis, this new form of "Constantinian" Judaism threatens Jewish life and the Jewish future. "The solution," he writes, "lies in a common struggle aimed at *overcoming national differences and barriers*, rather than increasing and heightening them, as strong trends within Israel and the Zionist movement demand"[13] (emphasis added). Ellis is adamantly opposed to religion becoming allied in any way with political power. He proscribes this for all religious groups, not only Jews, envisioning instead a future in which traditional religious boundaries will give way to "a broader tradition of faith...with other struggling communities in a common struggle for liberation."[14]

> Constantinian Christianity has now been joined by Constantinian Judaism. Constantinian Islam is also a reality. Yet there are Christians, Jews, and Muslims who also oppose and suffer under Constantinianism. Could it be that those who participate in Constantinian religiosity—whether Jew, Christian or Muslim—are, in effect, practicing the same religion, albeit with different symbol structures and rituals? And that those who seek community are also practicing the same religion?...Movements of justice and compassion across community and religious boundaries may be the vehicles for a better understanding of commonalities in religiosity that can no longer be defined by traditional religious labels.[15]

The Costs of Not Healing

In his 2011 *Encountering the Jewish Future*, Ellis turns to Jewish philosopher Hannah Arendt to bring this issue of Jewish identity into sharper focus. Arendt (1906–1975) was a German-Jewish intellectual, perhaps one of the most famous (and, to some, infamous) of her time. Not surprisingly, given that she was twenty-seven years old when she fled from the Nazis to settle in the United States, Arendt spills a lot of ink on anti-Semitism and the role it plays in Jewish identity. She is perhaps best known for her classic *The Origins of Totalitarianism,* in which she introduces the concept of the "banality of evil." In 1961, Arendt went to Jerusalem to cover the trial of Adolf Eichmann by the State of Israel, an event that was significant in bringing the Nazi Holocaust to the awareness of the wider world. It also greatly elevated the profile of the State of Israel as the representative of the Jewish people and bulwark against anti-Semitism—here were Jewish judges, sitting in Jerusalem, bringing the Nazis to trial, the flag of Israel prominently displayed on the wall behind the bench. In her highly publicized coverage of the trial, however, Arendt refused to describe Eichmann as a monster driven by hatred of Jews, but rather as an emotionless bureaucrat carrying out his duties. This alienated her from many Jewish intellectuals and from the Jewish community at large. In the decades following the trial, and especially after the Arab-Israeli War of 1967, Arendt found herself increasingly at odds with the Jewish mainstream, as the Nazi Holocaust and the State of Israel became increasingly dominant both in the public conception of the Jewish people and in Jewish self-perception. The issue of anti-Semitism loomed large for Arendt, but, observes Ellis, she "did not believe that anti-Semitism was defining or eternal." Instead, he writes, it was "as if the Jewish community needed the existence of anti-Semitism to make sense of itself. Arendt thought that these understandings of anti-Semitism almost always missed the real challenges confronting the Jewish people."[16]

Arendt had been a Zionist—after the war, she worked to help resettle Jews in Palestine. But writing in 1946, she observed that "Herzl's picture of the Jewish people as surrounded and forced together by a world of enemies has in our day conquered the Zionist movement and become the common sentiment of the Jewish masses." This was not going to work, she predicted—Palestine is "not a place where Jews can live in isolation."[17] Zionism must guard against a dangerous set of illusions: "Some of the Zionist leaders pretend to believe that the Jews can maintain themselves in Palestine against the whole world..."[18] Arendt saw this as a prescription for disaster: "If we actually are faced with open or concealed enemies on every side, if the whole world is ultimately against us, then we are lost."[19]

Arendt's warnings apply with an alarming degree of accuracy to the Jewish situation today. If we see anti-Semitism as ubiquitous and eternal, it limits Jewish options, particularly with respect to a future for what is now the State of Israel. Ellis observes: "To see anti-Semitism lurking around any and every corner is to assert that anti-Semitism is an eternal threat against which Jews need to mold and maintain their Jewish identity. Today, some Jewish commentators speak and write about the 'new' anti-Semitism, usually defined as those who support Palestinian human rights and criticize Israeli policies...In Arendt's language, the Jewish community has substituted a transcendent concept of Jew-hatred, now morphed into Israel-hatred, for a political analysis of why Palestinians, Arabs in general, and others, including some Jews, might support Palestinian human rights and be critical of Israel's policies."[20]

Precisely as Arendt feared, Jewish identity has today become inseparably connected to the threat of anti-Semitism. The State of Israel, stepping in to provide protection, has merged with what it means to be Jewish. In *The New Anti-Semitism,* for example, published in 1974 by the Anti-Defamation League of B'nai B'rith, the foremost Jewish advocacy organization in the United States, authors Forster and Epstein assert, "Israel represents the greatest hope and the deepest commitment embraced by world Jewry in two millennia... Jews in the Diaspora have come to feel that their own security and their own survival as a people, in a world from which anti-Semitism has never disappeared, depends in large measure on the survival of Israel."[21]

The position has only strengthened over the intervening four decades, due to the coordinated efforts of American and world Jewish advocacy organizations working in coordination with the State of Israel on both governmental and civil-society levels. This has gone a long way toward solidifying support in the West for Israel's policies of illegal expansionism and unbridled militarism. Tragically and ironically, this fixation on anti-Semitism has foreclosed a peaceful future for the State of Israel and the very people that the state is intended to protect. So Ellis poses the question that all Jews must ask, and in fact that must be asked by everyone, Jew and non-Jew alike, who is concerned with how to bring about peace:

What would Jewish identity be if the wounds of the Holocaust were healed rather than maintained?... Healing means a future beyond what Jews have known in the past. Arendt was a messenger of a future many Jews continue to reject... As I encounter Arendt, the cost of rejecting healing has become more and more obvious.

Where have our wounds brought us? Has our violation
of the Palestinians, ostensibly to secure the Jewish place
in the world, secured our place in the world? Or has
it brought a further wounding to Jewish being in the
world?"[22]

Healing is very much the issue. In my work as a clinical
psychologist, I specialized in the human reaction to traumatic events. We know that the most profound and po-
tentially damaging and long-lasting effect of psychological
trauma is the loss of the ability to trust. How, after experiencing (and sometimes simply by witnessing) the capacity
of human beings to hurt one another, to exhibit cruelty, and
to perpetrate violence, do we recover a sense of mutuality
and interdependency? How do we regain our ability to co-
operate and to establish harmonious, productive, and even
intimate relationships with others? What kind of existence
can we look forward to, as individuals and communities,
when these essential abilities and functions have been so
damaged?

It is only through relationship and in community that the
healing process can take place and trust can be restored. This
can be in one-on-one contact or in a group in any number of
settings—be they clinical, pastoral, or in rituals and practices
of a culture or a community. Whatever the form or setting, we
know, to use the clinical term, that the "treatment of choice"
involves the difficult emotional, cognitive, and often spiritual
processing of the painful experience. It is necessary to do the
work of finding a way to make meaning out of the event, even
when the questions seem to have no answers—to take the
often painful journey back into the ability to love and trust

again. And we know just as clearly what is *not* the treatment of choice: it is to enclose the injured community inside a fortress, station soldiers on the wall, and say to the traumatized people, "It's not safe out there. Trust no one. Stay safe, here within these walls—and we'll protect you." Ilan Pappé, the Israeli historian whose iconic *The Ethnic Cleansing of Palestine* has done so much to change the perceptions of Jews and non-Jews alike about the accepted narrative of the events of 1947–49, uses the phrase "Fortress Israel" to describe Israel today.[23]

Healing cannot happen under these conditions. In fact, under conditions such as these, the trauma response strengthens, threatening the health and even the life of the sufferer. If the healing process of meaning-making and positive reconnection with the world does not happen, depression or even a slow death can result. Often the individual or group will exhibit the same or similar violence, cruelty, or inhumanity toward others. It is only through the painful process of making sense of the experience that the person or the group can find its way back into relationship and community. The work of healing is difficult. Painful and difficult questions arise for traumatized people and communities: How can people do such things to other people? How could God have allowed this to happen? The questions raise issues of identity and faith that must be struggled with if the person or group is to go on in a healthy and productive manner. Often this can be the hardest part, because recovering from trauma means change: finding new ways of living in the interpersonal, political, and even spiritual realms that preserve what is precious and essential about the self but that represent a new and more adaptive way of being following the trauma.

Try to avoid or bypass this process, and you risk the consequences.

Frozen Identities, Frozen Futures

Arendt's life and work spanned most of the twentieth century. She understood trauma and the challenges of surviving it and somehow remaining human. In the postwar adjustment of the Jewish people, Arendt observed a fixation on anti-Semitism that had produced a "fixed identity" based on self-protection. Arendt saw this as highly problematic. Ellis sees Arendt's warning from those crucial years as delivering a clear message for today: "Clearly, Jewish identity evolves and takes on different formations at different times...Aspects of Jewish identity that have been carried over time might become irrelevant in certain contexts, when new ways of being Jewish come into being...The very concept of anti-Semitism as a viable construct independent of the changing world is, for Arendt, like a virus that blocks new beginnings. The same is the case when Jews adopt an outmoded nationalism as the age of nation-states recedes."[24]

Individuals, collectives, faith communities, and nations become stuck when their identities are frozen as the result of the trauma of oppression. But they can become unfrozen when exposure shocks them into awareness: Saul on the Road to Damascus; our own society when four girls were killed in the church in Birmingham, and when the television news reports showed us the fire hoses turned on the people protesting segregation; Rabbi Brant Rosen seeing the photos of the rubble of Gaza and the charred bodies of children. This is the beginning of healing; this is when we are challenged to grow into new, more resilient identities and when there is the need for the support of community and the guidance of spirit.

In my search for this healing, for signs of hope, I've found some heroes. Readers will have gathered that Brant Rosen is one of them. But Rosen would probably agree with me that whatever risks he has taken pale in comparison with what some Israelis are doing in an attempt to bring their country back from moral and political disaster. They are a tiny minority. But so were the black pastors and civil rights leaders who gathered in church basements in the United States in the 1950s; the local actions they undertook grew into a movement that changed our nation. So were the handful of pastors, academics, and activists who persevered through brutal repression to bring the global church eventually to take a stand against South Africa's apartheid regime. Let us remember this as we listen to the voices of these Israelis, and pray that they will remember this as well as they face a political and social situation in today's Israel that gives little cause for optimism.

A Village Was Here

Eitan Bronstein Aparicio has devoted his life to telling a story that most Israelis do not want to hear. Bronstein Aparicio, who emigrated from Argentina with his parents when he was five, founded Zochrot, an organization devoted to educating Israelis about the *Nakba*—the Arabic word means "catastrophe"—or the dispossession of more than 700,000 Palestinians between 1947 and 1949. "When it comes to the *Nakba* and what was there before Israel was created, it's a big hole, a black hole that people don't know how to deal with. It's perhaps the most important period of our life in this region and it's not really known," Bronstein Aparicio said in an interview in 2008.[25]

Bronstein Aparicio and his colleagues at Zochrot are committed to telling the story behind Israel's creation, a story that has been suppressed during the entire history of the state. They belong to a small but growing minority of Israelis who are questioning the ideological basis of Israel. Raised, as all Israelis, to believe in the idea of the Jewish state, Bronstein Aparicio nevertheless refused military service during the 1983 invasion of Lebanon, and then again in the military suppression of the First Intifada. His doubts deepened in 2000, at the beginning of the Second Intifada, when a group of Israelis shot and killed thirteen Arab demonstrators. "I understood then," Bronstein Aparicio told me when we spoke in late 2012, "that there was something more fundamental to be addressed. It wasn't just a matter of equal rights between Jews and Arabs. There is something very fundamental in the way Zionism effectively allows only Jews to be full citizens."[26]

Then something happened that changed the course of his life. He was doing research on a Jewish National Fund park located outside of Jerusalem. The JNF is a nonprofit corporation founded in 1901 by the World Zionist Organization to buy and develop land in Palestine for Jewish settlement. The JNF has established similar parks throughout Israel. Canada Park (so named because it was funded by donations from the Canadian Jewish community) sits on the ruins of three Palestinian villages. In the middle of the park is a forest planted to commemorate more than three hundred American and Canadian Jews who died in Israel's wars or who were victims of violent Palestinian resistance. The remains of a house, a short way into the park, wrongly identified by a visitor's sign as a Roman bathhouse, is all that is recognizably left of the Palestinian villages. The 5,500 inhabitants of these villages were expelled when the Israeli army captured this area of the West Bank from Jordan in 1967. Today, they and their descendants live as refugees, mostly in East Jerusalem and near Ramallah. In effect, the existence of these villages, and of the people who lived here, has been erased. Israeli historian Ilan Pappé has referred to this massive erasure of Palestinian history as state-organized "memoricide."[27]

"I came up with the idea of putting up signs in the park with the names of the three villages," Bronstein Aparicio told me, "and then suggested to people that there are hundreds of sites throughout Israel where these villages once existed, so let's go around the country putting up signs about the villages that were there. This simple act is very challenging for Israelis. It touches us at our core, because this Jewish state was established through the expulsion of most of the people who lived here. So these simple signs embody both—yes, this village was here, and was destroyed, and its people prevented from returning, but on the other hand, this new sign also expresses the denial that continues to this day.[28]

Zochrot now conducts a full range of activities, including educational seminars and tours of these sites. The organization has just completed a project of collecting testimonies of soldiers who served in the Israeli army between 1947 and 1949, who are now talking about the ethnic-cleansing operations in which they participated. These testimonies are very painful to listen to. But it is moving to see these men shed the burden of truth they have been carrying for over six decades. Like the memorialization of the villages, this is part of the recovery of a collective memory that is necessary if Israelis are to contemplate a future in which they are no longer colonizers.

Bronstein Aparicio and his colleagues at Zochrot are doing what they can to save their country. It is likely that they once believed that their work would have a political impact. Perhaps, they reasoned, once we Israelis better understand our past, we will demand that our government change its behavior. Perhaps when we know the suffering of the Palestinians, we who have suffered ourselves can empathize with them and cease seeing them as enemies. It may be that the members of Zochrot once believed that. But this has not been the direction of Israeli politics. "We may soon be operating outside the law," Bronstein Aparicio told me. Recently, a law passed the Knesset (Israeli Parliament) that imposes restrictions on donations to organizations such as Zochrot that promote a narrative threatening to the Jewish state. So, in addition to Bronstein Aparicio's work inside Israel, he is increasingly directing a message to us outside Israel. "I am an Israeli. This is my home," he told me as we concluded our conversation. "And I am asking for your help. I don't see that we can do it by ourselves, because the politics are taking us nowhere. What is needed is pressure from outside. It's the only realistic scenario. It's the only way to save us—and we are approaching the last chance. *As Americans you should care about the results of your support on our lives here.* You need to acknowledge the power that your government has."[29]

There are other Israeli voices like that of Bronstein Aparicio. They are crying out to the world for help. The voices are as powerful, as passionate, and as courageous as the Palestinian voices we have heard here, appealing to the world from the heart of their suffering and their grief over the waste of life, creativity, and human connection brought on by their situation.

It's Not My War, Bibi

Nomika Zion is one of the founders of Migvan, an urban kibbutz (a collective run according to socialist and egalitarian principles, on the model of the collective agricultural settlements founded by the original European Jewish settlers of what is now Israel). Migvan is located in Sderot, the Israeli city about a mile from the Gaza Strip that has been a primary target of rockets launched from Gaza since the beginning of the Second Intifada in 2000. Zion is a member of The Other Voice, a grassroots organization of citizens from Sderot and the surrounding region who call for a nonviolent solution to the ongoing conflict. She posted the following letter to Benjamin ("Bibi") Netanyahu during the Israeli bombing of the Gaza Strip in late November 2012.

Sderot, November 22, 2012 This wasn't my war, Bibi, and neither was the previous cursed war: not in my name, and not in the cause of my security... I didn't feel safer when two hundred homes were flattened on a cold winter night in 2004, leaving two thousand refugees without shelter; when the Gaza power station was bombed, leaving half a million people without electricity. I gained no sense of tranquility when the bulldozers razed homes, sweeping up fields, orchards, and chicken coops; when tanks fired without pause, when sonic booms went off over and over, rattling windows and sowing terror. And not since the siege placed on Gaza, not when the authorities have been trying to come up with scientific calculations for the number of calories a Gazan needs just in order to survive. And certainly not when a squadron of helicopters killed eighty-nine young men at a police academy...And not since tens of thousands of homes were pounded, infrastructure crushed, and bodies lined up, row by row, children without names, youths with no faces, citizens without an identity. There are a thousand and one ways to suppress violence by means of violence but not one of them has ever succeeded in annihilating it.[30]

Zion is asking questions about where Israel is going. She is wondering how to survive in such a society:

Life is hard when there's nothing left to believe in. It's hard in Sderot. It's very hard in Gaza. There is a price to hopelessness, Bibi. A blocked horizon. Closed-off consciousness. Life without hope exacts a heavy mental price.[31]

Zion's letter refers to Operation Cast Lead, which took place in 2009, the bombardment and land incursion that cost the lives of over 1,400 Gazans, 400 of them children. But along with Zion's grief about the loss of innocent lives, there was the horror of witnessing the deep illness at the heart of her society: "It frightens me to see my town lit up, as if for a festival and decked out with Israeli flags, groups of supporters distributing flowers in the street and people sounding their car horns in joy at every ton of bombs that's falling on our neighbours."

How did we, as a society, lose the ability to formulate questions about the feasibility of a political alternative? How did it happen that a person who suggests a nonviolent solution is the delusional one, the traitor, and the one who calls for the leveling of Gaza is the true patriot? And how did these dehumanizing processes seal us off from the suffering of others? How did we lose the capacity for empathy?[32]

Zion has refused to be caught up in the war spirit, either in the euphoria or in the demonization of the "enemy." Yet she is in despair about the "current of violence [that] seeps through the dark pores of Israeli society like a grave illness." She fears that although it is Palestinians, not Israelis, who are suffering the human losses, what is lost for Israel is far more fatal. What is left when the core values of a tradition are abandoned? "It is a kind of euphoria," Zion writes, "a joy of war, lust for revenge, drunkenness on power and burial of the Jewish command 'Do not be joyful when your enemy falls'" (Proverbs 24:17).[33]

"[This] was not my war, Bibi. The despair, however, is completely mine."[34]

Seeking a Livable Future

I met Rela Mazali in 2006, when I was serving on the board of an NGO that brought women from Israel and occupied Palestine to the United States to educate Americans about what is needed to bring peace to the region. Mazali was one of three extraordinary women I was privileged to accompany on a speaking tour. A Jewish-born Israeli, she was touring with two Palestinians: a Muslim woman from Gaza and a Christian woman from Bethlehem. Mazali was born in 1948, which made her my age, and that meant that in 1967, while I, a nineteen-year-old American, was watching the news of Israel's six-day conquest of the Sinai, Gaza, the West Bank, and the Syrian Golan Heights, Mazali was a soldier serving in the Israel Defense Forces. Stationed in the hills of the Upper Galilee, Mazali witnessed the bombardment and invasion of the Syrian Golan Heights by the Israeli military. Israeli forces conquered these heights during the 1967 war, while carrying out operations simultaneously against Egypt and in the West Bank against Jordanian forces. This latter campaign included the battle to take East Jerusalem, under Jordanian control since 1949. Multiple times during the speaking tour, I listened to Mazali tell the story of that time as the beginning of her awakening to the illness afflicting her society. Here is her account of that moment from a 2002 publication:

> I heard shouts from the cabins around me… "We have taken the old city!" (Ha'ir ha'atika beyadeynu—literally: "The old city is in our hands!"). I listened to the strange words. Listened and found them strange. Alien. Right then, in the middle of it all. I distinctly remember incomprehension. People. People—were killing people. Mechanically. Brutally. This old city—who cared? What difference did it make? I believed the systematic, premeditated, mass killing was supposed to be self defense, not about "taking" places. What difference did places make?… Looking on from the sidelines of the war, I knew I didn't understand. I knew I wasn't one of "we."[35]

Mazali, in a different generation from Nomika Zion's, experiences the same horror and despair as the younger woman about what militarism is doing to Israeli society. In a 2010 article, she asked, "What to do when the country I live in totally loses its compass? Totally loses its shame? What to do when the regime that collects my taxes uses them to deploy its high-tech military, armed to the teeth, against activists sailing to oppose a criminal siege[36] and then tell me they are protecting me? What to do when the governments of the world are too deeply implicated to hold this regime, this country accountable?"[37]

A Reality Check for Israel

I spoke with Mazali recently. We shared some bitter humor about the lack of success of her efforts and those of other organizations to rescue Israeli society from the evils of militarism and racism. The situation had worsened: the government was tracking toward policies even further restricting the rights of non-Jewish citizens, the siege of Gaza was unremitting, more settlements were taking Palestinian land in the West Bank, Jerusalem was increasingly "Arab-free," the infrastructure of the separation/land-grab wall and the segregated roads were moving ever closer to a system of enclosed, controlled Bantustans for Palestinians that rivaled the South African apartheid plan of the 1980s. What, I asked her, did she see coming, given this grim situation? Read my 2010 article, she told me. The conclusions she drew then in it appear even more compelling now.

"Today," wrote Mazali in that article, "BDS may be the only non-violent tool capable of moving Israel beyond its patterns of militarized brutality." BDS refers to the 2005 Palestinian civil-society call for boycott, divestment, and sanctions.[38]

> Courageously and creatively, BDS faces violence with a firm commitment to non-violence. It stands in solidarity first and foremost with Palestinians, and then with humanity—with the thousands of internationals and Israelis who have chosen nonviolent resistance as their means to oppose and end the oppression of Palestine.
>
> A tool, a strategy, not an end in itself, BDS is meant to work. As it did in the past when a 1953 boycott of segregated buses jump-started the crucial years of the Civil Rights Movement in the United States; ... when the world movement to resist South African apartheid gradually gained ground throughout the sixties to the dismay of successive US and British governments; when this movement kept growing, refusing to go away.
>
> Today, BDS can make it increasingly difficult for Israel's government to keep up the occupation and the internal repression...
>
> BDS is a means to justice for those to whom it has been denied. Not against, but rather for, both Israel and Palestine, it aims to end the policies destroying the lives of Palestinians and devouring the humanity of Israelis. BDS supports the livable, viable futures of all the people of this land.[39]

Mazali's conviction that support of BDS is the most effective strategy has only strengthened over the intervening years. When we talked, she added her voice to those of the other Israelis I had been speaking to in calling on the world to come to their aid: "I don't think Israelis will change course until there is this reality check from outside. We've done this and that, and things are getting worse and worse. It's a sad conclusion, and it's a tough conclusion."[40]

Saving Israel from Itself

In 2009 a young professor at Israel's Ben-Gurion University came to the same conclusion. In August of that year, the *Los Angeles Times* published this opinion piece by Neve Gordon, titled "Boycott Israel: An Israeli Comes to the Painful Conclusion That It's the Only Way to Save His Country." Gordon began the piece by citing recent examples of a growing international campaign to boycott Israel by criticizing well-known singers for performing there or for endorsing Israeli cosmetic products. He noted that even though the campaign has gained supporters, citing the success of similar actions against South Africa in the last century, many Israelis are not signing on because of the uncomfortable "echoes of anti-Semitism." Yet, Gordon continues, calling for a boycott is what he has decided he has to do.

It is indeed not a simple matter for me as an Israeli citizen to call on foreign governments, regional authorities, international social movements, faith-based organizations, unions and citizens to suspend cooperation with Israel. But today, as I watch my two boys playing in the yard, I am convinced that it is the only way that Israel can be saved from itself. I say this because Israel has reached a historic crossroads, and times of crisis call for dramatic measures. I say this as a Jew who has chosen to raise his children in Israel, who has been a member of the Israeli peace camp for almost 30 years and who is deeply anxious about the country's future.

The most accurate way to describe Israel today is as an apartheid state. For more than 42 years, Israel has controlled the land between the Jordan Valley and the Mediterranean Sea. Within this region about 6 million Jews and close to 5 million Palestinians reside. Out of this population, 3.5 million Palestinians and almost half a million Jews live in the areas Israel occupied in 1967, and yet while these two groups live in the same area, they are subjected to totally different legal systems. The Palestinians are stateless and lack many of the most basic human rights. By sharp contrast, all Jews—whether they live in the occupied territories or in Israel—are citizens of the state of Israel. The question that keeps me up at night, both as a parent and as a citizen, is how to ensure that my two children as well as the children of my Palestinian neighbors do not grow up in an apartheid regime...[41]

Gordon arrives at the same conclusion as Bronstein Aparicio, Zion, and Mazali. "I am convinced," he writes, "that outside pressure is the only answer...the only way to counter the apartheid trend in Israel is through massive international pressure. The words and condemnations from the Obama administration and the European Union have yielded no results, not even a settlement freeze, let alone a decision to withdraw from the occupied territories."[42] Over the nearly four years since the publication of this piece, the territory remaining for a Palestinian state resembles even more the disconnected Bantustans of the South African model. Indeed, as Gordon points out, apartheid is here. Gordon's 2009 call for "massive international pressure" so that his children do not "grow up in an apartheid state" speaks even more urgently today. Like the other voices from Israel, his is a cry for help that must not be ignored or deflected by appeals for patience based on political calculations that no longer correspond to current reality. Attention must be paid to such voices emerging from the struggle, as the lessons from South Africa and from the U.S. civil rights movement demonstrate.

Blemishes on a Dream: An American Rabbi's Journey

Rabbi Brian Walt's life has bridged all three of these struggles. Raised in South Africa during the apartheid years, Walt immigrated to the United States from his native South Africa as a young man. As a university student in Cape Town, Walt was the founding editor of *Strike,* a Jewish student newspaper on Jewish values and the struggle against apartheid. He has devoted his career to human rights work, serving as executive director of Rabbis for Human Rights North America and, most recently, as cofounder of the Fast for Gaza with Rabbi Brant Rosen. Walt was one of the coleaders of the Dorothy Cotton delegation to Israel and the West Bank described in a previous chapter. In June 2012, Rabbi Walt delivered an address to an audience of friends, colleagues, and longtime coworkers in Boston upon the death of a colleague. He used the occasion to recount his personal journey as a rabbi who had devoted most of his career to the Zionist dream and who had now arrived at a painful realization. "I have been a progressive, liberal Zionist for most of my life," Walt said as he began his speech. "Liberal Zionism and a deep connection to Israel remained a core part of my Judaism and Jewish identity...[it] meant that I believed the Jewish state would treat all with dignity, equality and respect." Liberal Zionists, he explained, "are deeply attached to the Jewish state, while viewing the oppression of Palestinians, the occupation and the settlement policy as deviations from the true intent of Zionism."[43]

Having grown up, in his words, "in a fiercely and passionately Zionist family," this was a comfortable outlook for Walt to assume, as he pursued a career devoted to confronting these "deviations" from Zionism that were, in his words, the "blemishes" on the dream of the Jewish state. The problem was that this work exposed him continually to experiences that were eroding these core and cherished beliefs about the Zionist project. Over time, a thought began to dawn on him: "These demolitions, settlements, violent dispossession of Palestinian homes were not 'rogue' acts. The Israeli state with all its military might enabled and supported these actions." Still, because of what Israel had always meant to him, and because it was so much a part of his community connections, it was hard for Walt "to even think of relinquishing my Zionism."

"Then in 2008," he said, "it came to a head." On a trip sponsored by Rabbis for Human Rights, Walt visited Hebron, a Palestinian city of 160,000 held hostage by a small Jewish settler community planted in its heart and protected by an Israeli army garrison. Walt described the moment:

For me this was the clincher: a deserted street restricted to Jews, in the middle of Hebron, passing by Palestinian homes where the residents are not allowed to walk on the street in front of their homes. When Michael Manikin, our guide, mentioned that this was a Jews-only street and showed us the apartments where Palestinians climb over the roof and then down a ladder to go to the store, the supermarket, the hospital, something in me had changed. Sadness and rage overwhelmed me. I realized that this was in some ways worse than what I had witnessed as a child in South Africa. Whenever I would compare my experience on the West Bank with my experience during Apartheid, Jews would get very angry. For many years I knew I should never use the A (Apartheid) word. At that moment I broke down crying and made a pledge that I would never again censor myself. I didn't know it then, but that was the moment when I crossed over.[44]

As a result of his exposure to the structural violence and overt racism of the Israeli occupation, Walt was forced to renounce that which had become for him, as for almost all other Jews of our generation, effectively an article of faith: allegiance to modern political Zionism. What is most significant about Walt's "crossing over" in this way is that it constituted not an abandonment, but rather, an affirmation of his faith and his commitment to its core values.

I finally had to admit to myself what I had known for a long time but was too scared to acknowledge: political Zionism, at its core, is a discriminatory ethno-nationalism that privileges the rights of Jews over non-Jews. As such political Zionism violates everything I believe about Judaism. While there was a desperate need in the 1940s to provide a safe haven for Jews, and this need won over most of the Jewish world and the Western world to support the Zionist movement, the Holocaust can in no way justify or excuse the systemic racism that was and remains an integral part of Zionism. In the past I believed that the discrimination I saw—the demolished homes, the uprooted trees, the stolen land—were an aberration of the Zionist vision. I came to understand that all of these were not mistakes nor blemishes on a dream; they were all the logical outcome of Zionism.[45]

It has been a long journey for Walt from the liberal Zionism of his childhood to a passionate reclaiming of his authentic Jewishness:

I believe that justice is the core commandment of our tradition. As a Jew I believe that we are commanded to be advocates for the poor, the oppressed, the marginalized. Prior to the 1940s, there was a vigorous debate about Zionism and Judaism. Within the Zionist movement there was a small but influential group of very prominent leaders—Martin Buber, Judah Magnes and others—who understood that imposing our will on the Palestinians would create an unending cycle of violence and violate our deepest values as Jews...Most Jews were not Zionists. The Holocaust transformed the Jewish world and Zionism won the sympathy of the world. Today, 60 years later, there is almost no distinction made between Zionism and Judaism. Zionism has become the religion of American Jews.[46]

New Questions for an Old Story

We have reached a tipping point. Faced with consequences of this pursuit of the Zionist dream, Jewish leaders are working to find a way back to the core values of their tradition. Brian Walt, together with Brant Rosen and about forty other American rabbis and several rabbinical students, have formed the Rabbinical Council of Jewish Voice for Peace.[47] Their numbers are still small, but this is the leading edge of an awakening that will be the salvation of our people. In a recent Passover reflection, Rabbi Margaret Holub, a member of this group, put it this way:

> How you tell your people's story depends on how you understand your people's place in the world. If you think that you are unique and that only your fate matters, then you can justify doing terrible things to another people. If on the other hand you see your own tribe as one player in a world craving peace and wholeness for every person, then you will move quite differently in our hurting world. With Passover coming in a few days, I look forward to eating and drinking with my friends and family and telling the story of our liberation from oppression. And at the same time I know we will be confronting the ways in which today we play the role of the Pharaoh in the ancient story, cruelly oppressing another people. An important part of my freedom as a Jew is the freedom to bring new questions to the old story.[48]

Like the Christian leaders we have met in these chapters, Rosen, Walt, Holub, and growing numbers of Jewish leaders, their eyes opened to the signs of times, have taken the painful, unpopular step out of the circle of fear-based conformity to nationalism, privilege, and "us and them." In so doing, they have stepped into another circle—one that is deep and wide; one that requires no credentials, no creedal rectitude, and no racial or historical pedigree, only a willingness to be "caught in an inescapable network of mutuality."[49] They have joined Martin Luther King Jr.'s "beloved community."

The Authentic Genius of Israel

As we consider this contemporary Jewish quest for reconnection with the precious and core values of our tradition, we turn again to Howard Thurman. In this startling insight about the true nature of Jesus in his Jewishness, Thurman's words speak directly to this contemporary Jewish struggle to turn back from the brink of disaster:

> Jesus did not consider himself as one who stood outside of Israel. If he had regarded himself as one who was starting a new religion, a new faith, then it would not have been hard to account for bitter opposition. With justice, the defenders of the faith could have opposed him because he would have been deliberately trying to destroy the very grounds of Judaism. But if it be true—as I think it is—that Jesus felt he was merely serving as a creative vehicle for *the authentic genius of Israel,* completely devoted to the will of God, then in order to love those of the household he must conquer his own pride. In their attitude he seemed to see the profoundest betrayal of the purpose of God. (emphasis in original)[50]

Jesus' conflict with the "household"—the "defenders of the faith"—sprang directly from his Jewishness. Out of his love for his people and their tradition, he challenged the establishment of his time to recognize how deeply that tradition had been betrayed and violated. Thurman speaks about those times in which it becomes necessary to let go of long-held convictions, and of a sense of self that you have claimed as your identity and have treasured as the legacy of a collective history. Here is Brant Rosen, refusing to celebrate a victory that has brought defeat and loss to the "other," now embraced as sisters and brothers. Here is Marc Ellis, who calls for a Judaism that can proudly claim its heritage as a true liberation theology, and Hannah Arendt summoning us to recognize the peril of remaining isolated within our own suffering. Here are the brave Israelis sending out a plea to the world to help them save their country from itself. All are standing alongside that authentic genius of Israel, unfurling the scroll and proclaiming the good news.

Welcome to our synagogue.

Chapter 11

KAIROS TIME: A CALL TO THE CHURCH

I have great affection for Dutch people. When I was practicing as a psychologist specializing in post-traumatic stress, my mentor was a brilliant psychiatrist from the Netherlands, and that country was one of the three or four in the world leading the way in the study of traumatic stress reactions. So it seemed right that in my present life as a member of an international and interdisciplinary network working on the Israel-Palestine question, I have found myself again in close contact with Dutch people. I meet them in Jerusalem bringing delegations of pastors and human rights workers to witness the nonviolent struggle of the Palestinian people under occupation. I meet them in Hebron and in the hill villages of the West Bank as "ecumenical accompaniers," protecting Palestinian civilians from Jewish settler violence and harassment and ensuring, as much as possible, that the Israeli army of occupation protects Palestinian civilians from the worst of this violence and abuse.[1]

Much, if not most, of this work is supported by the Protestant Church of the Netherlands (PKN), which, as a recent merger of the two reformed denominations and the Lutheran Church in the Netherlands, is the second-largest church in the country after the Roman Catholic Church. Besides supporting a full-time church employee in Jerusalem to lead visiting delegations and to work with local organizations, and providing stipends for ecumenical accompaniers, the PKN also provides substantial support for organizations at home. Two of these organizations are Kairos Netherlands and Friends of Sabeel in the Netherlands, Dutch organizations committed to education and action in support of a just peace in Israel and Palestine.[2]

And so it was that I found myself in Amsterdam in September 2011 for a conference on Kairos Palestine jointly sponsored by these two organizations. On this particular morning, I was seated in the audience, with the opportunity to experience what I have come to know as the Dutch affinity for fairness—it's part of that cooperative survival ethic—in the form of a panel on the Kairos Palestine document. The panel consisted of a number of speakers holding a range of opinions about the document, among them the administrative head of the PKN and a local rabbi. Much of what was said at the panel has faded from my memory, but the words of the church official and the rabbi are as vivid and immediate as they were that day in Amsterdam.

The church official stepped to the lectern. Like every other holder of this position, he was a pastor, cycling through a four-year term in service to the denomination. He held up a copy of the Kairos Palestine document and said, "The Protestant Church of the Netherlands is fully in support of the Palestinian struggle for self-determination and freedom. This is a fine and noble document. But as the leader of the denomination, I cannot support it because it endorses a boycott of Israel. This is an attack on an entire people. We have been down this road before," he said, referring to the anti-Jewish laws enacted in the early years of Nazi Germany,[3] "and we don't want to go in that direction." I don't remember the rest of his comments, because my head was spinning with thoughts and feelings in reaction to this statement. He may have made reference to the recent official declaration of the Dutch church's "indissoluble bond with the Jewish people," a phrase that I heard more than once during that week in the Netherlands.

Then the rabbi took the lectern. He, too, held up the Kairos Palestine document. "This is a fine document," he said. "It is an eloquent expression of the Palestinian desire for freedom and self-determination. But I cannot support this document. I cannot support it because although it talks about Palestinian suffering and Palestinian yearnings, the Jewish narrative is missing."

Those moments in Amsterdam have never left my mind, because contained in those two brief statements are the reasons peace in the Holy Land remains so far from us, and indeed appears to be receding daily. I had not been seated on that panel, and there was no opportunity to speak from the floor, and I don't know that I would have taken the opportunity had it been presented. I was completely occupied with the conversation going on in my head, and that is still going on, and (for this I am thankful) that is continuing to take place within the churches and in the Jewish community. It's my hope and expectation that it is a conversation that will begin to happen in the academy as well, and in the centers of political power. But if I had been given the opportunity to respond to these speakers, here is what I might have said:

To the rabbi, I would have made a simple, blunt, declaration: "Rabbi, you say that the Jewish narrative is left out of the Palestinian document, but you are wrong." The document that you hold in your hand, I would have told him, *is* the Jewish narrative of our time. If we Jews do not begin to understand the deep trouble we are in, then we are done for as a people. Someday, looking back on this period in our history, we will be in deep mourning. We will acknowledge the crimes that we committed in the name of Jewish safety and Jewish peoplehood, and we will feel horror, shame, and regret. Someday we will be on our knees in contrition for what we have done in the name of our own survival and our own redemption. Do not dismiss the Palestinian call for justice, do not put it away. Today the Palestinian story *is our story.*

To the leader of the Protestant Church in the Netherlands I would have addressed a simple question: "You say that because of the boycott you cannot support the Palestinian document. But can you actually tell me that you cannot distinguish between the anti-Jewish laws of the early years of the Third Reich in Germany and the Palestinian call to world Christians to stand for justice through this legal, nonviolent global movement to raise awareness of the plight of the Palestinians and to exert pressure on the State of Israel to comply with international law?" I would have pointed out to him that there are Jewish voices in Israel, in Holland, and elsewhere in Europe and in the world who are also in support of this movement, who understand that holding Israel accountable for its actions is an act of love, not of hatred, for the Jews of Israel and indeed for Jews worldwide. As a Jew, I understand how the trauma of the war years still affects the Dutch people deeply, even now, generations later. I understand all too well the persistence of this kind of memory. But reflecting on the statements of the Dutch church official and the rabbi, I wondered how long we were all to be trapped by these experiences, blocked from taking action now in response to the urgent conditions of our own times.

Several months later I was in Germany on a speaking tour. Several church groups eager to bring a message supportive of the Palestinian cause to German audiences had organized my visit. But this was Germany, and they were a bit nervous. On the evening of my first lecture, the local organizer took me aside and made a request: "Don't mention boycotts," he said to me. "You must understand that this is a very sensitive topic for Germans." I agreed to take his request seriously. After all, I was his guest, and I needed to honor his wisdom about what his audience was ready to absorb. I wanted this gutsy thing he was doing to be successful, and I didn't want to throw any bombs. But public speaking is a mysterious thing. There is a way in which you can feel your audience before you utter the first word. In fact, a successful speaker does just that—the first thing to do in stepping up to the microphone is to take a deep breath, look around the room, and allow yourself to connect nonverbally with the people who have come to hear you. I don't recall the moment I made the decision, but I realized quickly that this audience was hungry to hear what they felt but had not been allowed to voice. Five minutes into my talk I was telling them the story of the Dutch church leader and his reason for not supporting Kairos Palestine. Then I asked them the question I had not asked him: "How many of you here tonight," I said, "actually confuse the anti-Jewish laws of the Third Reich in the 1930s with the international movement to sanction Israel for its mistreatment of the Palestinians?" I didn't ask for a show of hands, but the nonverbal response was clear: It was relief. It was—I have no other word for it—gratitude. "I will make a deal with you," I continued. "If you as Germans will stop seeing yourselves as the worst criminals the world has ever known, I as a Jew will give up being the world's worst victim. It's time for all of us to move on."

The position of the Dutch church had surprised me. After all, this was not Germany; this was Holland—the Dutch had been the victims of the Nazis themselves, not the perpetrators of the crimes against the Jews. But I should not have been surprised. That had been a church bureaucrat speaking, not the people themselves. Given the opportunity, freed of institutional strictures and the burden of guilt or fear of noncomformity, human beings crave healing and want to move on from the pain of trauma and grief.

A few days after the Amsterdam panel, I had another encounter with this denomination official, at a private dinner for local pastors and international guests, given in honor of the Palestinian delegation that had attended the conference. The Palestinians, a South African man (a veteran of the antiapartheid movement), and I were each given a chance to speak for five minutes. We each addressed a strong challenge to the Dutch church to oppose Israeli apartheid as it had in the days of the struggle to free South Africans, black and white, from apartheid's sin and heresy. We challenged the church doctrine of a "bond" with the Jewish people that would stand in the way of prophetic, faithful church action. As a Jew, I added my sentiments that if the church really loved my people, it would stop enabling our crimes—and that it was time to courageously take the side of the oppressed. The church leader then stood to speak. He was visibly offended and angry. The church, he maintained, was being faithful to its principles. It had a responsibility to both the Palestinians and the Jews to maintain a balanced perspective and to extend a hand to both peoples. The church did not take sides; it worked for "reconciliation." I was seated next to a pastor from a small town to the east. He leaned over and spoke into my ear: "He does not speak for me."

Of course, it is the people who must speak. Church institutions, like governments, respond, eventually, to the voices of their constituencies. I remember a pastor from Ohio getting to his feet one day in response to a comment I had just made in which I called on clergy to speak boldly on this issue from their pulpits. "It's up to you!" I had said. He challenged me: "I need to hear from my congregation," he protested. "If only three or four people approach me on an issue, that's all I need."

I believe we need both. The call has gone out to all levels: to heads of churches, to clergy, to the people in the pews. What is clear is that the institutional churches, like governments, do not lead. *But they will follow.* Yes, the Dutch church official and the rabbi were both trapped in the past, unable or unwilling to find a way forward, either separately or together. But here is the good news, and I see it and hear it everywhere I go: people want to be free to create their futures, individually and collectively. When the stakes are highest, when the chains of the past are strongest, forged not only by an external oppressor but also by one's own institutions of church and government, the people create alternative communities or they demand change on the part of the existing structures. This is the story of the early church, local collectives guided by the vision of an alternative society, building God's kingdom in the midst of the most powerful tyranny in history. This is the story of the church under apartheid in South Africa, pulling itself out of the morass of its own self-betrayal to marshal the forces of the global church in support of its struggle to lead its country out of darkness. It is the story of the U.S. civil rights movement, born and nurtured in the church, channeling back into that same church the vision and spirit that had given it birth two thousand years earlier, reminding it of its faithful and courageous heart. And today, it is the story of the global Kairos movement, emerging in response to the call of the Palestinian churches to stand in solidarity with the Palestinian people.

A U.S. Call to Action

The churches are responding. Delegations from twenty-six countries were present in Bethlehem in 2011 at the second anniversary of the launch of the Kairos Palestine document. And, as described in an earlier chapter, a group from the United States was among them, inspired by the example of the Southern African Kairos group and asking the question: if the church in the United States does not step up to its responsibility to answer the Palestinian call, then who will? Within six months, American Christians—women and men, white and black, Catholic and Protestant, mainline and evangelical—produced a document titled "Call to Action: A U.S. Response to the Kairos Palestine Document, a Word of Confession and Faith from Christians in the United States."[4]

Declaring the mission of the newly formed Kairos USA "to mobilize the churches in the United States to respond faithfully and boldly to the situation in Israel and Palestine," the preamble to "Call to Action" describes the background and context for its creation:

> In June 2011, a group of U.S. clergy, theologians and laypersons, cognizant of our responsibility as Americans in the tragedy unfolding in Israel and Palestine, and mindful of the urgency of the situation, met to inaugurate a new movement for American Christians. We have been inspired by the prophetic church movements of southern Africa, Central and South America, Asia and Europe that have responded to the call of their Christian sisters and brothers in occupied Palestine. This is our statement of witness and confession—and our response as U.S. Christians to the Palestinian call.

"The tragic realities of Israel and Palestine today," the document continues, "would deeply trouble Jesus and the prophets. The land in which Jesus lived and was crucified by the Roman imperial rulers is again a place of violence, inequality and suffering. Palestinians and Israelis are trapped in a spiral of violence that is destroying their humanity, squandering their resources and killing their children." As Christians, the authors of "Call to Action" confess the tragic legacy of Christian persecution of Jews, recognizing that it is this history that gave rise to the modern aspirations of the Jewish people for a homeland. Having made this confession and acknowledged the right of the Jewish people to "security...free from the scourge of anti-Semitism," the document shifts its focus to the urgent realities of the present day, stating boldly that "the State of Israel's present course will not bring it the security it seeks nor grant the Jewish people freedom from fear." Even though violence visited against Israel has evoked profound feelings of fear and insecurity on the part of Israelis, the document continues, "the cause of the current calamity is not the result of any historic or natural enmity between the two peoples, or the presence of deep-seated hatred directed against the Jewish people. Rather, it is the overwhelming imbalance of power, Israel's practices of state violence, the ongoing abridgement of the human rights of the Palestinian people and the failure of the international community to hold Israel to principles of international law."[5]

Like the writers of the South Africa Kairos document written during the apartheid era, the authors of "Call to Action" felt a keen sense of responsibility as U.S. citizens for their government's massive and unconditional support for the historic and ongoing injustice toward the Palestinians. But as Christians, they were also aware of how closely intertwined U.S. national policies are with a theology, endorsed by so many American Christians, that has been used to justify these policies.

As individuals and as church institutions, we have supported a system of control, inequality and oppression through misreading of our Holy Scriptures, flawed theology and distortions of history. We have allowed to go unchallenged theological and political ideas that have made us complicit in the oppression of the Palestinian people. Instead of speaking and acting boldly, we have chosen to offer careful statements designed to avoid controversy and leave cherished relationships undisturbed. We have forgotten the difference between a theology that supports the policies and institutional structures of oppression and a theology that, in response to history and human affairs, stands boldly with the widow, the orphan, the poor and the dispossessed.[6]

Noting that the special relationship that has existed between the United States and Israel from the earliest days of the Jewish state "has crossed party lines and transcended political eras," Kairos USA challenges us to reflect deeply on what this says about the United States' own legacy as a conqueror and an occupier:

Our government's policy toward Israel has at times reflected our own religiously-tinged identity as a privileged society blessed by God. The notion, for example, that the Jewish people have a special claim on Jerusalem and a superior right to the territory of historic Palestine over the other inhabitants of the land bears a resemblance to our historic American notion of "Manifest Destiny"—our nation as the "shining city on a hill." As Americans and as Christians, we must carefully examine how our own deeply-rooted sense of privilege may affect our commitment to justice and equality in this and other human rights causes across the globe.[7]

Global Movement, Church Struggle

This quality of self-critical reflection, leading to an awareness of our responsibility to act not only within but outside our own context, is central to the Kairos movement. Liberation theologian, United Dutch Reformed pastor, and antiapartheid activist Professor Allan Boesak recently described Kairos consciousness in this way:

A Kairos consciousness is a critical consciousness. It discerns and critiques the situation in which we live...The crisis we are facing is not just economic, social and political, it is a moral crisis...Certainly choices are made on empirical evidence—social, political, economic analysis, and an understanding of the ways in which power and powerlessness work. But just as certain a Kairos consciousness makes these choices on the basis of faith. Much more than only the liberation of the oppressed is at stake here. Because Christians oppress others claiming faith in the God of Jesus who came to establish justice upon the earth, that faith, the integrity of the Gospel, and the credibility of the witness of the church are at stake here. The moment of truth is a moment to act for the sake of justice and humanity, but also for the sake of the integrity of the Gospel.[8]

South African theologian Charles Villa-Vicencio, one of the authors of the 1985 Kairos document, shared the following insight when we talked in Cape Town: "This is bigger than Palestine. It's the fault line running through Western civilization, the point of split in the first century between the followers of Jesus and those who clung to their Rome-granted power base in Jerusalem."[9] Today, hearing the call of the church in Palestine, we must ask ourselves, as we have at other critical moments in history, will we use religion to grant one group the right to dominate another, or to help bring humankind to a realization of our unity and interconnectedness? Being filled with the power of the Holy Spirit, the story of Pentecost reminds us, means being witnesses to Jesus' message of love and compassion not only in one's native land, "but to the ends of the earth," speaking all the languages of humankind.

The church was born to this struggle. Indeed, the church was born *in* this struggle. And the church is taking this on—in Africa, in the United States, and in a growing number of nations in Europe, South America, and Asia. It is the faithful action of the global church that will be critical in ending the system that is destroying Israeli society, has hijacked the Jewish faith, continues to fuel global conflict, and has produced one of the most systematic and long-standing violations of human rights in the world today. And to those who say that talk of "bringing to an end" an unjust political system in Israel indicates a wish to destroy the Jewish state and hatred of the Jewish people, the proper answer is the following (and here the use of irony can be excused): "Do you mean the way the world hated the South African people and wanted to destroy that nation?" The global movement to end apartheid in that country brought South Africa back into the community of nations, liberating its people, black and white, from the misery, violence, and soul-killing racism of the apartheid system.

As the examples of the South African antiapartheid struggle and the civil rights movement, and now the struggle for justice for Palestine demonstrate, in taking a stand against tyranny and injustice, church leaders often find themselves pitted against the very institutions of which they are a part. In their aptly titled *The Church Struggle in South Africa,* South African theologians John and Steve de Gruchy write, "The church is called to bear witness to the Kingdom of God in the world... This being so, *a faithful church will always find itself in tension with society.* For this reason, the church desperately needs the presence of prophetic movements... for these movements provide the critique that forces the church to a new assessment of itself. Such movements are part of God's way of renewing the church in every generation and situation"[10] (emphasis added).

The unwillingness to compromise on core issues, coupled with the willingness to step outside the strictures of the institutional church, characterizes the Kairos documents that followed the South African document of 1985. Kairos is a practical theology that emerges at those very times when it is most needed. In this, it hearkens back to the original *kairos,* the confrontation of a visionary, prophetic figure with the evil of empire—the man from Galilee standing up to the greatest power in the world. The first *kairos* embodied three key elements: (1) an urgent sociopolitical situation (the tyranny of Rome) that threatened the economic and social fabric of a village-based agrarian society; (2) a God-given ethical and spiritual tradition rooted in a civilization under mortal threat by that same tyrannical system; and (3) the appearance of a prophetic witness, teacher, and leader who called his people and their leadership to nonviolent resistance, a resistance based on faithfulness to their tradition. Jesus knew that the challenge of the historical circumstances required a return to the essential truths of the Jewish tradition, truths that had been betrayed by the monarchical/priestly system in power in Jerusalem working for the Roman occupier. It was this resistance, of course, that brought on the persecution by the authorities. Jesus' message threatened their power and privilege at the most fundamental levels. They acted, therefore, not only to preserve the existing power arrangement, but to suppress any challenge to the beliefs and values that served to legitimize the oppressive system. This story of *ideological* challenge to power and the attempt to repress it by reasserting prevailing beliefs characterizes freedom movements throughout history. It applies as well to today's struggle for justice in Israel and Palestine.

The Rules

As we've seen, beliefs play a major role in upholding the status quo in Israel and Palestine. Powerful attitudes and assumptions about Judaism, Jewish identity, and Jewish survival have operated as unspoken rules that control and limit the discourse. They have effectively become red lines; beliefs one may not challenge without being accused of being at worst anti-Semitic and at best naïvely and with good intentions reverting to Christian habits of denigrating Judaism and aiding the real anti-Semites. These unwritten rules are, with few but thankfully increasing exceptions, observed in the pulpits, in the academy, and in public discussion.

Rule number 1: "Sensitivity" to "the Jewish perspective" and Jewish self-perception (as defined for all Jews by some Jews who claim to represent them) is paramount. This includes two core beliefs: (a) the State of Israel is necessary to ensure the safety and survival of the Jewish people, and (b) the State of Israel and the values and tenets of Zionism are an essential and inseparable part of Jewish identity.

Rule number 2: The superior right of the Jews to the land is not to be challenged. You may acknowledge that the Palestinians have suffered and that their rights have been abridged, but you may not take any action or make any statements that might challenge fundamental Zionist assumptions or that might be perceived as compromising the security of the State of Israel.

Rule number 3: The third rule is more in the nature of a commandment: "Thou shalt bless the two-state solution." We are now approaching a consensus, even among those who have long championed the idea, that, according to Israeli peace activist Jeff Halper, "the two-state solution is dead, buried under settlements and infrastructure too massive and interlinked with Israel to detach, especially given the lack of will among international governments, led by the U.S. and Germany, to exert the pressures on Israel needed to force such massive concessions."[11] What remains are two options, both unacceptable to people occupying widely divergent ideological and political camps:

1. A continuation, indeed a strengthening, of Jewish rule over an occupied population in the West Bank and East Jerusalem and a second-class population inside pre-1967 Israel. This is a political arrangement that many agree meets the definition of apartheid.
2. A single state in which Jews, as a shrinking minority, will share power with non-Jews.

Both of these alternatives challenge the first two rules, which require the existence of a democratic majority Jewish state in historic Palestine. In order that The Rules not be challenged, the political mantra of "two states living side by side in peace and security" is chanted repeatedly, as if the act of saying "two-state solution" will somehow bring it about, despite the fact that successive Israeli governments have worked against this outcome and that the international community has been unable or unwilling to curtail Israel's expansionist and discriminatory actions. But as awareness about the situation in Israel and Palestine increases within the church establishment, the last decade has seen a growing challenge to The Rules on local, denominational, and ecumenical levels. We are witnessing a return to fundamental principles of human rights and a willingness to question theological and biblically based assumptions and beliefs that support Jewish privilege in the Holy Land. We are also seeing an increased ability on the part of Christians to withstand intimidation based on the charge that to challenge Israel's actions is an act unfriendly to Jews and is a betrayal of a half century of hard work in Christian-Jewish reconciliation.

Those who are interested in preserving the status quo perceive, accurately, that this challenge to The Rules threatens the flow of unconditional military aid and the practice of blanket diplomatic support for Israel on the part of the United States. Jewish scholars, working closely with American Jewish advocacy organizations with close ties to the State of Israel, have mounted a determined effort to counter this threat. They employ what has been so far a very effective method: changing the subject from advocacy for human rights to vigilance against anti-Semitism. Pivoting from compassion for the oppressed to the issue of Christian-Jewish relations, these voices claim that challenges to Jewish hegemony and privilege in Israel spring from anti-

Semitism.[12] For this reason, it is important for Americans to pay attention to the Palestinian context. The moral imperative originating so powerfully from their cry of suffering is slowly but surely overcoming the reluctance on the part of U.S. Christians to speak and act on behalf of justice for Palestinians for fear of being perceived as insensitive to historic Jewish suffering.

Do we really believe that the deeply felt Christian penitence over anti-Semitism is now being supplanted by a resurgence of anti-Jewish feeling? Far from it. Indeed, Christian awareness of historic sins has never been more acute. What is being swept away, rather, is sinful inaction and muzzling in the face of actions that violate not only the Palestinians' dignity and ties to their homeland, but the humanity and the dreams of freedom for which the original Jewish settlers of Israel sacrificed so much. What is being affirmed in Kairos Palestine, and in the international Kairos movement that has emerged in response to the document, is Christians' recommitment to compassion for the oppressed, willingness to speak truth to power, and the readiness to pick up the cross of what is right in the face of opposition and censure. It is time for the church to put its own house in order. It is time for the church to be the church.

And it is time for the Jewish establishment to leave off defending what cannot be defended, stop making rules for Christians, and look in the mirror. Is this not what Jesus would require of us—*his people*—today, if he were to stand on the Mount of Olives surveying the walls of exclusion and privilege we have erected? What would Jesus do if he came back to Jerusalem today? What temple of power and greed would he stand before, predicting how it will be thrown down? What kingdom would he proclaim in the face of these monuments to temporal power and military might? What suffering people would he then lead back to God?

The New Ecumenicism: Creating the Beloved Community

The act of writing a Kairos document brings people together. It creates a home for those who have been working for justice within their own congregations and denominations but in isolation from one another. This is not an "ecumenical" move-ment in the sense that the word is often employed—a kind of United Nations of churches, each delegate sitting at the table wearing his or her denominational or theological hat. Rather, it is ecumenical in the sense of a single body united in a faithful ministry. Charles Villa-Vicencio has posed this ques-tion: can a creative, prophetic drive penetrate the institutional church, a church conditioned by a history of compromise with the very structures of oppression? He asks: "Can religion truly break the iron cage of history? Can religion produce a qualitatively different kind of society? Is the Kingdom of God a real possibility?"[13]

The Church has done it before; the church can do it again. It is the mission of the emerging global Kairos movement to remind the Church, and all who are witnesses to the signs of our times, of its historic and sacred calling. Rev. Mitri Raheb, the pastor of the Christmas Lutheran Church in Bethlehem and a tireless warrior for justice, elaborated on this calling at the Kairos for Global Justice conference in Bethlehem in 2011, the same conference attended by the U.S. Kairos delegation. In reminding those assembled about the meaning of *kairos* and its significance not only for the Palestinian struggle but also for the future of humanity in these times, Reverend Raheb spoke about hope:

> The Kairos document has a whole section about hope, and for me this is the most powerful one. There is a big difference between optimism and hope. I'm not optimistic at all! In fact, my political analysis is saying that we are heading toward the most sophisticated apartheid system that ever existed in modern history. The West Bank will look more and more like a piece of Swiss cheese, where the Israelis will get the cheese and the Palestinians will get the holes. The facts are plain. Yet even so, the Kairos document tells us that we can and should have hope. Martin Luther said it best: even if we knew that the world were coming to an end tomorrow...even if we knew that the international community would not change tomorrow because of Kairos, even if we knew this, we would only have one option: we would go out today, into our garden, into our world, into our societies, and we would plant olive trees.

"This is what Kairos is about!" continued Reverend Raheb. "Planting olive trees when people think you're crazy. But I tell you, sisters and brothers, a crazy world like this needs crazy people like us. Unless we plant these olive trees today, there will be no shade for our kids to play in the day after tomorrow. There will be no oil with which to heal all these wounded Israelis, Palestinians, and everyone else. And there will be no branches to wave when peace comes. This is the spirit of the Kairos document, that it breathes a spirit of hope, a hope that springs from the resurrection of a culture of life." Reverend

Raheb then told the story of two American friends during the 2008 presidential election campaign. Each believed that his candidate would fix everything. "And I told both of them, you know what? Thank God our Messiah came two thousand years ago, said what needed to be said, did what needed to be done, and now the ball is in our court—either we pick it up or we leave it. Hope is to pick up the ball and say, yes, we will do it. In this sense, dear sisters and brothers, it is indeed the moment of truth. It is the time for action."[14]

A Call to Action

In the spirit of Kairos Palestine, which sees hope even when it seems most distant; of Kairos South Africa, which challenged its own church to remain true to its mission; and of the "Letter from Birmingham Jail," which required that faith be translated directly into action, the Kairos USA "Call to Action" lays out specific measures for individuals, churches, and organizations.[15]

Visit the land: "Come and see!" say the authors of Kairos Palestine, to "know the facts and the people of this land, Palestinians and Israelis alike." How many tens of thousands visit the land on pilgrimages every year? And how many limit themselves to the standard tourist itineraries, rather than seeing the occupation firsthand and meeting the Palestinians and Israelis working for justice and coexistence? Indeed, when pilgrims are allowed to see the real facts of the situation, they not only "walk where Jesus walked," they *see what Jesus saw.* And witnessing the suffering and seeing the injustice, like Jesus in his time and the prophets in their day, they are called to speak out and to act.

Learn: Move beyond stereotypes, long-standing prejudices, and biased reporting. There is a wealth of study materials and curricula available to churches, schools, and local organizations in the form of documents, videos, speakers' bureaus, conferences, and alternative media.

Enrich worship and congregational life: Pray for and preach justice and peace for Palestine and Israel. Pursue opportunities to learn and study about the situation, explore cultural and economic exchange, and challenge congregations to participate in the blessed calling of peacemaking.

Engage in theological reflection: Examine flawed biblical interpretations and theologies that have allowed injustice to continue unchallenged. Pursue open and active theological inquiry and encourage study and reflection, in order to guide our actions in striving to follow Jesus' injunction to "interpret the present time" (Luke 12:56).

Participate in nonviolent action: Translate concern into action. Support those in Israel, the occupied territories, and throughout the world who work for justice through peaceful means. Become educated about the Palestinian call for BDS (boycott, divestment, and sanctions), exploring this and other forms of legitimate, nonviolent action and other opportunities to become actively involved.

Advocate with the U.S. government: As Christians who are committed to justice, peace, and security for Israelis and Palestinians alike, hold the U.S. government and its elected officials accountable to the same principles. Support political candidates who do the same.

"Stop Killing Our Children"

It was the summer of 2006. In the company of a group of Americans, I was visiting the Palestinian village of At-Tuwani in the hill country south of Hebron in the West Bank. At-Tuwani is a village of about 350 souls—farmers and shepherds who draw their water from wells and graze their sheep in the surrounding pastures. This village is centuries old. Its inhabitants are now at the mercy of the occupying Israeli army, which blocks their access to pastureland, citing "military necessity," and face constant harassment from the residents of the nearby Jewish settlement of Maon. Since 1982, more than fifteen hundred *dunams* of land (one *dunam* is equivalent to one-quarter of an acre) have been confiscated from the village by the settlers of Maon. While the people of Maon are equipped with plentiful water and electrical power from newly installed water pipes and power lines, all such services are denied to the villagers. The taking of land and the denial of services have been only the prelude to Israel's plan to expel the historic inhabitants of this region from their farms and villages. At-Tuwani's flocks have been sickened, their milk spoiled by rat poison spread in the pastures by the Maon settlers, and the village's wells intentionally fouled by animal carcasses. At-Tuwani's children have been forced to take a circuitous route to the regional school, escorted by international peace workers and a reluctant Israeli army presence, because the settlers have physically assaulted them on their way to school.

Arriving in At-Tuwani, we visited with the villagers, drinking tea with them, listening to their stories, and meeting the international peace activists who live there as a constant presence to protect the villagers' human rights. As we prepared to leave, the villagers thanked us for coming. One man, however, stepped up and said, "It's fine to come and visit, but you must do something, you must speak up. Go home and tell your president to stop killing our children." I was struck by this statement. He did not tell us to call on the *Israeli government* to let his people live in peace. He directed us to *our own government,* which he understood to be the source of the evil he was experiencing. Indeed, the rest of the world, with the exception of the great majority of the American people, understands this. This issue is named directly in the Kairos USA document: "Rather than acting as an honest broker in negotiations between Israelis and Palestinians, our government has consistently supported, both financially and diplomatically, the actions of Israel that have brought suffering to Palestinians, continuing insecurity to Israelis and the declining prospect of a just peace."[16]

In the historic speech given in April 1967 at the Riverside Church, Martin Luther King Jr. fearlessly took on the thorny question of how, to use the words of the Kairos USA document, "our own deeply-rooted sense of privilege may affect our commitment to justice and equality in…human rights causes across the globe." It had not been an easy road for King on the way to delivering that speech. He had confronted strong opposition from his own ranks in the civil rights movement about speaking out against the Vietnam War. Perhaps he had to ask himself some of the same questions African Americans are asking themselves today about becoming involved in a struggle so far away. But we cannot imagine that he hesitated for long. Overwhelmed with shame, grief, and anger about the war, King realized that what we were doing abroad could not be separated from our business at home: "I could never again raise my voice against the violence of the oppressed in the ghettos without having first spoken clearly to the greatest purveyor of violence in the world today: my own government."

> Beyond the calling of race or nation or creed is this voca-tion of sonship and brotherhood. Because I believe that the Father is deeply concerned, especially for His suf-fering and helpless and outcast children, I come tonight to speak for them. This I believe to be the privilege and the burden of all of us who deem ourselves bound by allegiances and loyalties which are broader and deeper than nationalism and which go beyond our nation's self-defined goals and positions. We are called to speak for the weak, for the voiceless, for the victims of our nation, for those it calls "enemy," for no document from human hands can make these humans any less our brothers.[17]

Who arms Israel? Who funds the dispossession and daily humiliation of Palestinians in the West Bank and the military siege of Gaza? Who shields Israel from criticism on the inter-national scene? And who better to call our society to account in this matter than the church, equipped with the power of the Gospel to guide this prophetic movement?

Call to Discipleship

The church has done it before. The church can do it again. The church was born in the reverberations of Jesus' words spoken in the first chapter of the first Gospel:

> Now after John was arrested, Jesus came to Galilee, pro-
> claiming the Good News, and saying, "The kairos is
> fulfilled, and the kingdom of God has come near! Re-
> pent, and believe in the Good News."
>
> Mark 1:14–15

Think about what Jesus' declaration means. In arresting John, Rome was trying to put a stop to the momentous event that he was foretelling. The time has come, now as it was then, to step into history. The Greek word *metanoeite,* usually translated as "repent," means to change ourselves, to shift our focus radically, away from habitual concerns, and to turn our attention to the urgent needs of society. Kairos requires that we not be passive; to recognize that the kingdom is within our grasp, ours to create here on earth. In the words of the South Africa Kairos document, it is "a time in which God issues a challenge to decisive action." Theologian John Marsh puts it this way: "To embrace the opportunity means salvation, to ne-glect it disaster. There is no third choice."[18] "Hope," reads the Kairos Palestine document, "is the capacity to see God in the midst of trouble, and to be co-workers with the Holy Spirit who is dwelling in us."[19]

The call to discipleship was issued by Jesus, and then spread by his disciples. Today it is the Palestinians who issue this call. They summon us to acknowledge the brokenness of our own systems and the errors in our own beliefs, and to know that we receive the power to heal ourselves and to work for the Kingdom of God by hearing the call of the oppressed. In their "word of faith, hope and love," the Palestinians stand in the tradition of Jesus' original call to discipleship. They stand in the tradition of Martin Luther King Jr., who called for "a positive peace which is the presence of justice, not the negative peace which is the absence of tension,"[20] and of the South African and then the global church that declared itself in *status confessionis* in the face of the evil of apartheid.

There will be voices that urge us to ignore this call. As the movement to respond to the signs of the times grows, those voices will become louder, more strident, and more accusatory. The walls that have been built on Palestinian land to separate brother from brother and sister from sister will be built thicker and higher. But no one can build a wall in our hearts. Standing before the wall in Jerusalem, we hear the Good News: that we can bring down that wall. That it will fall, that in fact it is already coming down, as Jesus predicted to his followers on that Sunday in Jerusalem so long ago.

Martin Luther King Jr.'s charge to the church penned from that jail cell in Birmingham, Alabama, speaks as loudly and as clearly today as it did fifty years ago:

> ...The judgment of God is upon the church as never before. If today's church does not recapture the sacrificial spirit of the early church, it will lose its authenticity, forfeit the loyalty of millions, and be dismissed as an irrelevant social club with no meaning for the twentieth century.[21]

These words ring out across the decades, summoning the church to its destiny. Meanwhile, the Palestinians remain, in their villages, cities, and refugee camps—yes, at the doors of their tents—patient and steadfast, offering their hospitality, secure in their faith, calling on the conscience of the world.

ACKNOWLEDGMENTS

In chapter 10 of this book, I quote theologian Marc Ellis asking about where we are headed as a civilization. "The key issue," he writes, is "the continual struggle over our direction as individuals and as a people—toward the isolation of empire or toward the solidarity of community." Ellis was writing about the Jewish people, but he is making the point—one that is a central theme of this book—that our survival as a global society depends on all of us making the choice for community. This book is about the emergence of a community—one transcending national, ethnic, and religious boundaries, a community and a movement of which I am privileged to be a member, and to which I credit the genesis and the writing of this book.

The phrase "too numerous to mention" has become hackneyed, but it is true in reference to the names of the individuals who have supported, guided, and challenged me and whom I am extraordinarily blessed to call friends and colleagues. Special mention, however, goes to those colleagues who generously gave their time for interviews, whose work is featured in these pages, and who have provided many other means of support for the writing of this book. Some of their voices are heard directly in these pages, but all of them resonate. To the extent that I have found my own voice here, it is because they are singing, praying, crying, and even hollering a bit with me: Edwin Arrison, Hannah Schwarzchild, Brian McLaren, Rabbi Brant Rosen, Rabbi Brian Walt, Richard Horsley, Rev. Naim Ateek, Rev. Mitri Raheb, Rifat Kassis, Nora Carmi, Nomika Zion, Eitan Bronstein Aparicio, Tali Shapiro, Rela Mazali, Rev. Bob Roberts, Sr. Paulette Schroeder, Rev. Stephen Sizer, Marc Ellis, Rev. Carolyn Boyd, Rev. Lucas Johnson, Rick Ufford-Chase, Gary Burge, Tom Getman, Rev. Tinyiko Maluleke, John de Gruchy, Janneke Stegemann, Meta Floor, Giet ten Berge, Jan van der Kolk, Charles Villa-Vicencio, Fawzieh al-Kurd, Rev. Warren Bardsley, Rev. Walt Davis, Steve Haas, Hildegarde Lenz, Rabbi Lynne Gottlieb, Mike Daly, Munther Isaac, Daoud Nassar, Colin Chapman, Sami Awad, Neve Gordon, Rabbi Margaret Holub, Rabbi Lynn Gottlieb, Rev. David Good, Rev. Steve Hyde, GJ and Kay Tarazi, Ulrich Duchrow, Len Rodgers, Adam Estle, Todd Deatherage, Rick Malouf, Carl Medearis, Rev. Richard Toll, Rev. Steven Martin, Kay and Bill Plitt, Gloria and Bill Mims, Nadia Itraish, Steve France, Katherine Cunningham, Allison Schmitt, Pauline Coffman, Rev. Cotton Fite, Noushin Framke, Rev. Don Wagner, Rev. John Wagner, Michel Nseir, Rev. Cotton Fite, John Van Wagoner, Elaine and Jack Brouillard, Serge Duss, Beth Corrie.

Several organizations and congregations have played a major role in supporting and inspiring the experiences and work that went into this book: Interfaith Peace Builders, Friends of Tent of Nations North America, Sabeel Ecumenical Liberation Theology Center, Friends of Sabeel North America, Evangelicals for Middle East Understanding, Holyland Trust, First Congregational Church of Old Lyme, Ravensworth Baptist Church, Tent of Nations, Kairos Palestine, Kairos USA, U.S. Campaign to End the Israeli Occupation, Zochrot, New Profile, Israel Palestine Mission Network PC(USA).

My heartfelt thanks go to Wendy Grisham, Chelsea Apple, and the people of Jericho Books for their skill and professionalism in putting out such fine books, and for their courage and forward thinking in taking on this project. My association to the name of the imprint is strong: it is to the parable of the Good Samaritan in Luke chapter 10, which takes place on the road from Jerusalem to Jericho. "Who is my neighbor?" the lawyer asks Jesus. He who steps outside the strictures of class, privilege, and institutional boundaries to show compassion to those in need, Jesus teaches him. Jericho Books is doing important work in being willing to do the same, giving us eyes to see and ears to hear, and I feel honored to be part of this work.

Special thanks to Kathryn Helmers of Creative Trust for shepherding me through this entire process. Kathy's wisdom and professionalism has helped me navigate the most challenging stretches of the road from conception to publication. Her enthusiasm for and faith in the book has been key, and her commitment has been certain, steadfast, and perhaps above all, calming. It has been an honor to work with her.

This book is dedicated to my wife, Susan Braverman. I can cite Susan's skilled editing, her encouragement through the most challenging periods, and the sacrifices in time, finances, and family life that were made to support this writing. For all that, I am grateful. But that is not what the dedication is about. The dedication, "For Susie," is simply that. Like everything else, this is for her.

Portland, Oregon
June 2013

NOTES

Chapter 1: The Challenge to the Church

1 Aarne Siirala, quoted in Rosemary Redford Ruether, *Faith and Fratricide: The Theological Roots of Anti-Semitism* (Eugene: Wipf and Stock), 1996, p. 7.

2 Robert T. Osborn, "The Christian Blasphemy: A non-Jewish Jesus," in James H. Charlesworth, ed., *Jews and Christians: Exploring the Past, Present, and Future* (New York: Crossroad), 1990, p. 214.

3 Hans Joachim Iwand, quoted in Didier Pollefeyt, *Jews and Christians: Rivals or Partners for the Kingdom of God?* (Louvain: Peeters Press), 1997.

4 Paul van Buren, "The Jewish People in Christian Theology: Present and Future," in Darrell J. Fasching, ed., *The Jewish People in Christian Preaching* (Lewiston, NY: Edwin Mellon Press), 1984, p. 23.

5 James H. Wallis, *Post-Holocaust Christianity: Paul van Buren's Theology of the Jewish-Christian Reality* (Lanham, MD: University Press of America), 1997, p. 85.

6 "Declaration on the Relation of the Church to Non-Christian Religions, Nostra Aetate," proclaimed by his Holiness Pope Paul VI, on October 28, 1965, http://www.vatican.va/archive/hist_councils/ii_vatican_council/documents/vat-ii_decl_19651028_nostra-aetate_en.html, accessed February 5, 2013.

7 Paul van Buren, "The Jewish People in Christian Theology: Present and Future," in Darrell J. Fasching, ed., *The Jewish People in Christian Preaching* (Lewiston, NY: Edwin Mellon Press), 1984, pp. 19–33.

8 Shlomo Sand and Yael Lotan, *The Invention of the Jewish People* (London, Brooklyn: Verso, 2009); Shlomo Sand and Geremy Forman, *The Invention of the Land of Israel: from Holy Land to Homeland* (Brooklyn, NY: Verso, 2009).

9 Marc H. Ellis, *Beyond Innocence and Redemption: Confronting the Holocaust and Israeli Power: Creating a Moral Future for the Jewish People* (New York: HarperCollins, 1991).

10 Benny Morris, Avi Shlaim, and Ilan Pappé are among the chief names of the so-called New Historians, Israeli scholars who have challenged the traditional and accepted narrative of Israel's founding.

11 Ilan Pappé, *The Ethnic Cleansing of Palestine* (Oxford: Oneworld, 2007).

12 United Nations Resolution 194, adopted by the General Assembly on December 11, 1948, calls for the return of Palestinians who were made refugees by Arab-Israeli hostilities between 1947 and 1948. This resolution has not been implemented.

13 The causes and objectives of this war have been the topic of controversy. The Israeli claim, which until recently has been the commonly accepted narrative, is that Israel responded defensively to a threat of attack from Egypt following the closing of critical shipping routes through the Gulf of Aqaba and the massing of troops along its border with Israel. Recent writing

presents a picture of an unjustified and preemptive war initiated by Israel. See Miko Peled, *The General's Son* (Charlottesville, VA: Just World Books, 2012).

14 These settlements exist in violation of international law. The Fourth Geneva Convention, Article 49, stipulates that "[t]he Occupying Power shall not deport or transfer parts of its own civilian population into the territory it occupies." (http://www.icrc.org/ihl/WebART/380-600056, accessed June 15, 2013).

15 Walter Wink, *Engaging the Powers* (Minneapolis, MN: Fortress Press, 1992), p. 231.

Chapter 2: The Wall in My Heart

Huntington

1 Quoted in Douglas M. Johnston Jr., *Religion, Terror, and Error: U.S. Foreign Policy and the Challenge of Spiritual Engagement* (Santa Barbara, CA: Praeger Security International, 2011), p. 53.

2 Ibid., p. 54.

Chapter 4: Welcome to Our Synagogue

1 This argument for the necessity of the wall is suspect. It is estimated that approximately ten thousand West Bank Palestinians cross illegally into Israel (i.e., to the western side of the de facto border established by the wall) every day in order to work. A look at the wall's course on a map shows it clearly enclosing large, illegal settlement blocs, thereby suggesting that its function is to take land, effectively establishing a new border extending beyond the 1949 armistice lines that functioned as the recognized border prior to Israel's occupation of the West Bank in 1967. The wall also functions as a psychological barrier for Israelis.

2 In a March 21, 2013, *Los Angeles Times* opinion peace, Ian

Lustick, an American political scientist and specialist in the modern history and politics of the Middle East, reviewed recent data on Israel's image in the world outside the United States and Israel. He wrote, "How close is Israel to pariah status? Quite close…In a 2003 European Union–sponsored poll, Israel was seen as more dangerous to world peace than any other country. In 2006, an Israeli government poll conducted in 35 countries found Israel had the worst public image in every category it tested. In 2012, the BBC reported that 50% of 24,090 people polled worldwide thought Israel had a 'mostly negative' impact on the world, tied with North Korea and exceeded only by Pakistan and Iran." See "Israel Needs a New Map," http://articles.latimes.com/2013/mar/21/opinion/la-oe-lustick-zionism-obama-israel-20130321, accessed April 23, 2013.

Chapter 5: Jesus and Empire

1 Richard A. Horsley, in discussion with author, October 26, 2012.

2 Ibid.

3 Richard A. Horsley, *Jesus and Empire: The Kingdom of God and the New World Disorder* (Minneapolis, MN: Augsburg Fortress, 2003), p. 94.

4 Ibid., p. 114.

5 Richard A. Horsley, "Jesus and Empire," in Richard A. Horsley, ed., *In the Shadow of Empire: Reclaiming the Bible as a History of Faithful Resistance* (Louisville, KY: Westminster John Knox, 2008), p. 95.

6 Richard A. Horsley, in discussion with author, October 26, 2012.

7 Ibid.

8 Ibid.

9 James M. Washington, ed., *A Testament of Hope: The Essential*

Writings and Speeches of Martin Luther King, Jr. (San Francisco: HarperSanFrancisco, 1986), pp. 299–300.

10 Ibid.

11 Brian D. McLaren, *Why Did Jesus, Moses, the Buddha, and Mohammed Cross the Road?: Christian Identity in a Multi-Faith World* (Nashville, NY: Jericho Books, 2012), p. 82.

12 Ibid., p. 83.

13 Brian D. McLaren, in discussion with author, January 15, 2013.

14 McLaren, *Why Did Jesus, Moses, the Buddha, and Mohammed Cross the Road?*, pp. 83, 84.

15 Brian D. McLaren, *A New Kind of Christianity: Ten Questions That Are Transforming the Faith* (New York: HarperOne, 2010), p. 216.

16 Ibid.

17 Brian D. McLaren, blog entry of January 22, 2010, "More from the West Bank," http://brianmclaren.net/archives/blog/more-from-the-west-bank.html, accessed January 10, 2013.

18 McLaren, *Why Did Jesus, Moses, the Buddha, and Mohammed Cross the Road?*, p. 119.

19 January 12, 2009, at http://brianmclaren.net/archives/blog/the-conversation-is-changing-par-1.html, accessed January 16, 2013.

Chapter 6: To the Ends of the Earth

1 Gary M. Burge, *Whose Land? Whose Promise? What Christians Are Not Being Told about Israel and the Palestinians* (Cleveland: Pilgrim Press, 2003), p. 3.

2 Ibid., p. 6.

3 Gary M. Burge, *Jesus and the Land: The New Testament Challenge to "Holy Land" Theology* (Grand Rapids: Baker Academic, 2010), p. 126.

4 Ibid., pp. 126, 128.

5 Ibid., p. 126.

6 Gary M. Burge, in conversation with author, December 20, 2012.

7 Burge, *Jesus and the Land*, p. 89.

8 Gary M. Burge, in conversation with author, December 20, 2012.

9 Bob Roberts Jr., *Real-Time Connections: Linking Your Job with God's Global Work* (Grand Rapids, MI: Zondervan, 2010), p. 206.

10 Ibid.

11 Ibid., p. 207.

12 Ibid., p. 208.

13 Ibid.

14 Ibid., p. 27.

15 Stephen Brown, "Theologians Warn on 'Biblical Metaphors' in Middle East Conflict," *ENI Bulletin,* September 24, 2008.

16 *With God on Our Side*, Porter Speakman Jr., director/producer, http://www.withgodonourside.com/, accessed December 13, 2012.

17 "Prophets in Jerusalem," *Newsweek,* June 28, 1971, p. 62.

18 Proclamation of the Third International Christian Zionist Congress, 1996, http://www.internationalwallofprayer.org/A-013-1-Proclamation-of-Third-Intl-Congress.html, accessed January 16, 2013.

19 "Christians Call for a United Jerusalem," *New York Times,* April 18, 1997, http://www.cdn-friends-icej.ca/united.html, accessed January 16, 2013.

20 Steven Sizer, "Jerusalem: The City of God in Christian Tradition," Qatar International Conference on Jerusalem, February 26–27, 2012.

21 Gary M. Burge, "Why I Am Not a Christian Zionist, Academically Speaking," www.christianzionism.org/Article/Burge02.pdf, accessed January 28, 2013.

Chapter 7: My Legs Were Praying

1 Charles Marsh, *The Beloved Community: How Faith Shapes Social Justice, from the Civil Rights Movement to Today* (New York: Basic Books, 2005), p. 32.

2 Ibid.

3 Ibid.

4 Ibid., pp. 37–38.

5 Ibid., p. 38.

6 Marsh relates this to the then-dominant influence of Reinhold Niebuhr, "widely known in both religious and political circles as America's public theologian and as an intellectual architect of Cold War liberalism" (Marsh, *The Beloved Community*, p. 39). According to Marsh, Niebuhr did not support King's involvement in the boycott, counseling instead patience and the slow accumulation of small gains. Marsh cites Niebuhr's communication to the U.S. Supreme Court after the *Brown vs. Board of Education* decision, in which he "expressed hope that the nation would give the white southerner some time to accept the decision in a rational manner" (Marsh, *The Beloved Community*, p. 40).

7 Ibid., p. 34.

8 "A Call for Unity," http://www.stanford.edu/group/King// frequentdocs/clergy.pdf, accessed January 27, 2013.

9 Marsh, *The Beloved Community*, p. 42.

10 James M. Washington, ed., *A Testament of Hope: The Essential Writings and Speeches of Martin Luther King, Jr.* (San Francisco: HarperSanFrancisco, 1986), p. 295.

11 Howard Thurman, *Jesus and the Disinherited* (Boston: Beacon Press, 1976), p. 34.

12 Allan Boesak, *Farewell to Innocence* (Maryknoll, NY: Orbis, 1984), pp. 10–11.

13 Washington, *A Testament of Hope*, p. 290.

14 Marsh, *The Beloved Community,* p. 50.

15 Martin Luther King Jr., "Facing the Challenge of a New Age," in James M. Washington, ed., *A Testament of Hope: The Essential Writings and Speeches of Martin Luther King, Jr.* (San Francisco: HarperSanFrancisco, 1986), p. 140.

16 Visit the website for a complete report on the delegation, including biographies of the delegates and a list of the organizations they met with: http://www.dorothycottoninstitute.org/a-report-from-the-dorothy-cotton-institutes-2012-civil-and-human-rights-delegation-to-the-west-bank/. The Dorothy Cotton Institute develops, nurtures, and trains leaders for a global human rights movement, building a network and community of civil and human rights leadership. It explores, shares, and promotes practices that transform individuals and communities, opening new pathways to peace, justice, and healing.

17 Rev. Lucas Johnson, in conversation with author, December 24, 2012.

18 Ibid.

19 Martin Luther King Jr., "A Time to Break Silence," in James M. Washington, ed., *A Testament of Hope: The Essential Writings and Speeches of Martin Luther King, Jr.* (San Francisco: HarperSanFrancisco, 1986), p. 230.

20 "Vincent Harding Meets with Young, Nonviolent Protesters in West Bank," *Denver Post,* December 9, 2012, http://www.denverpost.com/news/ci_22154570/vincent-harding-meets-young-nonviolent-protestors-west-bank, accessed December 15, 2012.

21 http://www.interfaithpeacebuilders.org/.

22 "Interfaith Peace-Builders' African Heritage Delegation Arrives in Israel/Palestine," http://www.ifpb.org/del38/default.html, accessed January 5, 2013.

23 Rev. Carolyn Boyd, in conversation with author, January 7, 2013.

24 Ibid.

25 http://students.haverford.edu/kkoltunf/Ken/Religion_236_

Web/Civil_Rights/Freedom_Riders.html, accessed February 9, 2013.

26   Hannah Schwarzschild, "Why They Go: Freedom Riders Then and Now," last modified May 13, 2011, accessed January 11, 2013, http://thehill.com/blogs/congress-blog/civil-rights/161163-why-they-go-freedom-riders-then-and-now.

27   Beryl Cheal, "Refugees in the Gaza Strip, December 1948–May 1950," *Journal of Palestine Studies* 18:1 (1988): 138.

28   Hannah Schwarzschild, "Why They Go: Freedom Riders Then and Now."

29   Charles Marsh, *God's Long Summer: Stories of Faith and Civil Rights* (Princeton, NJ: Princeton University Press, 1997), p. 32.

30   "Vincent Harding Meets with Young, Nonviolent Protesters in West Bank."

31   Washington, *A Testament of Hope*, p. 295.

Chapter 8: How the Church Saved South Africa

1   Kairos Palestine document, http://www.kairospalestine.ps/sites/default/Documents/English.pdf, accessed January 14, 2013.

2   South Africa Kairos, 1985, "Challenge to the Church: A Theological Comment on the Political Crisis in South Africa," http://kairossouthernafrica.wordpress.com/2011/05/08/the-south-africa-kairos-document-1985/, accessed January 14, 2013.

3   Robert McAfee Brown, ed., *Kairos: Three Prophetic Challenges to the Church* (Grand Rapids, MI: Eerdmans, 1990), p. 3.

4   South Africa Kairos document.

5   Kairos Palestine document.

6   Edwin Arrison, in conversation with author, October 5, 2012.

7   The organization led by Arrison is living up to this principle. Established in March 2011 in response to the 2009 Palestinian call, Kairos Southern Africa was "established to reconnect and

nurture the prophetic voice that recognises God's face in the face of the poor and most marginalised people in Southern Africa." In December 2011, Kairos Southern Africa issued "A Word to the ANC, in These Times." This bold document included a confession that since the ending of apartheid in 1994, the churches had failed to "internalize the new culture of democracy and the values of our new democracy" (http://kairossouthernafrica.wordpress.com/2012/08/01/kairos-logo/). Racism and sexism still characterized the practices of many of the churches, the document alleged. It further challenged the government, led by the African National Congress party (ANC), on its factionalism, corruption, and failure to live up to its promises to bring social and economic equality to the people of South Africa. Although the document is addressed to the government of South Africa, it serves also to call upon the church to continue its struggle on behalf of the poor and oppressed.

8 Tinyiko Maluleke (University of South Africa deputy registrar), in discussion with author, April 11, 2011.

9 Charles Villa-Vicencio, *Between Christ and Caesar: Classic and Contemporary Texts on Church and State* (Grand Rapids, MI: Eerdmans, 1986), p. 241.

10 Ibid., p. 243.

11 John Allen, *Rabble-Rouser for Peace* (New York: Free Press, 2006).

12 John W. de Gruchy and Steve de Gruchy, *The Church Struggle in South Africa* (Minneapolis, MN: Augsburg Fortress, 2005).

13 Charles Villa-Vicencio, in discussion with author, April 12, 2011.

14 Charles Villa-Vicencio, *Trapped in Apartheid* (Maryknoll, NY: Orbis, 1988), p. 200.

15 Ibid., p. 201.

16 South Africa Kairos document.

17 Ibid.

18 Ibid.

19 Ibid.

20 The fact of Israelis' fear of annihilation is not in dispute. The question of the reality of the threat, however, is relevant. Israeli author Miko Peled talks about this in his memoir *The General's Son*, in which he chronicles how Israeli generals and politicians have traded on the powerful fiction of Israel's military vulnerability. Ira Chernus offers a compelling analysis of this issue in his April 18, 2011, piece in *The Nation*, "Three Myths of Israel's Insecurity," http://www.thenation.com/article/159998/three-myths-israels-insecurity.

21 According to most sources, between 750,000 and 850,000 Jews from Algeria, Egypt, Iraq, Libya, Morocco, Syria, and Yemen emigrated from the early 1940s through the 1970s as the result of discrimination and persecution, with the majority of emigration in 1948 resulting from retaliation on the part of Arab governments and anti-Jewish riots in some Arab countries over the establishment of the State of Israel. These facts are often cited to counterbalance Palestinian claims for repatriation or compensation for expulsions from Palestine in that same year. The issue is somewhat contentious, with some of those same Arab Jews who immigrated to Israel claiming that they came of their own free will, and some allegations of Zionist involvement in the persecution and violence that prompted Jewish immigration to Israel from Arab lands.

22 South Africa Kairos document.

23 Ibid.

24 Ibid.

25 Walter Wink, *Engaging the Powers* (Minneapolis, MN: Fortress Press, 1992), p. 4.

26 Ibid., p. 5.

27 "Press Statement on December 2012 Visit to Palestine by South African Ecumenical Delegation," http://kairossouthernafrica.wordpress.com/2012/12/05/press-statement-on-december-2012-

visit-to-palestine-by-south-african-ecumenical-delegation/, accessed January 25, 2013.

28 Ibid.

29 Charles Villa-Vicencio, in conversation with author, April 2011.

30 "Press Statement on December 2012 Visit to Palestine by South African Ecumenical Delegation."

31 Ibid.

32 Kairos Palestine document, http://www.kairospalestine.ps/ sites/default/Documents/English.pdf, accessed January 14, 2013.

33 "Press Statement on December 2012 Visit to Palestine by South African Ecumenical Delegation."

Chapter 9: Voices from Palestine

1 Arik W. Ascherman, "Armageddon, Straight Ahead," http://www. rhr.org.il/page.php?id=24&language=en&name=article, December 2, 2009, accessed January 21, 2013.

2 As described in chapter 1, *Intifada*—Arabic for "shaking off"—refers to two uprisings of Palestinians against the Israeli occupation. The first, lasting from 1987 to 1993, began in Gaza and spread to the West Bank. The second, from 2000 to 2006, began in Jerusalem following Israeli prime minister Ariel Sharon's visit to the Muslim holy site of the Dome of the Rock in Jerusalem. Ascherman here was wondering, fearfully, as have many others, when the next outbreak of widespread resistance resulting in an escalating spiral of violence might happen again.

3 Kairos Palestine document, http://www.kairospalestine.ps/ sites/default/Documents/English.pdf, accessed January 14, 2013.

4 Ibid.

5 Jonathan Kuttab, "Steps to Create an Israel-Palestine,"

http://articles.latimes.com/2009/dec/20/opinion/la-oe-kut-tab20-2009dec20, accessed January 16, 2013.

6 Ali Abunimah, "Israel Resembles a Failed State," *Al Jazeera,* December 28, 2009, http://www.aljazeera.com/focus/gazaone yearon/2009/12/200912269262432432.html, accessed January 21, 2013.

7 Kairos Palestine document, 3.4.1.

8 Ibid., 4.3.

9 Rifat Odeh Kassis, *Kairos for Palestine* (Palestine/India: Baday Alternatives, 2011), p. 100.

10 Ibid., p. 99.

11 Kairos Palestine document, 1.1.

12 Ibid., 3.4.3.

13 You can watch a video of Munther Isaac's thirty-minute address at www.christatthecheckpoint.com.

14 Munther Isaac, "Palestinian Christians," www.christatthecheck point.com, March, 2012.

15 Ibid.

16 Christians United for Israel (www.cufi.org) is a ministry in the United States devoted to providing political and financial support for Israel. CUFI founder and pastor John Hagee is a conservative Christian Zionist. In his preaching and public statements he promotes the belief that the State of Israel presages the fulfillment of biblical prophecies of the End Times and that it is the duty of Christians to support Israel as a Jewish state.

17 Munther Isaac, "Palestinian Christians."

18 Ibid.

19 Ibid.

20 Ibid.

21 Kairos Palestine document, 3.4.3.

22 Ibid., 4.2.1.

23 Ibid., 4.2.4.

24 Resonating but not made explicit in this section of Kairos Pales-

tine is the reality of the violent forms that resistance had taken on the part of some Palestinians. The document has been criticized because it does not directly reference or explicitly condemn the violence. But it is clear that the requirement for nonviolence is a centerpiece of the document. Given the suffering caused by violent resistance, and the repeated emphasis on and theological support for nonviolence contained within Kairos Palestine, it is hard to imagine that the document is not intended as a statement renouncing violence of any kind.

25 Kairos Palestine document, 4.2.3.

26 Ibid., 4.2.4.

27 Ibid., 4.2.6.

28 The name given to territories set aside for black inhabitants of South Africa as part of the policy of apartheid.

29 Available through Friends of Tent of Nations North America, www.fotonna.org.

30 Naim Stifan Ateek, *Justice and Only Justice: A Palestinian Theology of Liberation* (Maryknoll, NY: Orbis Books, 1989), p. 137.

31 Ibid., p. 138.

32 Ibid., p. 184.

33 Holy Land Trust Mission Statement, http://www.holylandtrust.org/index.php/about, accessed January 14, 2013.

34 Sami Awad, interview with author, January 3, 2013.

35 Ibid.

Chapter 10: Healing and Hope

1 Brant Rosen, *Wrestling in the Daylight: A Rabbi's Path to Palestinian Solidarity* (Charlottesville, VA: Just World Books, 2012), pp. 23–24.

2 Ibid., p. 23.

3 Ibid., p. 75.

4 Martin Luther King, Jr., "A Time to Break Silence," in James

M. Washington, ed., *A Testament of Hope: The Essential Writings and Speeches of Martin Luther King, Jr.* (San Francisco: HarperSanFrancisco, 1986), p. 230.

5 Howard Thurman, *Jesus and the Disinherited* (Boston: Beacon Press, 1976), p. 11.

6 Ibid., p. 15.

7 Ibid., p. 15.

8 Ibid., p. 15.

9 Ibid., p. 15.

10 Marc H. Ellis, *Toward a Jewish Theology of Liberation* (Waco, TX: Baylor University Press, 2004), p. 107.

11 Ibid., p. 192.

12 Ibid., p. 206.

13 Ibid., p. 54.

14 Ibid., p. 207.

15 Ibid., p. 216.

16 Marc H. Ellis, *Encountering the Jewish Future* (Minneapolis, MN: Fortress, 2011), p. 154.

17 Hannah Arendt, "The Jewish State: Fifty Years Later, Where Have Herzl's Politics Led?" in Jerome Kohn and Ron H. Feldman, eds., *The Jewish Writings* (New York: Schocken, 2007), p. 385.

18 Ibid., p. 386.

19 Ibid., p. 385.

20 Ellis, *Encountering the Jewish Future,* pp. 170–71.

21 Arnold Forster and Benjamin Epstein, *The New Anti-Semitism* (New York: McGraw-Hill/Anti-Defamation League, 1974), p. 17.

22 Ellis, *Encountering the Jewish Future,* p. 175.

23 Ilan Pappé, *The Ethnic Cleansing of Palestine* (Oxford: Oneworld, 2007).

24 Ellis, *Encountering the Jewish Future,* p. 179.

25 "Eitan Bronstein: Israelis Confront Nakba Denial," Institute for Middle East Understanding, March 10, 2008, http://imeu.net/news/article001240.shtml, accessed January 18, 2013.

26 Eitan Bronstein Aparicio, in discussion with author, December 30, 2012.

27 Ilan Pappé, *The Ethnic Cleansing of Palestine*, pp. 225–34.

28 Eitan Bronstein Aparicio, in discussion with author, December 30, 2012.

29 Ibid.

30 Nomika Zion, "It's Not Just About Fear, Bibi, It's About Hopelessness," http://www.nybooks.com/articles/archives/2013/jan/10/its-not-just-about-fear-bibi-its-about-hopelessnes/, accessed January 18, 2013.

31 Ibid.

32 Ibid.

33 "War Diary from Sderot," http://www.huffingtonpost.com/nomika-zion/war-diary-from-sderot_b_157497.html, accessed December 29, 2012.

34 Zion, "It's Not Just About Fear, Bibi."

35 Rela Mazali, "In Tow: A Mother's and Daughter's Gendered Departures and Returns," in Nahla Abdo and Ronit Lentin, eds., *Women and the Politics of Military Confrontation: Palestinian and Israeli Gendered Narratives of Dislocation* (New York/Oxford: Berghahn Books, 2002), pp. 207–33.

36 A reference to the 2010 Israeli attack on the high seas of the *Mavi Marmara,* a Turkish ship that sailed as part of one of a series of what have been called "Free Gaza Flotillas," organized to challenge the Israeli blockade of Gaza. Nine of the activists on board the ship were killed by Israeli commandos who boarded the ship.

37 Rela Mazali, "A Call for Livable Futures," http://www.huffingtonpost.com/rela-mazali/a-call-for-livable-future_b_625028.html, accessed June 28, 2013.

38 More information can be found at www.bdsmovement.net.

39 Rela Mazali, "A Call for Livable Futures."

40 Rela Mazali, conversation with the author, December 17, 2012.

41 Neve Gordon, "Boycott Israel," http://articles.latimes.com/

2009/aug/20/opinion/oe-gordon20, accessed January 16, 2013.

42 Ibid.

43 Brian Walt, "Affirming a Judaism and Jewish Identity without Zionism," http://palestiniantalmud.com/2012/06/01/affirming -a-judaism-and-jewish-identity-without-zionism/, accessed January 12, 2013.

44 Ibid.

45 Ibid.

46 Ibid.

47 Jewish Voice for Peace is a diverse and democratic community of activists inspired by Jewish tradition to work together for peace, social justice, and human rights. JVP seeks an end to the Israeli occupation of the West Bank, Gaza Strip, and East Jerusalem; security and self-determination for Israelis and Palestinians; a just solution for Palestinian refugees based on principles established in international law; an end to violence against civilians; and peace and justice for all peoples of the Middle East (www.jewishvoiceforpeace.org).

48 http://jewishvoiceforpeace.org/blog/passover-the-freedom-to-question-and-to-re-tell-our-stories.

49 James M. Washington, ed., *A Testament of Hope: The Essential Writings and Speeches of Martin Luther King, Jr.* (San Francisco: HarperSanFrancisco, 1986), p. 290.

50 Thurman, *Jesus and the Disinherited,* p. 90.

Chapter 11: Kairos Time

1 Ecumenical Accompaniment Programme in Palestine and Israel, www.eappi.org/en/home.html, accessed January 29, 2013.

2 Like its sister Friends of Sabeel organizations in other places such as North America and the United Kingdom, Friends of Sabeel in the Netherlands functions to help support Sabeel in Jerusalem

and to conduct conferences and other educational activities to increase awareness of Palestinian human rights issues and to educate about Palestinian liberation theology and nonviolence.

3 Soon after taking power late in 1933, the Nazi Party began to enact laws to isolate, marginalize, and impoverish the Jews of Germany. These included exclusion from positions of power and influence in government and the academy, prohibitions on intermarriage with non-Jews, and, much to the point here, what amounted to boycotts of Jewish businesses. These laws laid the groundwork for the program of extermination that has come to be called the Nazi Holocaust.

4 The full text of this document, along with study guides and other materials, can be found at www.kairosusa.org.

5 "Call to Action: U.S. Response to the Kairos Palestine Document," www.kairosusa.org., accessed February 5, 2013.

6 Ibid.

7 Ibid.

8 Allan Boesak, "Kairos Consciousness," March 25, 2011, http://kairossouthernafrica.wordpress.com/kairos-consciousness/, accessed January 26, 2013.

9 Charles Villa-Vicencio, in conversation with author, April 2011.

10 John W. de Gruchy and Steve de Gruchy, *The Church Struggle in South Africa* (Minneapolis, MN: Fortress, 2005), p. 111.

11 Jeff Halper, "The Israeli Elections: The Ball Is in Our Court," http://icahd.org/node/468, January 27, 2013, accessed February 3, 2013.

12 The most recent example is the Israel Action Network (IAN), created in 2010 to "counter the assault on Israel's legitimacy." Described as a strategic initiative of the Jewish Federations of North America in partnership with the Jewish Council for Public Affairs, the mission of the IAN as stated on its website is to "organize and mobilize the organized North American Jewish community to develop strategic approaches to counter-

ing these assaults..." http://israelactionnetwork.org/aboutus, accessed November 5, 2012.

13 Charles Villa-Vicencio, *Trapped in Apartheid* (Maryknoll, NY: Orbis, 1988), p. 209.

14 Rev. Mitri Raheb, "The Way Forward: From Kairos Palestine to a Kairos Movement for Global Justice," address presented at Kairos for Global Justice, December 2011.

15 Visit www.kairosusa.org for resources to assist individuals, organizations, and congregations in pursuing these actions.

16 "Call to Action: U.S. Response to the Kairos Palestine Document," www.kairosusa.org. For a disturbing and probing analysis of the United States' central role in enabling and perpetuating Israel's oppression of the Palestinians, see Rashid Khalidi, *Brokers of Deceit: How the U.S. Has Undermined Peace in the Middle East* (Boston: Beacon Press, 2013).

17 Martin Luther King Jr., "A Time to Break Silence," in James M. Washington, ed., *Testament of Hope: The Essential Writings and Speeches of Martin Luther King, Jr.* (San Francisco: HarperSanFrancisco, 1986), p. 230.

18 John Marsh, quoted in Robert McAfee Brown, ed., *Kairos: Three Prophetic Challenges to the Church* (Grand Rapids, MI: Eerdmans, 1992), p. 3. (Marsh cite in Brown: quoted in Alan Richardson, ed., *A Theological Word Book of the Bible* [London: Macmillan, 1962], p. 252.)

19 Kairos Palestine document, 3.2.

20 James M. Washington, ed., *A Testament of Hope: The Essential Writings and Speeches of Martin Luther King, Jr.* (San Francisco: HarperSanFrancisco, 1986), p. 295.

21 Ibid, p. 300.

RESOURCES FOR INFORMATION, CONNECTION, AND FURTHER STUDY

Denominational and Ecumenical Organizations

Churches for Middle East Peace. A coalition of twenty-two public policy offices of national churches and agencies advancing concerns, assessments, and advocacy positions on the Israel-Palestine conflict.
www.cmep.org

Episcopal Peace Fellowship Israel-Palestine Network. Dedicated to an Episcopal Church witness and advocacy for justice and peace for Palestinians and Israelis.
http://epfnational.org/palestine-israel-network

Evangelicals for Middle East Understanding. "Pray for and promote God's justice, peace, reconciliation, and religious freedom through solidarity with the people and churches of the Middle East and the West."
www.emeu.net

Friends of Sabeel North America. Supports the vision of Sabeel, cultivating the support of North American churches

through conferences, pilgrimages, and education.
www.fosna.org

Global Ministries of the United Methodist Church. Maintains ties with Christian communities in the Holy Land, conducts programs in support of religious freedom and human rights in Israel/Palestine.
http://www.umcmission.org

Israel/Palestine Mission Network of the Presbyterian Church (U.S.A.) "Engage, consolidate, nourish, and channel the energy in the Presbyterian Church (USA) toward the goal of a just peace in Israel/Palestine by facilitating education, promoting partnerships, and coordinating advocacy."
www.israelpalestinemissionnetwork.org

Kairos Palestine. Organization of Palestinian Christians for dissemination of "A Moment of Truth: A Word of Faith, Hope, and Love from the Heart of Palestinian Suffering." Promotes global understanding of the cause for Palestinian justice.
http://www.kairospalestine.ps

Kairos Southern Africa. Carries forward the legacy of Kairos theology in Southern Africa and expresses solidarity with others throughout the world.
http://kairossouthernafrica.wordpress.com

Kairos USA. Mobilizes Christians in the United States to respond faithfully and boldly to the situation in Israel and Palestine. Disseminates "Call to Action: A U.S. Christian Response to the Palestine Kairos Document," study materials, and resources for action.
www.kairosusa.org

Peace Not Walls. A campaign of the Evangelical Lutheran Church of America dedicated to advancing the efforts to-

ward a just peace for Israel and Palestine.
www.elca.org/Our-Faith-In-Action/Justice/Peace-Not-Walls.aspx

Presbyterian Peace Fellowship. "Called to be movers and shakers within the PC(USA) and beyond, encouraging one another to participate in God's nonviolent work of love, peace, and justice in the world."
www.presbypeacefellowship.org

Sabeel. An ecumenical grassroots liberation theology movement among Palestinian Christians. Sabeel seeks to deepen the faith of Palestinian Christians and to promote unity among them toward social action.
www.sabeel.org

United Methodist Kairos Response. Mobilizes United Methodists to align the church's investments with its resolutions opposing Israel's occupation of Palestinian land.
www.kairosresponse.org

Human Rights and Advocacy Organizations

Al-Haq is an independent Palestinian nongovernmental human rights organization. Al-Haq documents violations of the individual and collective rights of Palestinians in the occupied territories and advocates before national and international bodies.
www.alhaq.org

The BADIL Resource Center for Palestinian Residency & Refugee Rights. Rights-based approach to the Palestinian refugee issue through research and advocacy.
www.badil.org

Breaking the Silence. Organization of veteran Israeli soldiers that collects testimonies of soldiers who have served in the occupied territories.

www.breakingthesilence.org.il

B'tselem. The Israeli Information Center for Human Rights in the occupied territories. Documents human rights violations in the occupied territories.

www.btselem.org

Christian Peacemaker Teams. Works in Hebron and villages in the southern hills of the West Bank to protect Palestinians from harassment and violence by Jewish settlers.

www.cpt.org

Ecumenical Accompaniment Program in Palestine and Israel (EAPPI) organizes teams of international peace workers to monitor and protect human rights in the occupied territories.

www.eappi-us.org

Friends of Tent of Nations North America. Supports the work of Daoud Nassar, a Christian Palestinian farmer who is fighting for his land rights in the occupied West Bank. Sponsors U.S. speaking tours for Daoud and coordinates volunteer opportunities.

www.fotonna.org

Holy Land Trust. Offers unique travel and encounter programs in Bethlehem and the surrounding areas as well as comprehensive media and news programs related to life in occupied Palestine.

www.holylandtrust.org

ICAHD-USA. Supports the work of ICAHD in Israel/Palestine by organizing U.S. tours and educating North Americans about ICAHD.

www.icahdusa.org

Interfaith Peace-Builders. Sends delegations to Israel/Palestine so that U.S. citizens can see the conflict with their own eyes and connect with Israeli and Palestinian nonviolent human rights activists.

www.interfaithpeacebuilders.org

Israeli Committee Against House Demolitions. A direct action group established to oppose and resist Israeli demolition of Palestinian houses in the occupied territories.

www.icahd.org

Jewish Voice for Peace (JVP). A community of activists inspired by Jewish tradition to work together for peace, social justice, and human rights in Israel/Palestine.

www.jvp.org

Machsom Watch ("Checkpoint Watch"). Israeli women's organization that monitors human rights in the occupied territories.

www.machsomwatch.org

New Profile. Israeli organization devoted to uncovering and combating the pervasive militarization of Israeli society.

www.newprofile.org

Rabbis for Human Rights. The rabbinic voice of conscience in Israel. Founded in response to abuses of human rights by the Israeli military authorities in the suppression of the Intifada.

www.rhr.israel

US Campaign to End the Israeli Occupation. National coalition of more than four hundred groups working to end U.S. support for Israel's occupation of the Palestinian West Bank, Gaza, and East Jerusalem.

www.endtheoccupation.org

Yesh Din. Israeli human rights activists composed of academics, lawyers, former politicians, and military officers.

Documents human rights violations in the occupied territories, and works to change Israeli policy.
www.yesh-din.org

Zochrot. Organization of Israeli citizens working to raise awareness of the destruction of more than five hundred Palestinian villages in 1948 and the erasure of Palestinian culture.
www.zochrot.org

Websites and Web-Based Media

Alternative Tourism Group. Palestinian NGO specializing in tours and pilgrimages operating according to the tenets of "justice tourism."
www.atg.ps
See also "A Journey for Peace with Justice: Guidelines for Christians Contemplating a Pilgrimage to the Holy Land."
http://www.israelpalestinemissionnetwork.org/main/ipm
ndocuments/Guidelines_for_Christians_Contemplating
_a_Pilgrimage_to_the_Holy_Land.pdf.

Boycott, Divestment and Sanctions Movement. Website of the Palestinian BDS National Committee (BNC), a wide coalition of Palestinian organizations.
www.bdsmovement.net

Challenging Christian Zionism. Christian Zionism, from its historical roots to its influence on current events, politics, and culture. A wealth of articles and resources.
www.christianzionism.org

Electronic Intifada. A nonprofit, independent publication committed to comprehensive public education on the Israeli-Palestinian conflict.
www.electronicintifada.net

Haaretz. Israel's premier left/center newspaper, in print and online.

www.haaretz.com

JTA: The Global News Service of the Jewish People. Provides a wide-ranging selection of articles related to Israel and to Jewish life in general.

www.jta.org

Mondoweiss. News website devoted to covering American foreign policy in the Middle East, chiefly from a progressive Jewish perspective.

www.mondoweiss.net

+972. A blog-based website providing fresh, on-the-ground reporting and analysis of events in Israel and Palestine from an independent and progressive perspective.

http://972mag.com/

Palestine Remembered. Information and documentation on the Palestinian villages that were destroyed between 1947 and 1949.

www.palestineremembered.com

BIBLIOGRAPHY

John Allen, *Rabble-Rouser for Peace* (New York: Free Press, 2006).

Naim Stifan Ateek, *Justice and Only Justice: A Palestinian Theology of Liberation* (Maryknoll, NY: Orbis Books, 1989).

Allan Boesak, *Farewell to Innocence* (Maryknoll, NY: Orbis, 1984).

Robert McAfee Brown, ed., *Kairos: Three Prophetic Challenges to the Church* (Grand Rapids, MI: Eerdmans, 1990).

Gary M. Burge, *Whose Land? Whose Promise?: What Christians Are Not Being Told about Israel and the Palestinians* (Cleveland: Pilgrim Press, 2003).

Gary M. Burge, *Jesus and the Land: The New Testament Challenge to "Holy Land" Theology* (Grand Rapids: Baker Academic, 2010).

Marc H. Ellis, *Beyond Innocence and Redemption: Confronting the Holocaust and Israeli Power: Creating a Moral Future for the Jewish People* (New York: HarperCollins, 1991).

Marc H. Ellis, *Toward a Jewish Theology of Liberation* (Waco, TX: Baylor University Press, 2004).

Marc H. Ellis, *Encountering the Jewish Future* (Minneapolis, MN: Fortress, 2011).

Arnold Forster and Benjamin Epstein, *The New Anti-Semitism* (New York: McGraw-Hill/Anti-Defamation League, 1974).

John W. de Gruchy and Steve de Gruchy, *The Church Struggle in South Africa* (Minneapolis, MN: Augsburg Fortress, 2005).

Richard A. Horsley, *Jesus and Empire: The Kingdom of God and the New World Disorder* (Minneapolis, MN: Augsburg Fortress, 2003).

Richard A. Horsley, "Jesus and Empire," in Richard A. Horsley, ed., *In the Shadow of Empire: Reclaiming the Bible as a History of Faithful Resistance* (Louisville, KY: Westminster John Knox, 2008).

Rifat Odeh Kassis, *Kairos for Palestine* (Palestine/India: Baday Alternatives, 2011).

Rashid Khalidi, *Brokers of Deceit: How the U.S. Has Undermined Peace in the Middle East* (Boston: Beacon Press, 2013).

Martin Luther King Jr., "Letter from Birmingham Jail," in James M. Washington, ed., *A Testament of Hope: The Essential Writings and Speeches of Martin Luther King, Jr.* (San Francisco: HarperSanFrancisco, 1986).

Charles Marsh, *God's Long Summer: Stories of Faith and Civil Rights* (Princeton, NJ: Princeton University Press, 1997).

Charles Marsh, *The Beloved Community: How Faith Shapes Social Justice, from the Civil Rights Movement to Today* (New York: Basic Books, 2005).

Brian D. McLaren, *A New Kind of Christianity: Ten Questions That Are Transforming the Faith* (New York: HarperOne, 2010).

Brian D. McLaren, *Why Did Jesus, Moses, the Buddha, and Mohammed Cross the Road?: Christian Identity in a Multi-Faith World* (Nashville, NY: Jericho Books, 2012).

Ilan Pappé, *The Ethnic Cleansing of Palestine* (Oxford: Oneworld, 2007).

Miko Peled, *The General's Son* (Charlottesville, VA: Just World Books, 2012).

Bob Roberts Jr., *Real-Time Connections: Linking Your Job with God's Global Work* (Grand Rapids, MI: Zondervan Books, 2010).

Brant Rosen, *Wrestling in the Daylight: A Rabbi's Path to Palestinian Solidarity* (Charlottesville, VA: Just World Books, 2012).

Shlomo Sand and Yael Lotan, *The Invention of the Jewish People* (Brooklyn, NY: Verso, 2009).

Shlomo Sand and Geremy Forman, *The Invention of the Land of Israel: from Holy Land to Homeland* (Brooklyn, NY: Verso, 2012).

Howard Thurman, *Jesus and the Disinherited* (Boston: Beacon Press, 1976).

Charles Villa-Vicencio, *Between Christ and Caesar: Classic and Contemporary Texts on Church and State* (Grand Rapids, MI: Eerdmans, 1986).

Charles Villa-Vicencio, *Trapped in Apartheid* (Maryknoll, NY: Orbis, 1988).

Walter Wink, *Engaging the Powers* (Minneapolis, MN: Fortress Press, 1992).

ABOUT THE AUTHOR

Mark Braverman is a Jewish American with deep family roots in the Holy Land. Traveling to Israel and Palestine in 2006, he was transformed by witnessing the occupation of Palestine and by encounters with peace activists and civil society leaders from the Muslim, Christian, and Jewish communities. In his writing and speaking, Mark focuses on the role of religious beliefs and theology in the current discourse and the function of interfaith relations in the current search for just peace. He has been closely involved in the growth of the international Church movement to support the cause of Palestinian rights. In 2009 he participated in the launch of the Kairos Palestine document in Bethlehem. Mark is the program director for Kairos USA, a movement to unify and mobilize American Christians to take a prophetic stance for a just peace in Israel and Palestine. He lives in Portland, Oregon, with his wife, Susan.

More information, a blog, and additional writing can be found at www.markbraverman.org.